All on a Mardi Gras Day

All on a Mardi Gras Day

Episodes in the History of New
Orleans Carnival

REID MITCHELL

HARVARD UNIVERSITY PRESS
CAMBRIDGE, MASSACHUSETTS
LONDON, ENGLAND
1995

LIBRARY OF CONGRESS CATALOGING-IN-PUBLICATION DATA

Mitchell, Reid.
All on a Mardi Gras day : episodes in the history of New Orleans Carnival / Reid Mitchell.
p.   cm.
Includes bibliographical references and index.
ISBN 0-674-01622-X
1. Carnival—Louisiana—New Orleans—History.
2. New Orleans (La.)—History.   I. Title.
GT4211.N4M57   1995
394.2'5—dc20   94-28098
CIP

FOR E. A. BUURMA

Contents

Introduction   1

1. Creoles and Americans   10

2. African-Creoles   29

3. Americans and Immigrants   38

4. Rex   51

5. Comus   65

6. Northerners   82

7. High Society   96

8. Mardi Gras Indians   113

9. Mardi Gras Queens   131

10. Louis Armstrong's Mardi Gras   147

11. New Orleanians   165

12. Zulu   178

Epilogue   192

Bibliographic Note   205

Notes   209

Acknowledgments   235

Index   237

Illustrations

(Illustrations are courtesy the Historic New Orleans Collection, Museum/Research Center, unless otherwise indicated.)

An antebellum Comus parade

The invitation to the 1866 Comus ball

The 1873 Comus tableau

The 1879 arrival of Rex

The Independent Order of the Moon, 1887

The invitation to the 1891 Atlanteans ball

Mardi Gras, 1920s

A turn-of-the-century parade

A female pirate

A Zulu Social Aid and Pleasure Club parade

White children blackface to portray African-Americans

The 1946 arrival of the king of Zulu

   (William Russell, photographer. Hogan Jazz Archive)

Louis Armstrong, 1949

   (courtesy Don Perry, photographer. Hogan Jazz Archive)

All on a Mardi Gras Day

Introduction

IN NEW ORLEANS, during Carnival 1901, a group of revelers eating and drinking at a Begue's breakfast declared themselves to be the Carrie Nation Club, naming themselves for a combative prohibitionist. They agreed to return to Begue's, a culinary institution that introduced the lavish brunch to New Orleans, every Mardi Gras to hold their annual meeting. On their third anniversary, the Carrie Nation Club paraded through the streets en route to their meal. This was true carnivalesque logic: to announce an identification with one point of view—militant prohibition—while openly behaving in a contradictory fashion by pursuing almost militant self-indulgence. Burlesquing Carrie Nation appealed to them in part because she was a much-ridiculed figure at the time. But she probably also attracted them because by taking on masculine assertiveness, acting in a way thought by many to be beyond the bounds of womanhood, and reveling in extreme behavior, Carrie Nation was inherently a carnivalesque figure.

Whereas revelers used Mardi Gras to satirize prohibitionists and other reformers, early-twentieth-century reformers pointed to New Orleans Carnival as an example of just what needed reforming.

In 1908, the Reverend Charles L. Collins of the Kentucky Anti-Saloon League visited New Orleans to see Carnival. Collins proclaimed that "no city on the continent offers harder problems for the reformer." Much about the city's easy ways displeased him, including certain aspects of Carnival. "As to the Mardi Gras festivities proper," he wrote, "I am both delighted and shocked beyond measure." He had visited "the so-called restricted section"—the redlight district—at least twice, and found "vulgar exhibitions" on Mardi Gras. (One wonders what other kind of exhibitions he expected to find.) With a reformer's logic, Collins offered the city some stern advice: "New Orleans owes it to herself to place rigid restrictions upon many of the features of the Carnival and abolish many others, or the spirit of reform which is abroad in the land is sure to strike the whole Carnival idea and blot it out." Collins's attitude was similar to that of the Yankee chaplain who complained that "it is no easy matter to go to heaven by way of New Orleans."[1]

The design of this book is simple. I have selected several stories of Carnival, most of which took place on Mardi Gras itself. Each chapter or chapter division begins with such a story of lesser or greater length. After the story comes an explanation; each story will be placed in some context or even contexts. My explanations hardly exhaust the stories, but they reveal some of the stories' meanings. An episode is "a usually brief unit of action in a dramatic or literary work," "a developed situation that is integral to but separable from a continuous narrative," or "one of a series of loosely connected stories or scenes." At the very least, I will claim that the last meaning applies to the stories I tell.

The title of this book, *All on a Mardi Gras Day,* comes from the song by Dr. John; his recording is the best aural recreation of Mardi Gras I know. I have unabashedly borrowed my subtitle—*Episodes in the History of New Orleans Carnival*—from Robert Darnton's *The Great Cat Massacre and Other Episodes in French Cultural History.* Darnton's "episodes" are odd stories and odder texts from which he elicits an interpretation of French culture; some of the stories that follow are just as odd.

Some of these stories will be familiar to anyone interested in Carnival in New Orleans. Such stories include those of the first Rex parade or the organization of Comus. Although less well known, others have been the subject of considerable discussion—such as Timothy Flint's description of "the great Congo-dance," which provides a rare glimpse into African-Creole festive traditions in antebellum New Orleans. Others, including a 1908 brawl between black and white New Orleanians, are strays, collected from contemporary newspapers. Some stories occurred in living memory—the organization of King NOR and of the Elks Krewe of Orleanians in the 1930s, as well as the 1960s boycott of Zulu. And one was still going on as I finished this book—the attempt of the New Orleans City Council to desegregate Carnival and the resulting backlash and backpedaling.

The reader might be surprised at how many of these stories are ones of violence: a brawl in 1856, a "race riot" in 1908, an arbitrary arrest in 1918. The link between Carnival and criminality, Carnival and violence, has long been recognized in New Orleans. It has also been recognized by historians of Carnival in early modern Europe; perhaps the best-known work connecting festivity with deadly violence is Emmanuel Le Roy Ladurie's *Carnival in Romans*, an account of a massacre that occurred in France in 1580. Natalie Zemon Davis, who is fascinated by the connections between ritual and violence, finds violence between Catholics and Protestants associated with religious rites, particularly processional days, and with festivities.[2]

Just as in early modern Europe, Carnival in New Orleans often revealed social conflicts. Sometimes the conflict was between Creoles and Americans, sometimes between natives and immigrants, sometimes between the respectable and the revelers. Often the conflict was the one most deeply rooted in New Orleans society— that between white and black. As Carnival permits the display of antagonisms, it is hardly surprising that many of the stories that follow are stories of violence.

There are practical reasons people might act violently on Mardi Gras. Often they are disguised, making identification difficult. Often they travel in small groups, relying on one another as a situation mounts toward confrontation and violence. Often they are drunk, and more prone toward anger. The use of drugs other than alcohol also characterizes Mardi Gras. Yet such drink, drugs, and disguises also possess ritual elements. I am reluctant to call this behavior religious or to characterize Carnival in New Orleans as offering access to the sacred. But the masquerade, the playacting, the intoxication, the explicit sexuality, the dance and parade and strut all set the day apart from the normal world we usually inhabit. Historians of culture, following Victor Turner, often refer to this ritual state as "liminal." During New Orleans Carnival, men and women are playacting, pretending to be what or who they are not. In this realm they perform actions from which they would ordinarily refrain. They might do so not only because they are unrecognizable to others but because they are unrecognized by themselves. The transformation of individual into masker, of self into character, separates people from their actions and permits extravagances—extravagances of consumption, of eros, of physical movement, of noise and music and speech, but extravagances of assertion and violence as well.[3]

Yet I am not entirely comfortable applying the term "ritual" to Carnival. Trying to distinguish among "ritual," "spectacle," and "festival"—all of which can be applied to New Orleans Carnival—John J. MacAloon notes one crucial distinction: "Ritual is a duty, spectacle is a choice." On the one hand, most participants in New Orleans Carnival are there as a choice, not as a duty. On the other hand, the city's annual Carnival is really no longer a matter of choice, but an obligation. We might think of the Carnival activities of individuals and associations—masking, parading, merrymaking—as "performance," while regarding the annual event as a "civic ritual."[4]

Carnival is a competitive performance, one characterized by exclusion, teamwork, and assertion. The same Carnival groups that embrace some New Orleanians by definition exclude others. Sometimes what determines those included and those excluded is simply personal ties, but even networks of acquaintanceship reveal political, racial, cultural, and class conflicts. The competition is frequently over space—over who has a right to be where at what time, who should have access to the central public spaces of the city. And assertion is key to Carnival: it is a performance in which one demands, "Look at me."

Among the many examples of assertion, consider Creoles and Americans fighting over which dances belong in the New Orleans ballroom; enslaved Africans and African-Americans preserving a sense of their culture in processions and dances only fleetingly recorded; antebellum thugs demanding treats and searching out fights—and postbellum thugs looking for treats and fights; white supremacists battling Reconstruction; working-class blacks creating the Mardi Gras Indians and the Krewe of Zulu—as well as jazz; the social elite symbolically ruling the city as they imitated a royal progress through its streets; the fathers placing their daughters into fictitious courts; Chris Valley organizing the vaguely populist Krewe of Orleanians; the gay community holding lavish balls; women putting their bodies on display and claiming so-called male prerogatives; and the American tourist purchasing an authentic experience according to the dictates of our commercial culture. Even the buffoonery of the Carrie Nation Club, marching proudly toward the sybaritic delights of a Begue's brunch, asserted the rights of the flesh over the social vision of prohibitionists such as Carrie Nation and the Reverend Charles L. Collins.

Despite its competitive aspects, Carnival also serves New Orleans as a ritual of integration. Indeed, it has been a ritual of civic self-definition. While Carnival provides a chance for competition and assertion, it is a chance offered to everyone. Furthermore, Carnival is seen as asserting a New Orleans ethos that sets the city and its people apart from the rest of the United States.

For some in the city, Carnival has come to symbolize a particular New Orleans racial harmony. Despite all the evidence to the contrary, they insist that Carnival shows the fundamental satisfaction of all New Orleanians with the city's social arrangements. Even in 1991, when some black New Orleanians made an effort to reform Carnival, conservatives sometimes argued for beating back the reforms so that Carnival could return to its role as a symbol of racial harmony. One reaction to the controversy has been sincere surprise that a symbol many believed unified the city no longer unifies.

Carnival has served New Orleans so well as a symbol because in one sense it has remained undefined and in another it has continually been redefined. This continual process of redefinition is one reason for a historical approach to Carnival in New Orleans. Carnival has meant different things to different people at different times. Beyond that, these people have challenged one another over the public space in which Carnival occurred. One method of telling the history of Carnival is to tell the story of these various contests.

The social upper class of New Orleans in particular has tried to define Carnival. In the antebellum era, many upper-class voices called out for a reformed Carnival or dismissed the Carnival that existed in the streets of the city as ill-bred. During the middle and late nineteenth century, the upper class attempted to appropriate Carnival by organizing it. They were somewhat successful within the city—they claimed the central public space of the city for their parades—but they were wildly successful in the national arena: their definition of Carnival became widely accepted throughout the United States. This conquest and gentrification of Carnival, never as thorough as the elite wished, was part of a larger international pattern in which folk forms were seized and pseudofolk forms invented by the upper classes of the late nineteenth century; it was an example of what Eric Hobsbawm and Terence Ranger call "the invention of tradition." Yet the nature of Carnival is such that upper-class dominance has always been weak; the festival itself not only celebrates disorder but invites raucous participation from all New Orleanians. The rise of middle-class Carnival, the creation of lavish new parades and balls by wealthy New Orleanians not accepted by the social upper class, the demands of commercial Carnival with its national audience, and the endurance of folk Carnival, particularly within the black community, have all confounded upper-class efforts to define and dominate Carnival in New Orleans.[5]

The persistence of black folk Carnival—as distinct from black elite Carnival—is another major theme of this book. Our first glimpse of black Carnival is in 1823, when Timothy Flint saw the "King of the Wake" leading the "great Congo-dance." Here the retention of African forms among African–New Orleanians is made clear, as is their seizure of what had been a white holiday for their own purposes. The late-nineteenth-century rise of the Mardi Gras Indians shows this African–New Orleanian sensibility integrating American elements into African traditions and creating a new cultural form. The early-twentieth-century invention of Zulu, a parade that commented directly on white attitudes toward black people and on white Carnival itself, may be viewed as an example of the phenomenon that Henry Louis Gates, Jr., discusses as "Signifyin(g)": "repetition and revision, or repetition with a signal difference"; in this case, black repetition and revision of white cultural forms.[6]

Because of the ongoing disagreements about the meaning of Carnival, its history is also a history of public debate. Every Carnival season has brought recurring laments—from the mid-nineteenth century on, some New Orleanians have greeted each Mardi Gras with the proclamation that the Mardi Gras of their childhoods was the "real" Mardi Gras, that things used to be better. This book ends during a moment of such debate: the 1991 Carnival ordinance. Frequently, the public debate over Carnival focused on the question of disorder. At various times throughout Carnival's history, respectable New Orleanians have argued that the holiday had become too rowdy. The battle between the rowdy and the respectable often reflected existing racial, ethnic, and class conflicts. Respectability was often defined in racial terms and rowdiness associated with certain ethnic and racial groups. Throughout Carnival's history some New Orleanians have found the celebration threatening. The threat is usually discussed as if it originates in Carnival itself, but generally it proceeds from other sources. In the 1800s, Carnival represented the conflict between Creoles and Americans; in the 1850s it represented the political violence associated with nativism; before the First World War, it reflected the tensions produced by the rigidity of constitutionally mandated Jim Crow; in the Vietnam war era, Carnival assimilated the confrontation between "hippies" and "straights." All these conflicts were grounded in social reality. Carnival had little to do with causing them, a lot to do with displaying them.

The social conflicts, the competitive performance, the need for symbolic integration, the different races, religions, and cultures suggest a crucial fact to consider about New Orleans and its Carnival. New Orleans began as a plural society. It might appropriately be called a "creole society," but the word "Creole" has various local meanings that make the term slippery when applied to New Orleans. Although Carnival has sometimes been made to function as a symbol of integration, the word "Creole" has too often indicated the drawing of boundaries, sometimes the desperate drawing of boundaries. Although Creole should be an inclusive term, it has been used as an exclusive one. But the point to make here is that, ever since French settlers established a colony with African slaves in a New World environment surrounded by indigenous Amerindian people, New Orleans has been multiracial and multicultural. That might be the starting place for most studies of New Orleans; it certainly is the place to begin any study of its culture.[7]

And this is a book about New Orleans. It is not a book about theory. I do not wish to join any debate over the meaning of "ritual" or "performance"; my brief remarks on these and other terms are only intended to help the reader understand my stories of New Orleans Mardi Gras. This book is not a contribution to any of the ongoing debates about the nature of Carnivals; it does not fit into the genre of "Carnival Studies." Although my interpretation has benefited from reading studies of other Carnivals, I have not usually chosen to follow their questions.

In part, I can make this decision because of a recent book on Carnival in New Orleans, Samuel Kinser's *Carnival, American Style: Mardi Gras at New Orleans and Mobile*. *Carnival, American Style* is heavily informed by Kinser's knowledge of European Carnivals, by historical anthropology, and by semiotics. In any case, the existing scholarship on Carnivals can suggest but cannot dictate how any scholar studies any individual Carnival. In fact, the notion that all scholarship must conform to a given model is in itself anticarnivalesque. What I bring to this book is less a model than a historical sensibility—or, at least, one historian's sensibility.[8]

Sometimes I let the narrative itself convey meanings, rather than drawing analytic conclusions that the reader can draw equally well. I am an author, not a critic. Narrative, after all, has long been successful in communicating the complexity of our experience. When my narrative fails, it is my fault, not the fault of narrative.

※

Scholars have a highly developed vocabulary with which to criticize and a tiny, awkward one with which to celebrate. This leads to a final question. David Nirenberg, a former Princeton graduate student, a medievalist, and a friend of mine, read an earlier draft of this book and asked me, "What do you like about Carnival?" Since this book focuses primarily on social tensions and their display, I worry that readers other than David will wonder if there is anything I like about Mardi Gras in New Orleans. Much of the history that follows is painful. There has been a lot of thoughtless celebration written down and called New Orleans history, and it has done nobody any good.

So let me be explicit. I see in Mardi Gras much what I hear in a really good jazz band: a model for the just society, the joyous community, the heavenly city. I see a recurring ritual devoted to spontaneity, a festival in which collective display is impossible without individual creativity, a form in which innovation is grounded in tradition. In short, a model for community where individual expression is the basis for social harmony and where continuity is the basis for creativity. And, despite considerable evidence to the contrary, I trust I will find in my hometown the creativity and good humor that will allow the best to endure, even if it must endure side by side with old troubles that should be long gone and human failings that will last till Gabriel's horn. Few people in New Orleans look for the millennium, but when the millennium comes, it will look a lot like New Orleans.

1

Creoles and Americans

1804. The first carnival season New Orleans celebrated after American annexation found Governor W. C. C. Claiborne a nervous man. What sort of conflict might erupt in a city that had had three regimes—Spanish, French, and American—in the last year? The tension between the new American administration and the French citizens was palpable. Then, at one of the public balls, a *"Fracas"* broke out. "It originated," Claiborne reported to Secretary of State James Madison, "in a contest between some young Americans and Frenchmen, whether the American or French dances should have a preference." When one American interrupted a French dance with an English quadrille, a voice cried out, "If the women have a drop of French blood in their veins, they will not dance." The women left the ballroom. It was a battle between reels and waltzes. Worse, rumor had it the new American regime intended to deprive New Orleanians of their customary amusements—a rumor that led Claiborne to attend a few balls himself to reassure the people.

The cultural conflict between Creoles and Americans, French-speakers and English-speakers, already evident, now became a matter for public policy. Claiborne hesitated to bother Madison with such a trivial affair, "but being desirous at the present juncture of communicating every circumstance which might have a political tendency, I have deemed it worthy of mentioning." Besides informing the Secretary of State about the politics of culture in the new U.S. territory, Claiborne stationed militia at the public ballroom. At a later ball, the Americans and the French divided into two parties, one singing "Hail Columbia" and "God Save the King," the other "Enfants de la Patrie, Peuple français, peuple de freres." Claiborne told Madison, "I fear you will suppose that I am wanting in respect in calling your attention to the Balls of New Orleans, but I do assure you Sir, that they occupy much of the Public mind, and from them have proceeded the greatest embarrassments which have heretofore attended my administration." Claiborne was later ridiculed in the press as "a certain American governor, who could not converse with the French society; who could not dance French Country Dances!"[1]

In antebellum Louisiana, Creole meant native-born. As Joseph G. Tregle has shown, a Creole could be "white, black, colored, French, Spanish, or Anglo-American." But in 1804, the Creole community was overwhelmingly French-speaking. Furthermore, the Creole political community was composed of French-speaking white people native to the state of Louisiana—black people in antebellum Louisiana had no political rights. If a politician was a "leader of the Creoles," he represented the native-born, French-speaking white community, the so-called *ancienne population*. In political terms, then, Creole was sometimes used as a form of shorthand for the French-speaking white community. In cultural terms, Creole might be used to designate values and practices indigenous to Louisiana at the time of American annexation.[2]

The conflict between Creoles and Americans was hardly limited to the ballroom. They disagreed over forms of civil law, over matters of language, over politics. Yet the ballroom became a public space where the two groups competed and a performance space where they could reproduce each culture's music and dance. Given the centrality of dancing to New Orleans culture, it was perhaps predictable that Claiborne should first see conflict within the ballroom.

At the center of Carnival—indeed, at the center of early New Orleans social life—was the dance. Carnival was the season for dancing, but, in fact, so was every other season in New Orleans. Creole women loved to dance, and travelers commented on the addiction to amusements shown by Creole men. Claiborne complained that "the attainments of *some of the first people* consist only of a few exterior accomplishments." "Frivolous diversions," he said, "seem to be among their primary pleasures, and the display of Wealth and the parade of power constitute their highest objects of admiration." This observation revealed Claiborne's distaste for Louisiana culture and was itself an example of the cultural conflict within the new territory. Claiborne's comment also identified a New Orleans fascination with making power and wealth visible by indulging in theatrical presentations of social status. Critics would continue to point to "the display of Wealth and the parade of power" as the essence of elite culture and, eventually, of Carnival. Claiborne's very censure shrewdly suggested that New Orleanians' "frivolous diversions" were not entirely frivolous.

Other observers joined Claiborne in designating "frivolous diversions" the center of Louisiana culture. In 1807, M. Perrin du Lac observed that Creoles "yield themselves to pleasure in excess." Amos Stoddard noted in 1812 that Louisianians possessed "native vivacity," adding that "they are particularly attached to the exercise of dancing, and carry it to an incredible excess." According to Stoddard, balls lasted from early evening to early morning, and the irrepressible, apparently inexhaustible Louisianians would attend balls two or three nights in a row. It was a taste shared by black Creoles, both slave and free. In 1806, Governor Claiborne complained to the mayor of the city about the black-owned taverns and cabarets "resorted to by Slaves who passed most of their nights in dancing and drinking."[3]

So New Orleanians danced, apparently at every chance they had. The newspapers throughout the nineteenth century were full of advertisements for balls and ballrooms. Some of the establishments were genteel and decorous; others were the objects of deserved gossip and scandal. Some ballrooms, such as the Globe, the Louisiana, and the Orleans in the 1850s, specialized in rough crowds. Indeed, one newspaper referred to the Globe as "that most villainous of all establishments." Besides dancing, the patrons at these ballrooms could drink and (illegally) gamble. Some of the most notorious dance halls had rooms above the ballroom for the use of prostitutes. Most famous—and most romanticized—were the "Quadroon Balls," which were essentially markets for interracial sex.[4]

Although public balls typified Carnival, they hardly distinguished it from the rest of New Orleans social life. Balls were held year round, not just during Carnival. The end of Carnival and the arrival of Lent meant only the end of masked balls; public balls continued. What distinguished dances between Twelfth Night and Ash Wednesday was that they were *bals masque,* or costume balls. It was the element of disguise that separated the Carnival ball from the ordinary, just as it was the element of masquerade that helped distinguish the Carnival parade from other public processions. The popularity of bals masque created a thriving market for costumers. For example, in 1828, an individual could prepare for the balls at the shop of Lise Douviller on rue St. Anne. There customers could buy costumes and, if they chose, change into them in a special apartment, "where the eyes of the curious cannot penetrate."[5]

Yet even though the masked balls defined New Orleans Carnival in its earlier years, their association with Carnival was not absolute. In the 1830s, some ballroom operators who held masquerades during Carnival season did not bother to describe the events as Carnival balls. Furthermore, although the end of Carnival meant the end of the profusion of masked balls, it did not always mean the end of all masked balls. The Salle d'Orleans made this quite clear in 1833, even in its ad for "Bal de Mardi Gras" on "Derneir Jour du Carnaval." This was its last Carnival ball, but its livelier clientele need not have worried: the dance hall would hold costume balls every Saturday until St. Joseph's Day, in March. After Carnival, the revelry continued—with interruptions during yellow fever season—and even "Carnival" entertainments stretched beyond that Carnival.[6]

Ballrooms were not merely arenas for entertainment. In the late eighteenth and early nineteenth century, they were cockpits of ethnic association and even cultural conflict between the incoming Americans and the native population—witness the fracas described by Claiborne. People representing both cultures attended the public balls, met socially, learned each other's music and dances, and courted. Nathaniel Cox, an American, wrote home in 1807, worrying, "I fear you suppose me lost to you and all my former acquaintances because I am settled among the French." Yet, he explained, except in the ballrooms, one could live in New Orleans without mixing with Creoles. "And even at the ball room the Americans only become spectatory as much to see the French boys & girls dance as you would visit a theatre to see the actors perform."

Carnival balls also reflected the cultural division of the city's white people. Immediately after the Louisiana Purchase, George W. Morgan, an American, commented on the impact that the influx of Americans had on Carnival: "The Carnival is carried on with harmony, tho not as formerly, in public Balls." Morgan thought there were now too many people in the city to have a generally attended Carnival ball in any case, but what replaced the open dances showed signs of ethnic division. Each week two "subscription" balls were held. The dance at the French coffee house was attended almost exclusively by French-speakers; the other was a mix of the two rival groups.[7]

The Americans arrived in New Orleans with an arrogance that caused immediate political conflict within the city. They looked down on the Creoles as Catholic, Latin indolents and ignoramuses who had no traditions of republicanism. They attempted to replace indigenous political and legal institutions with Anglo-American ones and tried to supplant French as the language of Louisiana. To a certain extent, the immigrant Americans thought of the Creoles in New Orleans as the native-born Americans thought of the immigrants in the Northeast. The American program of remaking Louisiana in the image of Anglo-America inspired political resistance among the Creoles. Ethnic rivalry grew so extreme that, in 1836, the Americans in the city cajoled the Louisiana legislature into dividing New Orleans into three separate municipalities with a common mayor and police force. The city remained divided until 1852, by which time the division between Creole and American was overshadowed by that between Creole and American New Orleanians and foreign-born immigrants.[8]

Socially, Creoles and Americans, legend to the contrary, got along well. They often lived side by side, and intermarriage between the two groups was common. Creole society, after all, had long been used to the intrusion of outsiders, particularly the arrival of Spanish authorities in 1763. As early as 1819, Benjamin Latrobe reported that there were three societies in New Orleans—one French, one American, and one mixed. He also said that society, not surprisingly, was in flux. "On the whole, the state of society is similar to that of every city rapidly rising into wealth, & doing so much & such fast-increasing business that no man can be said to have a moment's leisure. Their business is to make money."[9]

Two things are notable about Latrobe's statement. First, it appears to contradict the earlier statements of Claiborne, Perrin du Lac, and Stoddard. Were people in New Orleans so addicted to pleasure that they had no time for business, or were they so busy earning money that they had no time for pleasure? In 1819, the stereotypical answer would have been that Creoles danced, Americans made money. Thus Carnival could be viewed as the apotheosis of Creole values as opposed to American ones—a simplistic rendering of Creole and American characters that was hardly accurate. Second, Latrobe's statement, like that of George Morgan, also reveals how quickly Creoles and Americans began to mix socially, so much so that they created what Latrobe called a mixed society. Furthermore, Cox and Morgan both described the sometimes uneasy presence of Americans at Creole recreations. Governor Claiborne may not have known how to perform French country dances, but nevertheless, he attended the Carnival balls. Clearly, many New Orleanians, American and Creole alike, found time for leisure despite their pursuit of business.

And the Carnival ball, as indeed Carnival in all its forms, became a symbol of this new mixed society in New Orleans. More than forty years after Claiborne's anxious Carnival experience, the *Daily Delta*, an English-language newspaper, discussed the 1849 Mardi Gras balls at length, as a means of examining society in New Orleans. The newspaper bragged that, on Mardi Gras night, "there were balls in all directions and every room was crowded." The paper found much to be proud of in the city's Carnival balls. It boasted of the absence of social distance; no phony aristocracy marred the holiday. "The newness of our population, and the circumstances under which we all start in life, here preclude anything like the creation of a *soi-disant* aristocracy—an upper ten thousand, such as we read of, and laugh at, as having a real existence in some of the northern cities. Here, the only distinctions (and they are the only proper ones, in a Republican country) are between respectability of deportment, propriety of conduct, decency of behavior, and the reverse."

The newspaper portrayed the balls as attracting all the good citizens of New Orleans, whatever their ethnic background. Anglo-Americans, Irish, Creoles, and Jews—the women "pensive-browed, dark-ringleted daughters of Israel"—attended the balls at the St. Louis Theatre and the Armory. Thus the ballrooms represented the plural nature of New Orleans society, a pluralism the *Daily Delta* celebrated.

Nonetheless, the newspaper also revealed itself as a partisan of American New Orleans, for it used the Mardi Gras balls particularly to praise the newer mixed society at the expense of the older Creole society. In this respect, the cultural rivalry that Claiborne had acknowledged still lingered. The newspaper judged the ball at the Armory, which had been managed by Americans, more successful than the St. Louis ball, overseen by Creoles. The American ball attracted a larger and more diverse crowd. Furthermore, in the *Daily*

Delta's opinion, the American ball was the livelier of the two. "Our Saxon ladies added to the spirits, the gaiety and good taste of the Creole, a degree of vigor, energy and devotion, which were bound to achieve in this, as in all their other endeavors, complete success."

The dancers at the St. Louis ball showed more restraint and too much dignity; they were more concerned with proprieties than they should have been at Mardi Gras. But "at the Armory . . . the enjoyments were characterized by more vivacity—the dancing by more vigor and abandonment—the music was louder and stronger—and the whole affair went off with infinitely more earnestness than at the St. Louis." The newspaper thus used the two balls as symbols for two societies in New Orleans—a languishing Creole society and a growing, plural American society—and it invited the Creoles to join the latter. The *Daily Delta* actually seized upon the ballroom, where in 1807 Americans had stood and watched "the French boys & girls dance," as a symbol of American cultural strength.[10]

1846. Charles Lyell witnessed the Mardi Gras celebration. He found the spectacle a relief: it was the first time since arriving in the United States that he saw people take a holiday, and he noted that "several unmasked, stiff, grave Anglo-Americans from the North" viewed the revelry with surprise and contempt. "There was a grand procession parading the streets, almost every one dressed in the most grotesque attire, troops of them on horseback, some in open carriages, with bands of music, and in a variety of costumes—some as Indians, with feathers in their heads, and one, a jolly fat man, as Mardi Gras himself." Both members of the crowd and people stationed on balconies wielded bags of flour, delighting in coating anyone "who seemed particularly proud of his attire." In the midst of the good-humored crowd came a team of horses and a wagon carrying cotton, the helmsman of which drove straight through the parade. Lyell saw "this rude intrusion" as "a kind of foreshadowing of coming events, emblematic of the violent shock which the invasion of the Anglo-Americans is about to give to the old *regime* of

Louisiana." Thus Lyell, too, characterized Carnival as Creole. He believed that the American spirit—"stiff" and "grave"—was antithetic to its celebration. Business, in the form of the crucial cotton trade, had no time and no use for the parade.[11]

Governor Claiborne's dispatches to James Madison identified the conflict between Creoles and Americans as key to Carnival 1804. This cultural rivalry manifested itself in the streets as well as in the ballrooms of New Orleans. But by the time of Lyell's observations in the streets of the city, the Creole-American rivalry was almost fifty years old. "The invasion of the Anglo-Americans," which had begun before the Louisiana Purchase, had yet to erase the Creole character of New Orleans or its Carnival. Lyell was wrong: the Americans of New Orleans did not reject Carnival; indeed, although they could not resist reforming it, in the 1850s they would embrace it as their own. New Orleans and its Carnival would succeed in "creolizing" the Americans.

Despite the claims of the *Daily Delta* in 1849, until the 1850s Carnival was generally considered a holiday of the New Orleans French. Indeed, in 1852, L. U. Gaienne, a clever defense attorney, hoping for light judicial treatment of his clients who had been arrested on Mardi Gras, appealed to Creole patriotism. Gaienne argued that "no innovating puritanical principles" should replace "old Creole customs," insisting that "the Mardi Gras celebration" was "under the protection of the police." "The license of the day," according to the account in the *Daily Delta*, "should be almost unrestricted according to his ideas, as it was necessary before starting on the narrow road to heaven, to pluck some flowers on the wayside of the earth."

Albert J. Pickett, a travel writer whose description of New Orleans focused on the French and Spanish "because," he declared, "being the more novel and strange, they are the most interesting," identified Mardi Gras as a Latin custom—and one he hoped "the eminently pious portion of the Catholics shunned." Newcomers to the city had the wildest misapprehensions about the celebration. John Dunlap wrote home in 1845, "I am told that the Catholic

Carnival that takes place sometime during February or March is the greatest curiosity of all the [shows?] of the place." He thought the day was marked by a procession of priests and worshipers through the streets and markets, and that Carnival itself was a religious observance.[12]

Although wrong about the religious nature of the procession, Dunlap was nonetheless right about its importance to Mardi Gras day itself. Attending masked balls was the traditional Carnival activity, and New Orleanians also celebrated the season with what might be called "normal" entertainments: they went to plays and concerts or to the circus. Only on Mardi Gras itself did Carnival take to the streets. There an old custom of individual masking developed into a parading tradition that for many came to define first Mardi Gras and later Carnival.

This street celebration had clear European origins. The early French settlers of New Orleans brought with them the tradition of celebrating Mardi Gras. In France and elsewhere in Europe, Mardi Gras was a day of feasting and festivity, of disguises, of theater, dance, drinking, and public mockery. Eighteenth-century Paris, from which many New Orleanians came, had a vigorous tradition of popular entertainment that probably influenced New Orleans Carnival, particularly its range of costumes and characters. Many of the other early European settlers of Louisiana, including the German Catholics and the Spanish, came from areas with traditions of Carnival. If there was any one single model for the festival, however, it was the Carnival in Venice—perhaps the model Carnival for Italy and France. Renaissance Venice boasted an exuberant Carnival where Venetians celebrated sexuality with masquerades, pageants, plays, and other amusements. Maskers, some of them prostitutes who dressed in male clothing to escape detection, roamed the streets. Companies of nobles organized plays and pageants that were lavish, sexual, and full of classical allusion. Although the government attempted periodically to reform this Carnival, it was not particularly successful.[13]

In New Orleans, semiorganized parades grew naturally from

street masking; they simply required maskers, some of whom already indulged in elaborate costumes and group costumes, to march together, perhaps masquerading around a common theme. The earliest parades took a minimum of organization and inspired maximum participation, at least among those already prone to masquerade. Someone—sometimes a theatrical entrepreneur seeking publicity for his masked ball—would place an advertisement in the papers, calling on all maskers to assemble at a certain time and place and then march along a route chosen in advance. Legend has it that the organizers of the first parades were young Creole gentlemen who decided to model New Orleans Carnival on the Carnival of Paris, or perhaps the Carnival of Venice. Whether they were Paris-educated or even gentlemen, they were probably French-speakers, as they placed notices in the French press more often than in the English. For example, in 1842, the French-speakers organized a parade in the guise of a funeral procession; the reveling mourners were to help bury "l'Honorable, venerable et estimable confrere MARDI-GRAS." (Funeral processions for Mardi Gras himself were common in Paris Carnival.) The Mardi Gras procession seems to have remained Creole longer than the Carnival balls.[14]

Carnival activities organized by small groups of young men had been traditional in French Carnival. In early modern France, the Carnival abbeys had been composed of young men. In the sixteenth century, a town along the Rhone usually supported a *Maugovert*—a mock abbey that regulated balls and Carnival masquerades and conducted charivaris when weddings they believed inappropriate were celebrated. In Toulouse, bands of young men dominated Carnival in the streets as well. There the strongest Carnival organization was the Basoche, an association of young law clerks. During Carnival the Basoche transformed themselves into the "confrerie des Baises-Cus"—the Confraternity of Kiss-Ass, referring to their practice of stealing purses and demanding a posterior kiss for ransom.[15]

As rowdy as New Orleans Carnival was, nothing on the order of the "confrerie des Baises-Cus" developed there. But the centrality of informal organizations of young men in early Carnival, particularly in presenting street processions, is clear. Young French-speaking men were reputed to be behind the earliest processions; and young English-speaking men organized the Krewe of Comus and its parade. Furthermore, a few additional traditions of the Carnival abbeys survived in attenuated form. Young men organized some of the Carnival balls. And the charivari persisted. In 1804, when Madam Don Andre, "an old widow" with an annual income of forty thousand dollars, married a young man, other young men decided "to prosecute the Married pair with charivari, until they [agreed] to give a splendid fete to the genteel part of Society, and one thousand dollars to the poor of the City." As late as the 1850s, Captain Ric and the Sheet Iron Band, led by a local notary and composed of young clerks, serenaded newly married couples in New Orleans whose age difference was significant; the charivari was called off only when the couple gave the Sheet Iron Band money for charity. In nearby Carollton, similar serenades by Cowbellion societies were used to raise money for the local orphan asylum. Charivaris were perfectly congruous with Carnival processions; in fact, the two events were indistinguishable.[16]

Informal Mardi Gras parades were held, not quite on a yearly basis, from the late 1830s until the mid-1850s. The first Mardi Gras parade may have been the large procession of 1837. The *Picayune*, which failed to mention that the parade took place on Mardi Gras—either because it was too obvious or because the editors did not consider the parade an integral part of Carnival—treated the procession as a great oddity. "A lot of masqueraders were parading through our streets yesterday, and excited considerable speculation as to who they were, what were their motives, and what upon earth could induce them to turn out in such grotesque and outlandish habiliments." The masqueraders distributed sugarplums, kisses, and oranges to the crowd that followed them. The most striking feature of the procession was a six-foot rooster riding in a vehicle, crowing and flapping its wings.

The next year young gentlemen put on another "grand cavalcade," and it looked as though a new Mardi Gras tradition was beginning. They may have been influenced by the spectacles put on at the Camp Street Theatre earlier that year by the Ravel family, one of whose popular shows featured "the Venetian Carnival." The procession was large, splendid, and ludicrous, with bands playing music, "personations of knights, cavaliers, heroes, demigods, chanticleers, Punchinellos, & c. & c. all mounted," faces hidden behind masks. Transvestism provided the most popular disguise, as the young men "dressed in female attire and acted the lady with no small degree of grace." Crowds accompanied the parade, running ahead, following behind. The next year, 1839, the parade was even more lavish. Because people anticipated the procession that year, they filled the windows and balconies overlooking Royal Street. From there spectators heard discordant music—"everyone having an instrument adapted to his fancy, and playing such tunes as came first in his head or no tune at all." They saw banners, fishing poles, men on Arabian chargers, men on donkeys, "heathen and Christian, Turks and kangaroos, ancient Greeks and modern Choctaws; friars and beggars; knights and princesses, hard-favored ones at that; polar bears and chicken cocks."[17]

The organizers of the procession hoped to attract their fellow French as audience and as participants. Sometimes they did not bother placing notices in the English-language section of the newspapers when they advertised the parade route. In 1840, the English-language *Picayune*, not having received a copy of the march route, could only "humbly hope, and most especially request" that the parade pass by its office. In 1840, the "Promenade de las mascarde du Mardi Gras" traveled along Orleans Street to Royal Street; along Royal it ran uptown to Canal; then from Canal to Chartres, where it ran all the way to Esplanade. From Esplanade the parade went up to Bourbon until it reached Orleans Street and the Orleans Theatre. Thus the Carnival procession kept within the bounds of the old city—within what is now known as the French Quarter. These processions of the late 1830s and the 1840s, however, were the last occasions when the French-speakers dominated New Orleans Carnival.[18]

It is worth describing briefly the streets in which the people celebrated. New Orleanians had built their houses in various styles, including French plantation, but the houses that lined the streets of the old city generally were Creole cottages and town houses. These were low-slung dwellings that opened up directly onto the street or sidewalk. The cottages were two stories high—consisting of a ground floor and an attic—and usually tiny, with only four rooms and no hallway on the street level. The town houses, which also fronted the street, were fancier affairs, sometimes three or four stories high, with slave quarters and a courtyard in the back. Business was conducted on the ground floor of some houses. The buildings were frequently stuccoed and often painted pastels. The streets themselves were unpaved and narrow. Later, as the streets grew broader, the buildings higher, and public space more suitable for spectacle, Carnival displays grew more elaborate. But in the late eighteenth and early nineteenth centuries, the streets in which Carnival took place were hardly imposing public spaces; masking and processions occurred very much in a neighborhood setting.[19]

1859. Mardi Gras night saw the third parade of a new Carnival organization, the Mystic Krewe of Comus, which had made its first appearance in 1857. Comus was founded not by Creoles but by Anglo-Americans, men who earned their living as commission merchants, cotton factors, and, in one case, a dealer in art supplies. They were familiar with the tradition of informal processions. The theme of Comus's first parade was "The Demon Actors in Milton's Paradise Lost," and they flocked the streets with devils. That night, Comus not only continued the tradition of parading on Mardi Gras but also established two new traditions: first, choosing themes for the parades; and second, displaying the pageant on stage as a series of tableaux after the procession had passed.[20]

After the first parade, Comus admitted thirty-eight new members and organized a closed social club named after an English literary character—the Pickwick Club. The krewe itself decided to remain transparently secret, creating another tradition that its successors continue to follow. In 1858, the Mystic Krewe paraded again, arrayed as Greek gods and goddesses and illuminated with torches, passing through the streets Mardi Gras night and staging a masque at the Gaiety Theatre. The streets were jammed with people who reportedly showed "opened mouth wonder." The theater was filled with invited guests; invitations were not transferable. At the theater, the gods and goddesses voted to return the next year, weather permitting. "Jupiter, who had opened the ball with Venus, and who, at the conclusion, had kindly consented to take the chair, then returned thanks to our citizens in behalf of his fellow divinities for the very handsome manner in which they had been treated. . . ." After the last tableau, the dance began and continued until midnight.[21]

Unlike earlier processions, the Comus parade was closed to the individual maskers who populated the streets on Mardi Gras. Earlier parade organizers had published a meeting place and a route, thereby inviting all maskers to unite. Choosing a theme in advance and designing elaborate costumes and tableaux meant restricting participation. Only members of Comus could march with Comus; the rest of the world was relegated to the role of spectators. This krewe began to redefine public spectacle in a way that created a hierarchy in the streets. Comus was the first organization to insist on the division between parade and people, maskers and audience, as essential to its identity. At a time when Carnival threatened to become so disrespectable and disorderly that some advocated outlawing it, the Mystic Krewe offered a way to return it to the respectable, to impose a kind of order on chaos.[22]

In 1859, the motif of the parade and the following tableaux was English folklore and holidays. The holidays portrayed were, to be sure, European: Twelfth Night, May Day, Midsummer's Eve, and Christmas. And never before or after did a New Orleans Carnival feature such a traditional, even medieval cast of characters. The Twelfth Night division of the procession, led by a knight on a white steed, had both a lord of misrule and an abbot of unreason, personages that would have been familiar to European confraternities in the early modern era. Games attended Twelfth Night, with revelers representing chess, cards, dominoes, billiards, dice, backgammon, ninepins, and other games of chance, wit, and skill. There was nothing particularly English about the representation of Twelfth Night, but May Day brought with it Robin Hood, Maid Marian, Friar Tuck, Tom the Piper, Tabor Man, Jack in the Green, and the figures of Morris dancers. Midsummer's Eve was represented by England's patron saint, St. George, and the Dragon, the Lion, and the Unicorn, as well as characters from Shakespeare's play—everyone noticed that when the tableaux were presented, a more slender Titania substituted for the "stout, well-conditioned young gentleman who performed the severe march over half" the city. Christmas was "Christmas in Old England," with Santa Claus "surrounded by live flagons, dancing bottles of champagne, swaggering and portly decanters with an expressive boar's head, a savory mince pie and plum pudding."[23]

Comus was aggressively English in its celebration of what New Orleans had always considered a French festival. It is hard to think of a clearer assertion than this parade that the lead in the holiday had passed from French-speakers to Anglo-Americans. This was not Mardi Gras, this was Shrove Tuesday. The list of Comus's founding members includes not one French or Spanish surname, and its membership apparently drew little upon the French-speaking community. In 1858, Comus's published route ran from Lafayette Square up Camp Street to Julia, down Julia to St. Charles, and only then across Canal onto Royal Street, down which they would go only "as far as their time and other attendant circumstances" would permit, before returning to Canal Street and the Gaiety Theatre via Chartres. In 1859, they began at Royal and Orleans, marched the few blocks out of the old city, and kept to the central uptown streets. Whereas earlier processions had taken place within the old city, Comus's incursion into the French Quarter was secondary to the parade through the American sector and the arrival at the theater. Furthermore, Comus, by making its parade and tableaux the climax of Carnival, asserted symbolic authority over the whole celebration. The Krewe of Comus claimed the central streets of New Orleans for Americans; beyond that, it appropriated Carnival itself for Americans. Yet, this new parade that the Americans created to assert their primacy within the city was modeled after the old Creole forms, thus implicitly pledging the city some cultural continuity. The Americans' conquest of Carnival was also their conquest by Carnival.[24]

New Orleans Mardi Gras is so often traced to its French or African-Caribbean origins that it is sometimes forgotten that Anglo-Americans arrived in Louisiana with festive traditions of their own. Most Americans who moved to New Orleans in the antebellum era came from the Middle Atlantic states. Despite their reputation in New Orleans, Americans were hardly without festive traditions. True, the Americans who came to Louisiana had little idea what Carnival was about. Most of them were Protestants who viewed Mardi Gras as a remnant of Catholic—read "pagan"—superstition and ceremony. Even so, Americans brought to New Orleans both important civic observances, such as Washington's Birthday and the Fourth of July, and a British folk tradition of Christmas and New Year's revelry. Indeed, the British traditions that fit best with Louisiana Carnival were associated with Christmas and New Year's. Mummers or masqueraders would dress in outlandish costumes, perform dances and plays, and travel from house to house.

And there was a courtly tradition as well. The creation of mock courts, governed by a lord or abbot of misrule, had been a feature of English festive celebrations. In parts of England, there was a tradition of Twelfth Night kings, selected when, by chance, they got the bean in a special Twelfth Night cake—the same custom as the French kingcake.

In Philadelphia, this wintertime masquerading continued in the form of the annual Mummers Parade. Other Americans to the north had similar traditions; in the Middle Atlantic states, there was the Dutch holiday of "pinkster" (Pentecost), which was adopted by black people as well. In New Orleans, these observances migrated to the already existing Carnival celebration, although Twelfth Night remained a significant day in New Orleans Carnival throughout the nineteenth century.[25]

Although few American cities had such a large French population, what sets New Orleans off from other American cities of the early nineteenth century is not its cultural diversity or its range of ethnicities. What is different about New Orleans is that the English-speakers, the Anglo-Americans, were the immigrants. The usual models of immigrant adaptation and assimilation do not sit comfortably on either the newcomers or the Creoles. On the one hand, the Creoles were not immigrants to their own city. On the other, the Americans had access to political, economic, and cultural power far beyond, for example, the Irish who were coming to both New York and New Orleans by the 1840s. These two groups, Creoles and Americans, were far more evenly matched than in the usual American ethnic confrontation.

To a certain extent, Americans "Americanized" New Orleans and its Creoles. To a certain extent, New Orleans "creolized" the Americans. Thus the wonder of Anglo-Americans boasting of how their business prowess helped them construct a more elaborate version of the old Creole Carnival. The lead in organized Carnival passed from Creole to American just as political and economic power did over the course of the nineteenth century. The spectacle of Creole-American Carnival, with Americans using Carnival forms to compete with Creoles in the ballrooms and on the streets, represents the creation of a New Orleans culture neither entirely Creole nor entirely American.

But Carnival in New Orleans was not entirely white, either. The division most commented on in early-nineteenth-century New Orleans was between those who spoke English and those who spoke French. That rivalry did shape much of the conflict in New Orleans at the time, but its resolution was already clear, and not simply because the growing American community would overwhelm the French (in fact, soon both groups would be numerically overwhelmed by new immigrants). Beneficially, this division would be overcome by a cultural exchange between Americans and Creoles. Poisonously, it was resolved also by a shared racism that became New Orleans's greatest source of unrest. The French and English split paled next to this racial division within the city.

No matter what the cultural differences between some French-speakers and some English-speakers, they could unite in agreeing that they were white. And no matter what cultural differences—indeed, no matter what differences there were in skin color—between other French-speakers and English-speakers, the broader society defined them as black. The definition of white and black, by far the most divisive in New Orleans, was also the most comprehensive; it mitigated cultural and ethnic divisions among white people. The ideology of race would unite French-speakers and English-speakers by the Civil War, and it would also draw in other immigrant groups, including the Germans, the Irish, and, in the twentieth century, the Italians. As important as the cultural division was, in the long run, Carnival in New Orleans would be more significant as an arena for the display of racial concerns. And as thorough as the legal separation between white and black would be, Carnival itself would be a form where white and black cultures mingled.

2

African-Creoles

VISITING NEW ORLEANS in the winter of 1823, Timothy Flint witnessed a black holiday. "Every year the Negroes have two or three holidays, which in New Orleans and the vicinity, are like the 'Saturnalia' of the slaves in ancient Rome." Unfortunately, Flint's account does not specify whether or not these holidays ever took place around Mardi Gras. As his stay in the city lasted from January until March, however, it seems likely that the "Saturnalia" he saw occurred during Carnival. It is hard to imagine when else the white citizens of New Orleans would have granted black people festive license to dance and masquerade through the streets of the city, as Flint describes.

On this Saturnalia, black New Orleanians performed "the great Congo-dance." "Some hundred of Negroes, male and female, follow the king of the wake, who is conspicuous for his youth, size, the whiteness of his eyes, and the blackness of his visage." The king wears a cro n—"a series of oblong, gilt-paper boxes on his head, tapering upwards, like a pyramid . . . From the ends of these boxes hang two huge tassels, like those on epaulets." The king "wags his head and . . . grimaces." His followers "have their own peculiar dress, and their own contortions." They wear streamers that wave and bells that tinkle as they dance. "Every thing is license and revelry."

This was black Carnival in New Orleans. It may have had some relationship to white Carnival; perhaps it took place at the same time. But the "king of the wake" and the "great Congo-dance" were hardly imitations of white festive customs. Unlike the twentieth-century king of Zulu, the king of the wake had no white Carnival kings to mock. In the future, black Carnival in New Orleans would serve as a commentary on white Carnival. But in 1823, Timothy Flint glimpsed black ceremonies that existed independently of white Carnival.

By this time, it is no longer accurate to speak of such a festivity as strictly "African." Whatever African heritage the Congo-dance and the king of the wake drew on, they were also the product of long development within New Orleans—and perhaps some borrowing from other New World slave societies. This tradition, then, might well be called African-Creole. An African-Creole festive tradition was played out during Mardi Gras and emerged most clearly with the Mardi Gras Indians in the late nineteenth century. For it to appear at that time—to white reporters—the African-Creole tradition must have been cultivated within the black community long before.[1]

New Orleans was never exclusively French, and its cultural traditions were therefore not the product of French culture alone. The most important reason for this was the large African population of the original city. Africans came to colonial Louisiana as early as 1719. By 1746, African and African-Creole New Orleanians outnumbered white New Orleanians roughly two to one. These Africans, imported as slaves, were largely Bambaras from the interior of West Africa. Africans and African-Caribbeans fit the European festivity of Carnival into the structure of their own culture. Dena J. Epstein has argued, in *Sinful Tunes and Spirituals*, that African culture survived more thoroughly in New Orleans than anywhere else in mainland North America; indeed, she asserts that "only in Place

Congo in New Orleans was the African tradition able to continue in the open." Gwendolyn Midlo Hall goes further, claiming that "New Orleans remains, in spirit, the most African of cities in the United States."[2]

Were the Congo-dance and the king of the wake derived from African traditions? Flint certainly thought so. For example, the king's crown was not based on a European-American model; presumably it had African sources. What Flint characterized as "contortions" and "grimaces" also originated in an African aesthetic. Can we identify any specific traditions that this performance evoked? Perhaps.

Much of Bambara society was organized around initiation associations, or *dyow*. The function of the dyow was fundamentally educational. Each dyow initiated its members into some form of religious knowledge. But the dyow served other functions as well. Some acted as police, combatted sorcery, staged agricultural rituals, or buried the dead. They were organizations both secular and religious that governed individual communities. Conceivably, there are echoes of the dyow in the mutual benevolent societies that have come to characterize the life of black people in New Orleans, for these organizations too hold parades, aid their sick members, and bury them when they die.

For the study of Carnival, one particular dyow, the *Kwore*, is especially interesting. In a ritual display of the absurdity of life, the *Kwore Duga*—masked buffoons on hobbyhorses—performed antics described by Western observers as comic, lascivious, cruel, and obscene. All the dyow employed music, the mask, and dance as part of their public performance. This was a serious tradition indeed, but one with certain resonance for New Orleans and its Carnival. Did Flint understand the implication of the phrase "king of the wake"? Did this festivity stem from the old burial societies?[3]

Immigration from the Caribbean reenforced the African traditions of New Orleans. And many Caribbean societies developed festive traditions similar to those in New Orleans. On islands dominated by French planters, Mardi Gras provided the space for African-Creole celebration; on islands dominated by the English, the period from Christmas to New Year's served as the occasion for such celebration. Both French Mardi Gras and English Christmas festivities also provided models of European culture, including dances, costumes, and theater, which the islands' slave populations incorporated into their Creole traditions.

New Orleans received substantial numbers of people from the Caribbean, particularly refugees from Saint Domingue; after Cuba expelled many French colonials in 1809, more than a thousand of the refugees—white people, free people of color, and enslaved black people—came to New Orleans. And they brought their culture with them. As Louisiana possessed the same cultural mix found in the islands, it is not necessary to postulate Caribbean sources for New Orleans practices. The presence of Caribbean immigrants did, however, contribute to the city's culture.[4]

Who was the king of the wake? Unfortunately, the answer is not clear. We do not know if he was slave or free, African or Creole. Flint's language is suggestive: "Some hundred of Negroes, male and female, follow the king of the wake, who is conspicuous for his youth, size, the whiteness of his eyes, and the blackness of his visage." Flint implies that this Congo-dance was a ritual, not a unique event. He lists the attributes of the king as if they were requirements for the office as well as peculiarities of the king he happened to observe. But perhaps this particular king was always the king in this ritual. Flint witnessed only one Congo-dance.

Henry C. Castellanos's *New Orleans as It Was* provides a clue to understanding the dance. In this memoir, Castellanos describes dances at Congo Square during his youth—roughly ten or fifteen years after the dance Flint witnessed. According to Castellanos, certain African performers at the dances did claim descent from kings and received appropriate respect from the other slaves. "Two of these that I saw were blacksmiths, and were called by all the African womanhood *candidos*, which means kings." Castellanos identified these men as the leaders of the dances at Congo Square. "Selecting their female mates, they would place themselves in the midst of a ring of yelling, yelping and stamping crowds, who looked upon their saltatory feats with every manifestation of delight." "King of the wake" seems to have been a recurring role that required a combination of skill and the regard of the crowd.[5]

What was the king doing? The performance clearly required athleticism and excited admiration. As king, this black man asserted himself; indeed, he acted out a role of command and leadership almost certainly denied him in his mundane life. He also wore ceremonial attire. The many other performers shared in the glory of this Congo-dance. Their black audience enjoyed the spectacle and its African-derived aesthetic, and they understood it better than either Timothy Flint or we could ever hope to. Very likely, all the elements that Flint identifies—the bells, the streamers, the crown, the contortions—had significance to both performers and audience. This was a ceremony of integration, one that united actors and audience. Possibly, this performance, which Flint identified as "license and revelry," was also a religious rite. Christian Schultz, who witnessed "twenty different dancing groups of the wretched Africans" in New Orleans in 1808, believed that they were "collected together to perform their *worship* after the manner of their country." Perhaps there was an element of worship in the dance of the king of the wake as well. These African-Creoles may have seized the white New Orleans festive calendar not for Carnival so much as for religious observance, just as the dances in Congo Square may have been worship and not merrymaking.[6]

This raises another question: How did the white audience of this black performance understand it? Flint was not alone as a white observer. He mentions that "even the masters of the negroes" watched the Congo-dance. The white audience witnessed a ceremony that they could not comprehend on its own terms, but that nonetheless intrigued them. White New Orleanians and their guests sought out black performances, particularly the famous dances at Congo Square. Castellanos observed that "white people, from motives of curiosity or fun, invariably attended these innocent pastimes." They did not need to know what the king of the wake meant by his performance to extract their own meaning from it. This multivalence, the way a performance can mean different things to different people, must be recognized if Carnival in New Orleans is to be understood, because so many of the city's Carnival performances address plural audiences. The king of the wake did not perform knowingly for Timothy Flint's benefit, yet Flint's observations remain our only account of his performance. The king's presentation itself, the dancing and the grimacing, the wagging of his head, also remains close to the heart of New Orleans culture, passed down by means other than the written word.[7]

For black people who strove to keep African traditions alive, Carnival, like Congo Square, presented a festive space in which to do so. Carnival can represent some of the reasons New Orleans permitted more retention of African culture than did other places in the United States—for example, the openness to festivity and the plural nature of its society. It can also represent the space in which various cultures interacted and blended. Indeed, Carnival not only displays Creole culture but also points to its creation.

In *Carnival, American Style*, Samuel Kinser argues that, in early-nineteenth-century New Orleans, "black people's sense of Carnival was opportunistic." He observes, "They had no use for its Christian religious or European seasonal meanings." Carnival was a licensed holiday to be used for their own purposes. By using Carnival, they claimed it as well. It was more than just an empty form into which black New Orleanians could inject African or African-Creole culture. The New World holiday developed a meaning beyond African retentions. The black people of the city welcomed the yearly festival as a chance to escape some of the burdens of their slavery and their social status. Carnival in itself became their holiday.

Here the black abolitionist Martin R. Delany's discussion of Mardi Gras is suggestive. In his novel *Blake*, Delany comments on some of the meanings of Mardi Gras for black people. The novel is set in the 1850s, but Delany is probably describing New Orleans as it was during a tour he took in 1839 and 1840. On Mardi Gras evening, black people were permitted to ignore the firing of the curfew cannon; both free people and slaves took advantage of

Carnival license to promenade through the streets "in seeming defiance of the established usage of Negro limitation." They walked down Chartres, which Delany thought "more lively, gay, and fashionable than usual." They patronized the fancy stores that stayed open for business on Mardi Gras night. The spectacle entranced Delany, and he intended it to entrance his readers. Indeed, on Mardi Gras night, it was not just the black population who walked openly through the streets of New Orleans: "Freedom seemed as though for once enshielded by her sacred robes and crowned with cap and wand in hands, to go forth untrammeled through the highways of the town."

Clearly the black people Delany watched enjoyed the freedom Mardi Gras offered. Yet the range of images we have of antebellum black Carnival is noteworthy. On the one hand, there are the king of the wake and his followers, preserving and modifying—"creolizing"—traditional culture; on the other, there are black New Orleanians promenading down Chartres, enjoying the fashionable district much as white New Orleanians did. Rather than reconciling these two images, we should regard the distance between them as representing choices open to antebellum black New Orleanians. It is important to glimpse the range of possibility now in order to avoid characterizing one set of behavior or the other as the only authentically "black" choice. Both choices—the great Congo-dance and claiming the fashionable streets of the city—were ultimately acts of assertion by black New Orleanians.

What Delany found remarkable—the way Carnival license extended even to slaves—some white people viewed benignly. Others observed the license with foreboding. The possibilities for disorder with black participation in the festivities struck them as far too great. And, in a way, Martin Delany agreed. He portrayed black people using this Mardi Gras license to assemble to plot an insurrection.[8]

Some black New Orleanians found satisfaction in employing Carnival to subvert momentarily the city's racial order. Mardi Gras permitted masking, and it offered a range of public balls to which a purchased ticket brought admission. Masking hid one's race. During Carnival, a black New Orleanian could mingle with white New Orleanians, drink with them, dance with them, deceive them about his race. This was a potent source of fear and titillation for white people, and a source of gratification for black people. Efforts were made to prevent maskers from crossing racial lines. For example, in 1842, the Louisiana Ball Room specified that its Society Ball was "For White Ladies" ("Pour les Dames Blanches"). Other ballrooms required a brief examination of all maskers before entry, partly as a method of racial filtration.

These regulations were easy enough to dream up, but difficult to enforce. How could someone tell quickly and positively who was "white" in a society as racially and ethnically mixed as New Orleans? New Orleans was too large for everyone to be identified by sight. Furthermore, "demasking" the balls contradicted the Mardi Gras spirit. A Carnival ball was to be safe and unsafe simultaneously. The ball could not have the license associated with disguise if the disguise was ripped from the masker's face. Yet how could the Carnival festivities give license to one group of people—white men—and deny it to others—most conspicuously slaves and free black people? If only for a few nights of masked balls and one day of street mumming, Carnival broke down the city's system of racial control. Indeed, this may have been part of its allure for white New Orleanians as well as black.[9]

Yet Carnival should not be imagined as pure joy for black New Orleanians. If Carnival can be a form of social release, it can also display social tensions. Black New Orleanians took advantage of Carnival to celebrate amid slavery and white supremacy. But white racists used the license of the day as an excuse to abuse black people. This negative aspect of Carnival should also be acknowledged, all the more so because it would continue. For example, during the 1850s, what was known in Rio de Janeiro as *entrudo*—the practice of throwing flour, sometimes adulterated with dirt or even lime, on passers-by—was a Carnival custom. According to the *Daily Orleanian*, white thugs particularly enjoyed employing the adulterated flour against black people; using Carnival license, they mocked those they regarded as inferior, and, by making black people literally white, applied a visible form of Carnival inversion. The *Daily Orleanian* also protested that antiblack violence went far beyond mere entrudo, stating that "more than one poor and unoffending African was prostrated and beaten" on Mardi Gras day. If black people chose to walk the streets of New Orleans, even during Carnival, they did so at some risk. There was a contest for the streets of the city.[10]

Nonetheless, most black New Orleanians welcomed the annual arrival of the Carnival season and, in particular, Mardi Gras itself. Carnival offered them space in which to develop traditions that originated in Africa, as well as a chance to defy racial conventions. It also gave enslaved New Orleanians the illusion of freedom. Throughout the antebellum period, newspaper reporters and editors insisted that black adults and all children were the ones most devoted to Mardi Gras masking. Admittedly, in many cases this claim was part of a strategy of denigrating Mardi Gras. It is unlikely, however, that a newspaper would straightforwardly lie about a public event that many of its readers witnessed. And it is plausible that many black New Orleanians did love masking. Most of them were enslaved, and those who were not lived in a racist society. Masking on Mardi Gras offered them a chance to escape this society through fantasy, assert themselves through performance, and explore white society and confound it through disguise. Mardi Gras became an annual celebration of black self-expression and African-Creole culture. As Timothy Flint suggested, Mardi Gras was a "black Saturnalia."[11]

3

Americans and Immigrants

ON MARDI GRAS 1856, a half-dozen Irish masqueraders stopped two American ship captains and demanded that they "treat the crowd" to drinks. After the captains bought a round at a nearby liquor store, they tried to leave, only to be stopped again. Peter Dunican, the masqueraders' leader, "stepped up and told them they could not go until they had contributed money to assist [the masqueraders] in celebrating the day." The two captains refused, and the drunk mummers attacked them. One of the captains fled successfully, but the masqueraders overwhelmed the other, beat him, took his pocketbook and watch chain, and then threw his unconscious body out on the sidewalk.[1]

This nasty incident concerns both treating, a festive tradition, and violent assertion, characteristic festive behavior. In the British Isles, rowdy maskers demanding treats had long been part of Halloween, Christmas, New Year's, and May Day folk celebrations. Traditionally, Irish holidays had been marked by brawls between rival gangs. Thus the Irish masqueraders behaved in a time-honored manner. The confrontation between Peter Dunican and the American captains was in some ways a cultural confrontation—though it is important to note that however reluctant the captains may have been to buy a round of drinks, they were not so offended by that demand as by the one to contribute money. The second demand may have struck them as simple robbery. Treating, however, had long been a tradition when social "betters" encountered their "inferiors," and ship captains would certainly have been familiar with the ritual from their dealings with their crews.[2]

The incident also reflected ethnic divisions within New Orleans and the introduction of a new cultural group to the city. The same Irish and German immigration that had such a great political, social, and cultural impact on Northern cities also washed into New Orleans. By 1850, the free population of New Orleans was almost half foreign-born. Terms such as French Quarter and American sector became meaningless. In 1850, the white population in the heart of the American sector was more than 50 percent foreign-born, 19 percent Louisiana-born, and only 30 percent born in the United States but outside of Louisiana. The French Quarter, too, had a majority of foreign-born inhabitants.[3]

The most visible immigrants of the antebellum period were the Irish, who still constitute a distinct community within New Orleans. Their influence on New Orleans speech has been immense, giving rise to that New Orleans accent that sounds to outsiders like Brooklynese. They have been a powerful political force, particularly in the police department and the assessor's office, and they gave their name to the best-known white working-class neighborhood: the Irish Channel. The Irish Channel is the center of New Orleans's St. Patrick's Day celebration, a celebration modeled less on Irish customs than on New Orleans Mardi Gras.

In 1850, roughly one-sixth of the city's population had been born in Ireland. The Irish settled throughout New Orleans, not just in the Irish Channel. They filled a wide variety of occupations, but, just as in other American cities, they were found most often doing menial jobs. Probably more so than in most American cities, this put them in economic competition with the black population, both free and slave. Notoriously, Irish laborers were hired for tasks considered too risky for valuable slave workers, such as digging the New Basin Canal. Furthermore, the Irish were subject to prejudice. Although they lacked characteristic American anti-Catholicism, respectable New Orleanians looked down on the Irish as a dangerous criminal element. Yet, unlike slaves and even free black people, the Irish were white and the Irish could vote.[4]

The Irish brought their own festive traditions to New Orleans. Shrove Tuesday was observed in Ireland with lavish feasts; it was also a traditional wedding day. But the patronal days are more important for understanding Irish behavior during New Orleans Carnival. These saints' days were associated with pilgrimages and fairs. Like Mardi Gras, the patronal days combined piety and license; but they reversed the order. The pilgrims did penance to receive the blessing of the saint, then they allowed themselves a day of general revelry. The revelry certainly included good poteen and sexual license, but it also had a measure of recreational violence. Fighting between rival gangs was commonplace. Of course, the most famous fair gave the language an idiomatic expression for a free-for-all—a donnybrook. It was this violence that led a church increasingly concerned with Victorian respectability to abolish gradually many of the festivals.[5]

It could not have been much of a comfort to the American captain that he was beaten up according to Irish festive tradition. But holiday violence was not simply some cultural baggage brought by immigrants from the Old World. In New Orleans, Mardi Gras violence had become so common that it was almost an integral part of the holiday. The phenomenon continued, year after weary year. In 1845, two cooks stabbed each other, another cook slashed his boss (a woman) and a fellow employee, a man was killed in a street fight, and a fight broke out in the hat room of the St. Louis Ball Room between Mr. H. F. Hatch and Mr. Jackson, the nephew of a local judge, "in consequence of some alleged insult received in the ball room, which resulted in Mr. Jackson's receiving three dangerous dirk wounds in the side after having slapped Mr H's face."

In 1849, the judge of the Fourth District Court, out for a walk on Mardi Gras day, intervened to protect a masked man whom the Carnival crowd had attacked. He was almost beaten himself. Fortunately, a man in the mob recognized the judge and dissuaded the crowd from mishandling him. In 1851, a masker named John Hawkins stabbed a free man of color, Charles Butler, on the street; and one ball-goer stabbed another at a dance. Four years later, Pierre Dufour, "a famous Mardi Gras mummer," rode down a woman and child crossing the street; John Kelly, also mounted and masquerading as a wild Indian, first rode into a man and then hit him over the head with a stick. John Flett stopped a man in the street, demanded money or a treat, and threatened him with a beating. In 1857, a masker stabbed the barkeeper at a drinking house, an incident that the paper called "Grim Mardi-Grasing." In 1858, three murders or attempted murders were perpetrated on the streets by maskers. Charles Mackay, a visiting Scotsman, noted that no one was very upset by these crimes: "Human life is a cheap commodity, and the blow of anger but too commonly precedes or is simultaneous with the word. And among the counterbalancing disadvantages of a too warm and too luxurious climate, this predisposition to the stiletto or the bowie-knife is not the least disagreeable or the least remarkable."[6]

It was but a short step from the immediate violence of the streets—a real or fancied insult, drunken tempers, a knife at hand—to the more regulated mayhem of the duel. At least some duels took place as a result of Mardi Gras aggression. At a ball on Mardi Gras night 1855, two young men offended each other. The next evening they met at the dueling oaks and exchanged pistol shots. Both were wounded, one severely. In 1859, Mr. Canonge and Mr. Hiriart fought a duel on Mardi Gras itself. Neither was hurt and each went home with honor satisfied, and, in Mr. Canonge's case, with new holes shot in his coat.[7]

There was also the Mardi Gras custom of throwing flour on passers-by (entrudo). One observer wrote, "Every Mardi-Gras man has his pockets filled with flour, and as he passes the well-dressed stranger, who excited by curiosity gets near, throws handfuls upon him, to the amusement of those bystanders who fortunately escape." In 1853, James Bruys went before the recorder to complain that, on Mardi Gras evening, James Wallace had thrown flour in his face, "nearly blinding him for the time." The court issued a warrant and Wallace had to post bail, ensuring that he would "appear for explanation." Now, certainly Mr. Bruys was annoyed by the assault, and he had a right to be. But revelers were probably surprised to learn that the respectable would actually try to enforce the laws on the books against traditional Mardi Gras license. In 1855, a less litigious man beat two maskers who had thrown flour on him; he then "turned around and swore he could whip any body that would take their part." A few years later, another reveler took extreme umbrage: when a man hit a masker for throwing flour on him, the masker in turn stabbed the man. But those who practiced entrudo were not always harmless revelers; some maskers began to add quicklime to the innocent flour.[8]

Thus Dunican's assault on the American captains could have stemmed either from Old World festive traditions or from New Orleans's own propensity for Carnival violence. It could have resulted from class antagonisms as well. The masqueraders saw the captains as well-to-do, men with pocketbooks and watch chains— men who certainly could afford to stand a round of drinks and finance the maskers' celebration. The captains' reasonable refusal to contribute to the Carnival purse may have struck Dunican and his gang as an insult. Or they may have intended to goad the captains to the point of violence from the very beginning.

It is unlikely, however, that there was an overt political content to the Irishmen's encounter with the Americans. Nonetheless, this brutal incident instantly became a piece of political propaganda in the contest between the Democrats and the Know-Nothings. The 1850s were years of nativism, both in New Orleans and in the nation at large. In the 1850s, the conflict that most threatened the city was not between white and black or between French-speaking and American. Rather, it grew out of the tension between immigrants, particularly the Irish, and older Americans, as well as the use that politicians made of the conflict. When the New Orleans *Bee* told the story of the Dunican mummers, the editors fit it into this pattern of antebellum political rivalry.

Immigration changed New Orleans dramatically. In some ways, it added even more exoticism to a city Americans already found strange. Most antebellum immigrants were Catholic, but their Catholicism, particularly that of the Irish, was much different from the Creole variety (though even the "indifferent" Creole Catholics on the New Orleans police force quickly joined their Irish fellow officers in arresting a masker dressed "in the full canonicals of a Catholic prelate" on Mardi Gras 1855). They certainly enjoyed the "continental Sabbath" that American Protestants found so shameful in New Orleans—bars, ballrooms, and theaters open, people actually enjoying themselves. Still, they were not French, and they were far more likely to assimilate to the more powerful English-speaking society than to the Creole one. At the time, the Irish and the Germans made the city seem less "American." Looking back, however, we see that their arrival increased the ethnic diversity of an already polyglot city, making it less "Creole" and more "American."

The political ironies of this situation were great. The Creoles found the Irish and the Germans as threatening as they had the Americans. The Americans, through the Democratic Party, proved far more adept than the Creoles at managing the immigrants politically. So some leaders of the French-speaking Catholic Creole community made common cause with the American Party, or the Know-Nothings. The fact that the American Party was violently anti-Catholic made the Louisiana variety of Know-Nothingism an odd animal indeed. Eventually, the refusal of the national party to moderate its anti-Catholic stand led most Creoles to quit the party.[9]

During the 1850s, politics in New Orleans became the politics of violence. Mobs dominated the polls. At first, Democratic mobs and ballot-box stuffers were the most successful, but, by the mid-1850s, the Know-Nothing mobs controlled elections. Respectable Creoles and Americans were horrified by the level of political violence and corruption. Indeed, the 1858 election witnessed the formation of a remarkably ineffectual Vigilance Committee, modeled on the one in San Francisco and sworn to protecting the vote of Creoles and foreign-born Americans. It seized the city arsenal and then sat idly by while the Know-Nothings won their greatest municipal victory.[10]

When the Creole *Bee* reported the beating of the ship captain, it used the immigrant status of the criminals and the "American" caste of the victims to draw an oblique political conclusion: "We would recommend this case—which is but one of the many other outrages of a similar character of recent occurrence—to the gentlemen who do the 'Thug' articles in some of the journals of this city, whereby the native-born portion of our population have gained such a high reputation abroad." This was an attack on the *Daily Delta*, a Democratic party newspaper that spotlighted Know-Nothing "thugging" of immigrants. In light of the ethnic divisions and political rivalries in the city, it was inevitable that this Mardi Gras confrontation would be understood immediately in nativist terms. Carnival violence was transformed into political rhetoric.[11]

In the 1850s, Mardi Gras itself became associated with political violence. After the Civil War, the New Orleans *Republican*—a Republican newspaper in the heady and dangerous years of Reconstruction—looked back on the 1850s, "the reign of Know-Nothingism," as a time when Mardi Gras "was often polluted and disgraced by the acts of men, who, feeling safety in disguise, did not hesitate to murder those who were politically opposed to them." (I have yet to find, however, a specific example of a politically motivated murder occurring during Carnival.) At the time, in 1858, the Creole *Bee* pointed out how easily men in masks could get away with murder. "Every honest resident of the city—every man who here earns his living—who owns or seeks to acquire an independence for himself or his family—is directly and personally interested in the suppression of the rampant rowdyism that defiles our streets with the blood of our fellow men."[12]

The identification of Carnival with violence, particularly political violence, led some to argue for its abolition. The *Bee* argued that, even if New Orleanians felt personally safe, they still ought to protect their commercial interests: "The reputation of a city, like that of an individual, has vast influence in making or marring its fortunes, and should be carefully guarded by every member of it." In fact, the *Bee* suggested that outlawing Carnival might be necessary. "Better no celebration of Mardi Gras than have our dreams filled with the shades of murdered men and helpless orphans."[13]

In the years before the Civil War, Mardi Gras stood in no very high repute with many respectable New Orleanians. The mobbing of the ship captains by the mummers was the sort of incident that turned many against the festivity. The respectable claimed that the crowds were made up of their social inferiors, particularly young white boys and black people, both slave and free—or, as the *Daily Orleanian* claimed in 1857, "fruitsellers, low *marchands*, and the canaille." In the 1850s, some called for outlawing Mardi Gras; others hoped that the celebration in the streets was dying out naturally. The violence of the streets repelled some potential revelers, as it surely attracted others. Newspaper editors printed mock-woeful or truly nostalgic laments for the holiday. Mardi Gras, they predicted mournfully or gleefully, was passing; it would soon be gone entirely. In 1850, the *Daily Crescent* found that only "a few juveniles delighted themselves with painted pasteboard and a pint of flour each" that rainy, disagreeable Mardi Gras. Its editor announced, "The Carnival has flitted back to the land of its birth, and its parti-colored shadow only remains to amuse our children. The gayeties of that pleasant time of yore have been driven away by the matter of fact population that has built up this city. . . ." In 1854, the *Bee* was less mournful: "We are not sorry that this miserable annual exhibition is rapidly becoming extinct. It originated in a barbarous age, and is worthy of only such."[14]

This kind of complaint about Carnival and crowds was not limited to New Orleans. At the same time in Trinidad, the respectable and their newspapers were waging a campaign against street parades and public masking. There, the years after the 1834 emancipation had seen a decorous, upper-class French festivity become a boisterous, folk African-Caribbean one. Whereas in New Orleans the elite viewed immigrants, workers, and slaves as dangerous riff-raff, in Trinidad the upper class feared the freed people. The language employed against the people and the festivity sounded much the same in Trinidad as in New Orleans: Carnival was an "orgy indulged in by the dissolute of the town," "an annual abomination," "a wretched buffoonery [tending] to brutalize the faculty of the lower order of our population." The government made several efforts to ban the street parades, only to be met with violence.

Such complaints could also be heard in places other than New Orleans, the Caribbean, and Latin America. Philadelphia had no Mardi Gras, but from the 1830s on, its respectable classes were claiming that public holidays brought a disreputable, racially mixed mob into the streets. Christmas masking frequently led to violence, even death. The parades of Philadelphia were also associated with political violence, particularly nativism. For that matter, the antebellum shift from public to private executions throughout the United States, which eliminated a grisly form of public spectacle, was motivated by similar complaints.[15]

To be sure, the respectable celebrated Carnival away from the streets. Masked gentlemen paid their friends visits. Aline Valeton de St. Bris remembered years later that "New Orleans gentlemen used to take their carriages and go calling on Mardi Gras—just as they did on New Year's—while the lady of the house stayed at home to receive the guests." Even so, one man of the family stayed home "to ask the masked callers who they were." "Usually the men took turns at this task, so necessary, to guard against intrusion." Clearly, the possibility always remained that the streets might invade the households of the ladies and gentlemen.[16]

Some of the laws that New Orleans enacted in December 1856 against "offenses and nuisances" give a vivid sense of the kinds of unruly behavior to which some people were prone. New Orleanians were to stop defacing buildings with paint, mischievously ringing doorbells, and removing nameplates from buildings; they could no longer beat drums, blow horns, or sound trumpets in the streets and public places, let alone fire guns and set off firecrackers. Public drunkenness was outlawed, as was appearing masked and disguised in public: "It is unlawful . . . to make any charivari . . . No person on Mardi Gras, or at any other time, shall throw flour or any other substance on any person passing along the streets or any public place."[17]

The City Council also thought it necessary to regulate balls. The very thing that made dances Carnival balls—the disguises and the masks—also made them dangerous to the city's social order. When men and women were disguised, could they be held account-able for their actions? When both sexes, all classes, even all races could go masked, could social hierarchy be enforced? In 1825, for example, according to the Louisiana *Gazette* respectable citizens were offended by the sight of "a drunken apprentice boy, not yet sixteen years old, who was chatting familiarly with a married lady, whose standing in society, we know to be second to none," at a masquerade ball at the St. Philip Street Theatre.

Wearing masks to the balls was insufficient to ensure the women's anonymity. "Who could have been at the ball, and not have seen ladies with their face covered it is true, but every other part of the body exposed, if not to the sight, at least to the touch, of every drunken fellow that thought proper, by examining the rings of the fingers, the ornaments of the neck, or the drops in the ears, (and how much further I do not know, for this is all I saw) to discover the person of the wearer." That respectable women could expose their bodies to drunken apprentices made the Carnival ball a dan-gerous, if attractive, place. The Carnival balls also threatened racial mores. The author of *New Orleans as It Is*, an antislavery account that focused on the horrors of racial amalgamation, told of prostitutes recruiting clients at the masked balls. He also claimed that mis-tresses and wives donned masks to attend these balls so they could spy on errant lovers and husbands. Part of the release that Carnival offered New Orleanians was a momentary escape from propriety and hierarchy; by definition such escape jeopardized social order.[18]

Furthermore, as noted earlier, the ballroom could too easily become a place of violence. In an atmosphere of drink and sexual allure, fights sometimes broke out, and the local propensity for carrying arms could make them deadly. Consequently, the St. Philip Street Ball Room in 1828 assured the public that "managers [would] be appointed to keep good harmony." Also, some ballrooms, to maintain "le bon order," not only hired peacekeepers ("quarte personnes chargees d'y serveiller") but also refused to admit women unaccompanied by men. Proprietors of ballrooms insisted on peeking under patrons' masks so they could identify the masqueraders. In 1830, the Orleans Ball Room began announcing that only women with invitations would be admitted. It also required masqueraders to remove their masks and have their identity confirmed. This would keep out undesirables—or at least allow them to be identified if they displayed undesirable behavior.

In 1838, advertisements for the Mansion House Ball Room and the Marine Ball Room reassured their customers—or warned them— that gentlemen with concealed weapons would not be admitted. Another policy to prevent heterogeneous social mingling was segregation by price of admission. In 1855, the Orleans Theatre restricted admission to the dress circle to those who bought special, expensive tickets. Compare its charge of $5.00 to that of the Salle de Bal du Globe, where admission was $1.00 for men and 50¢ for women, or even to the ball at the Armory, where admission was $2.50.[19]

Despite the efforts of ballroom managers to reassure their clientele by establishing admission policies, in the end the city government felt obliged to intervene. A second set of regulations soon followed the December 1856 ordinances. These applied to balls and other public events. New Orleanians were not to give balls without a license from the mayor; unlicensed balls would be closed immediately by the police, and if a ball ran longer than the license permitted, the manager would pay a fine. Those who attended the balls were to check their canes, sticks, swords, and other weapons at the door: "At every public Ball, there shall be a person appointed to receive and take care of such articles." In case disarming the dancers was not enough, or if some weapons were smuggled in, the mayor would also station police at all licensed balls. Finally, the color line was to be rigidly enforced at all public balls: "It shall not be lawful for any white person to occupy any of the places set apart for people of color and the latter are likewise forbidden to occupy any of the places reserved for white people at any public exhibition or theatre, and any person offending against this section shall immediately leave the place so unduly occupied, or if he refuse or neglect to do so, shall pay a fine of five dollars."[20]

If enforced, the December 1856 regulations would have eliminated Mardi Gras on the streets. Masks and disguises, drums and trumpets, public drunkenness—these were Carnival. But the laws were not enforced. Indeed, had they been, the first Carnival after these regulations were promulgated, that of 1857, would have seen the celebrants in the first Comus parade in jail. That year those who were arrested for traditional Carnival behavior were treated with leniency. The next year, Recorder Solomon in the Third District "magnanimously discharged those brought before him for the offense of being too funny on Mardi Gras." In 1859, the *Bee* noted that in Recorder Summers's court "the drunken cases were benevolently disposed of, as the day previous was Mardi Gras, and the Recorder was in a good humor." Whatever the law, officialdom was usually charitable about Mardi Gras revelry.[21]

Nonetheless, the annual holiday did pose a threat to the city. While some Carnival raucousness was socially licensed, no matter what the law said, violence to the point of murder was not generally condoned—although Charles Mackay suggested that it was not vigorously condemned, either. Certainly, the problem of violence has never been eliminated from the celebration of Carnival. But in the 1850s, when the city was riven with ethnic tension and political conflict, fears of Carnival violence reached their peak. Unrest was only barely beneath the surface. There was the riot that threatened to break out over the phony priest in 1855—only his arrest prevented the masker from being mobbed—the assassinations that people claimed took place during Carnival, and the possibility of masked ruffians disturbing the streets and the ballrooms and even penetrating genteel households. This is the context in which the affray between the ship captains and Peter Dunican's gang must be situated; this is the context in which many of those who read the *Bee* would have placed it. No more than Governor W. C. C. Claiborne, when he posted militia in the ballrooms during Carnival 1804, could New Orleanians of the 1850s ignore the relationship between ethnicity, politics, violence, and Carnival.

4

Rex

MARDI GRAS 1872 was lively. Maskers came out in force, and some people thought their costumes were more than ordinarily grotesque, although, as usual, an estimated three-quarters of the revelers disguised themselves as "irrepressible plantation hands." But there were other costumes—for example, one man came as a knight, carrying a pasteboard shield. The "chief wonder," according to the *Republican*, was "where the boys came from. They scrambled under the legs of bystanders, to the imminent peril of their secure footing. They climbed up inaccessible awning posts, shinned up to the feet of the Clay statue, got up on window sills that overlooked the streets, ran after every cart and wagon containing maskers, slinked under the bellies of standing horses, and were in the way on every side, besides manifesting a great indisposition to clear out when told, and wherever they dared, making faces at policemen. . . ."

By mid-afternoon, crowds had gathered at the traditional spot, the Henry Clay statue at St. Charles and Canal. Clerks and other employees who had been given the afternoon off now augmented the morning revelers.[1]

Part of the excitement this Mardi Gras was the scheduled

appearance of a new Carnival personage. Edicts had been placed in newspapers and delivered to local authorities, all of them issued in the name of Rex, who called himself the king of Carnival. As the *Louisianian* observed, the edicts were designed to make the yearly masquerade "pleasurable and orderly." Rex instructed the city's mayor on his duties; ordered Governor Henry Clay Warmoth to close his office and "to disperse that riotous body known as the Louisiana State Legislature" at three o'clock; and directed that all private businesses be closed so that "none of our beloved subjects may be debarred from participating in the honors to be accorded their liege Sovereign." The *Louisianian* concluded, "There is no doubt that the amusements will this year be conducted on a grand and more orderly style than has obtained latterly. This mythical sovereign of the realm will doubtless be quietly obeyed." Thus the large crowds and the expectant gathering around the Henry Clay statue. The first Rex began his progress between three and four o'clock.[2]

It was a gaudy and wonderful display. Although the Rex parade was perhaps the best-planned daytime parade to date, and a harbinger of things to come, it also reveled in its impromptu grotesqueries and splendors. Rex—Lewis J. Salomon dressed as a king and riding on horseback—came with music, mounted police, a section of artillery, attendant lords, and a fatted ox. He led an estimated three hundred maskers. The marchers in the first division inevitably included white people masquerading as black people. The blackfacing this year was tinged with politics; several maskers impersonated legislators, and "one ambitious old Moke" paraded with the label "Our future Governor." Another set of maskers attracted particular attention, the organized group that called themselves "the Pack." This group, wearing white cotton stretched across light wooden frames, represented a deck of cards. They stopped to visit Mayor Flanders and presented Governor Warmoth and the grand duke Alexis each with a pack of cards. "The Pack is composed of gentlemen all fully identified with New Orleans," one newspaper explained.[3]

Next came the lord of the carriages, leading an estimated sixty carriages with maskers. "Feminine looking individuals aired their pedal extremities on the dash board and waved their handkerchieves to the crowded galleries. . . . Or they sat magnificently in the rear of their conveyances and made themselves sick smoking and partaking of other enjoyments particularly masculine." These may have been men dressed in women's clothes, a common Carnival practice, but more likely they were women dressed as men, a more disreputable Carnival tradition, one indulged in by the demimonde. In other carriages people dressed shabbily, in "gunny-bag suits imitating dress coats." Vans followed the carriages, including a hundred carts, milk wagons, and other vehicles. The lord of the horses led 120 mounted maskers, among them the Dan Rice cavalry from the Dan Rice circus, and young men on horseback, with brooms for lances and tin pots for helmets. A little political satire crept in here as it did so often during the parade: "One of the maskers rode on a mule nearly buried under a circular chapeau of the Napoleon time, and carried for a banner a Republican ticket made up in his own fashion." Among the riders was also "a gentlemen in a very red suit, and who was possessed of a face ugly and ferocious enough to frighten a common, low white man, let alone a respectable negro"; he represented "that mysterious order of negro exterminators, the K.K.K."

An "indiscriminated and miscellaneous rabble" followed the riders. There were people dressed as Indians, people blackfaced, people dressed as baboons, people wearing funny hats or dressed in cambric of garish colors. And there was a commercial element to the parade as well: this was too good an advertising opportunity for local businessmen to pass up. So one van showed a womanly figure laboring at a Singer sewing machine. Also among the marchers were Southern Express Company packages delivering themselves.[4]

Mardi Gras evening saw the usual round of balls, including a splendid one at the St. Charles, where an odd assortment of mythological, historical, and contemporary figures appeared, including Jupiter, Apollo, Peter the Hermit, Luther, Joan of Arc, Cleopatra, Mephistopheles, Achilles, Horace Greely, and an array of kings, earls, ghosts, gorillas, black people, and Irishmen. Louisiana Fire Engine Company Number Nineteen had their own ball at Turner Hall. There were also the usual petty crimes. The recorder, however, showed leniency to the "impecunious drunks who appeared before him, as His Majesty Rex had urged mercy upon sinners; warning them to obey both city ordinances and Rex's promulgations, he sent them out to enjoy the rest of carnival."[5]

Who was Rex? Tradition holds that the Rex parade stemmed from coincidence, that it was improvised because the grand duke Alexis of Russia, a scion of European royalty, visited New Orleans during Carnival 1872. New Orleanians cite this visit as the reason for the formation of the Krewe of Rex. Some public-spirited individuals, the story goes, felt obliged to provide truly magnificent entertainment for the duke, so they invented Rex and stage-managed his first parade. The story, however, is wrong.

The duke's visit did stimulate considerable excitement and civic display. Mayor Flanders and other prominent citizens greeted Alexis and his entourage when they arrived, arranging for a thirty-gun salute and for carriages to escort him to the St. Charles Hotel. When in the city, the grand duke attended the opera—he entered the theater during the Anvil Chorus of *Il Trovatore*, which the orchestra interrupted to play the Russian national anthem; he received six foreign consuls, most of them in their official uniforms; he went to two Mardi Gras balls—at the first, the orchestra interrupted their program at his entrance to play the Russian national anthem; he was serenaded by a band as he sat with Governor Warmoth on the piazza of his hotel; he visited the circus. Large crowds gazed on him. But the grand duke entered New Orleans lore when he watched the first Rex parade from a platform before city hall with his suite, the mayor, the governor, and General James Longstreet. Legend has it that when the parade reached city hall, the band played "If Ever I Cease to Love," the song that became Mardi Gras's theme. In fact, it played the Russian national anthem.[6]

Indeed, the duke received such lavish treatment that it occasioned grumbling. The *Louisianian* protested Americans groveling before a grand duke: "The Grand Duke Alexis is not much of a Republican, but he is more a man of the people than those who make professions of the fact." Pay Alexis "decent respect," but don't become a "fawning sycophant." The black editors read in the "snobbery" of their political enemies—the mayor and his party—values inimical to republicanism. Colonel Valery Sulakowski, formerly of the Fourteenth Louisiana Infantry, C.S.A., found the visit of the Russian autocrat offensive as well; a native-born Pole and a veteran of Kossuth's rebellion against Austria, he wanted to assault the duke on the streets.[7]

Alexis's role in Mardi Gras has always been portrayed as passive. He was either the dignified recipient of New Orleans's attentions or the slightly pompous, lovesick duke courting the mocking Miss Lydia Thompson. If the bands did play "If Ever I Cease to Love," a song Thompson made popular, it was to mock the duke in the traditional fashion of the charivari. Thompson herself was something of a carnivalesque figure—among other things, she played male roles, and once she and a fellow actress horsewhipped a Chicago newspaper editor—but her burlesque successfully fit the carnivalesque into commercial culture. Traditionally Alexis has been treated as a catalyst whose presence caused the creation of Rex, something with which he had nothing to do and which left him unaffected.[8]

Actually, Alexis had even less than that to do with the formation of Rex. The idea that Rex was a procession organized especially for the grand duke was developed after the fact. The notion of organizing the so-called promiscuous maskers—viewed both as rabble requiring discipline and as a natural Carnival resource awaiting exploitation—was an old one; indeed, it had been attempted during Mardi Gras 1871. When Lewis J. Salomon, the first Rex, discussed the parade's origins in 1921, he did not even mention Alexis. According to him, the purpose behind the first Rex parade was to "put some life into" Carnival, something particularly needed in the postwar era. He explained that "Carnivals were talked of as a tonic for the war-wearied South, but there were no street pageants, parades or things of that sort, just an occasional ball or dance." When E. C. Hancock, the managing editor of the New Orleans *Times*, suggested an organized daytime parade in January 1872, he appointed Salomon, the son of a private banker, to handle the money. Salomon had two weeks to raise the five thousand dollars that he estimated the parade would cost. Hancock publicized the coming of Rex through the *Times*, while Salomon collected one-hundred-dollar contributions from "all the public-spirited men and our friends." "'But what do you want $100 for, Lewis,' they would say and [he] would reply, 'I am going to make you a duke in the Carnival.'" Salomon called these "holdup calls."

Possibly because of his successful begging, the group elected Salomon king of the parade. Thus, organized Carnival, an activity later notorious for excluding Jews, had a Jewish monarch for its first Rex. Salomon dressed in a Richard III costume borrowed from a local theater. The parade had no floats, but it did have a theme: the Arabs. The dukes "were all mounted and wore flowing robes—almost like the Ku Klux Klan." Behind the self-appointed court of Rex came individual masqueraders and members of Carnival clubs. Almost inevitably, the old man's reminiscences in 1921 ended on the traditional eulogistic note: "Yes, the Carnivals in those days were the real thing, the people masked more promiscuously than they do now, and the spirit of revelry was absolutely unconfined."[9]

Salomon remembered Rex as the first true Carnival parade, which suggests either that he forgot Comus altogether or that he thought of it as belonging to a different category. Since Salomon was in his eighties at the time of the 1921 interview, it is certainly possible that his memory was unreliable, and that this accounts for the absence of both Alexis and Comus in his tale. It is equally possible that "Mardi Gras" was considered a daytime event, distinct from the nighttime parade of Comus. Newspapers in the 1850s, 1860s, and 1870s devoted separate columns to Mardi Gras and to Comus on Mardi Gras night. In any case, J. Curtis Waldo, another of Rex's original founders, also gave little prominence to the grand duke in his 1882 account of the creation of Rex.[10]

Rather than crediting the happenstance of the grand duke's visit, Salomon identified a perceived need for civic ritual as a "tonic for the war-wearied South" as the impetus behind the Rex parade. This "tonic" would soon give rise to civic boosterism, as Carnival became entwined with the New South rhetoric of sectional reconciliation and prosperity. But the people of the South required the "tonic" of pageantry and parade because of the defeat suffered during the Civil War. That there should be a relationship between Carnival and the Civil War is hardly obvious, yet the invention of Rex and the rise of what was called "organized Carnival" during the post-war era suggest that some New Orleanians sought release from mourning through celebration. For them, recovery from the war required the revitalization of Carnival. Furthermore, the assertion of the rule of Rex and the order that he brought to the crowd in the streets met a desire for a kind of symbolic victory amid actual defeat.

Later, many New Orleanians would deny that Mardi Gras was celebrated during the Civil War. This was only true if organized parades defined Carnival—which they never had in antebellum New Orleans. True, during the Civil War no organized procession marched on Mardi Gras night (the young men of Comus had joined the Confederate army), but such processions had come and gone before. To say that Mardi Gras could not take place without them was to redefine Carnival; it was to apply a late-nineteenth-century definition to the earlier folk festival. Furthermore, the absence of Comus and other parades did not mean that nobody in New Orleans wanted to parade; first the Confederate, then the federal authorities forbade parading during Carnival. During Carnival 1862, when New Orleans was still in rebel hands, the mayor and the city council outlawed processions and public masking: "No masquerade procession or masked individuals will be allowed to parade the streets of the city of New Orleans on TUESDAY, 4th day of March, 1862 (the same being Mardi Gras.)." The Union army, imposing martial law in May 1862, banned public gatherings. "All assemblages of persons in the street, either by day or night, tend to disorder and are forbidden."[11]

But during the federal occupation, the public held masked balls, and the Carnival bills at the theater continued as before; indeed, with a larger transient population seeking amusement than the city had ever seen before, they flourished. For example, the Orleans Theater presented a grand festival on Mardi Gras night 1863—with admission two dollars for men, one dollar for ladies. The Orleans Ball Room held a masked ball, and there were several other, small masquerade dances. In 1864, the Globe Ball Room boasted of its brass band and the elaborate list of dances that it would play: marches, polkas, quadrille, mazoorka, scottisch, lancers, waltzes, reels. And 1865 was much the same, with the resumption of special theatrical programs for Carnival. The St. Charles Theatre offered "the Streets of New York, a piece full of sensational incident and spectacular interest," more likely aimed at Northern soldiers and civilians than New Orleanians. After the play, the theater hosted a masked ball, "of which the promise is given that it shall be select without being cold and stiff, and abundantly gay without abusing festival privileges."[12]

Most important, promiscuous masking continued during the war years. In 1863, a Union soldier noted, "Today is Mardi Grasday and is celebrated by people dressing themselves up and making fools of themselves generally." As usual, children donned masks; and, as usual, "a few females of questionable standing" wore male clothing. With the rain and the flooded streets, there were not many people out, and, perhaps because of the high price of foodstuffs, for once there were no volleys of flour. Or maybe the celebration was subdued because federal troops, not local police, enforced the law that year. At least two masqueraders, P. Tobias and L. Wyman, ended up in provost court, where the judge fined them ten dollars each for fighting. In 1864, the Era predicted a repeat of 1863—"Africans" and children would costume "and there [would] be crowds of disreputable women in male attire, or in gaudy and tinseled garments of their own wear, mingling in the throng, swearing like troopers, drinking like tops, and bearded like pards."

The next day, the Era proclaimed—surely without a double

meaning—that "the orgies of Mardi Gras were revived yesterday, and the day was more generally devoted to pleasure and enjoyment than for several years past." Once again, there was flour thrown, maskers on foot, horseback, and in carriages, little boys scampering. There was even a tendency toward organization. The maskers promenaded on Canal Street in particular, and spectators gathered around the Henry Clay statue to cheer them as they passed. But, as the *Bee* pointed out, "There appeared no unity of action to give effect or make a grand display as in former times." The *Era*, however, boasted that Mardi Gras was lively without any squabbles or fighting—"which was not wont to be the case, in days when the morals of the city were judged by the chivalric standard."[13]

Nathan B. Middlebrook, a soldier from Connecticut, had just arrived in the city when Mardi Gras 1864 took place: "It put me in mind of the Fourth of July north when the Fantasticks were in vogue[,] only on a large scale. The streets was full of Masked faces and there dress was acording to the mask. Some were [dressed] magnificent." Middlebrook believed, erroneously, that it had been General Benjamin Butler, not General Nathaniel Banks, who had canceled Mardi Gras the year before: "They came out as usual and he had them all arrested which I think was hardly right as it has always been the custom to celebrate that day, the citizens are down on Butler but they like Gen. Banks the present commander of this department." Middlebrook declared, and presumably many other Union soldiers shared the sentiment, "I [saw] more fun that day than I have since I came in the army."[14]

Such fun continued with increased vigor after the war. In 1867, *L'Avenir* reported that every possible place was transformed into a ballroom for Mardi Gras night. People returned to the streets during Mardi Gras day, cavorting in grotesque costumes, some traditional, some not. Several of the newly favored costumes had clear political overtones. In 1869, one visitor noted that Yankee carpetbaggers and "enormous apes" were two of the costumes favored by maskers in the streets: "Some of these apes went about in waggons, whence they sprang upon the balconies of the houses, and one of them jumped upon a waggon laden with cotton bales, and so terrified the negro driver by his sudden apparition, that he took to flight, whereupon the ape seized the reins and drove the mule-team some blocks before the driver recovered his senses."

In 1870, the mildly censorious New Orleans *Republican* commented that "the utter paucity of inventions" among the maskers "was amply shown by the astonishing number of Ethiopian minstrels." The editors complained that "character dressing appeared to be above their comprehension and the prevailing idea seemed to be that the most fun could be got out of a few old rags thrown over the shoulders and a cheap mask perched on the nose." But the *Republican* also acknowledged, "The fact that our citizens so generally participated in the celebration is ample proof that Mardi Gras is a vent quite necessary to the pent-up passions of our people."[15]

This tradition of masking was the rough material that the organizers of Rex planned to mold into a parade; the "pent-up passions" they wished to direct and to restrain. The vitality of the festival in the streets would be used to energize a new parade while the new parade would reorganize the streets in favor of order and hierarchy. The Krewe of Rex could have used Comus for their model but they chose a different approach, one influenced by the old Mardi Gras processions. They took the atomistic, promiscuous maskers and organized them into a parade. Thus, they imposed order onto disorder, hierarchy—complete with a mock king—onto individualism, planning onto spontaneity. This may have been a trivial arena to celebrate the values of order, hierarchy, and planning, but the values were very much those of their class and times, not just in the South, but in Gilded Age America. What is ironic is that they did this in a context that traditionally celebrated the opposite of these values, that celebrated disorder. Like Comus, they also helped change Carnival from something in which people participated or not on an individual basis into something in which audience and actors were clearly delineated. In 1872, the organizers of Rex asserted the usefulness of Carnival as a civic ritual and claimed both Mardi Gras day and the central spaces of the city for the respectable.

As if suspicious of the organizers' designs, the New Orleans *Republican,* a newspaper owned by Michael Hahn, who came from an old Louisiana German family, complained on Ash Wednesday 1872: "The matter with this procession is simply this: There was too much order about it. Confusion, disorder and discord, both of colors and of sounds, is the great beauty of a carnival procession, which does not intend to represent a single idea, nor to tell a story, but means to play and make fun. Every crowd should have gone on its own hook." The editorial continued, "To control a carnival procession by general orders defeats the object of the day. Hence the procession yesterday was a disappointment." The paper also complained that the parade was too slow and stopped too often, subjecting the costumes to scrutiny under which they could not bear up. Five years later the *Republican* observed of the new, reformed Carnival, "Mardi Gras is too high toned for poor people."[16]

Republicans were not the only ones to complain. Some old New Orleanians continued to dissent from the new Carnival order. As late as 1876, one editor protested that St. Rex's "showy military parade" did not "replace . . . the old time Mardi-Gras procession of maskers, in which hundreds of our best citizens participated." And in 1882, the society column of the *Times,* saying that individual maskers had been "the strictly carnival feature of the day," argued that "the magnificent parades of Rex and of Comus are yearly increasing in splendor—but I am afraid they are doing so at the expense of the general jollity of the home public . . . The masses, who formerly deported in the attire of monks, or devils, or princes of the realm, are gradually dropping back into the ranks of the quieter spectators."[17]

Rex, however, had come to stay. It would not be too many years before the self-proclaimed king of Carnival, the new usurper, would be identified as the essence of Carnival throughout the United States. With utmost composure, Rex had begun issuing

orders from the very first; forever after he insisted on his right to
rule. Rex created his parade by inviting all maskers to join him. But
for those who wished to organize Carnival, this cheap, effective,
and time-honored method had drawbacks. It was hard to control
these promiscuous maskers, hard to ensure that they would maintain
the dignity of the mock sovereign. Almost as soon as Rex invented
the daytime parade, he began to reform it. For example, the advertising element had drawn national criticism; indeed, Edward King's
sympathetic articles on New Orleans in *Scribner's* had complained of
it. So in 1874, Rex ordered advertisers out of the parade unless their
shows were novel.

In 1876, St. Rex continued to urge the reform of Mardi Gras.
He maintained the ban on flour—thus substituting his own mock
authority for the legal but failed authority of the city; he prohibited
maskers from marching out of their "proper division"; and he excluded "all indelicate or improper displays" from his parade. In sum,
the krewe wanted to transform the old, vulgar street festival into
something seemly. Individual maskers, however, continued to use
the day and Rex's new parade as an opportunity to assert their
vulgar, sexual, disrespectful natures. This was hardly what an elite
who wished to reestablish social hierarchy wanted to see. Rex finally
drew the logical conclusion. If the promiscuous maskers could not
be disciplined, they would have to be eliminated. In 1877, Rex
prohibited "promiscuous maskers" from participating in his Royal
Pageant. What had started as a way of organizing maskers now
excluded them. In order to march with Rex, maskers had to organize
themselves and apply in advance for permission—and keep in their
assigned places. Advertising vans were also forbidden.[18]

Rex required a more permanent organization for planning
Mardi Gras on the streets than the one that had so quickly but
successfully put together the 1872 parade. After the success of that
initial parade, the men of Rex made more businesslike arrangements.
Using "patents of nobility as Dukes of the Realm, emblazoned with
the seals of the State of Louisiana, city of New Orleans, and the
King of Carnival," as lures, they encouraged "the merchants and

bankers intrusted with our city's welfare" to form a public sustaining organization for the "secret" krewe, the Royal Host. The Royal Host's role was to finance the krewe so they could put on more elaborate Carnival shows. In 1873, with the aid of the Royal Host, the krewe sent an agent to Paris to buy costumes in advance, and rented the Exposition Hall for three nights. The patents of nobility were now "found framed in the offices of our most prominent business houses." At a time when many white Louisianians were complaining that they had no chance to participate in government, they took on the tasks and glory of government by organizing a fictitious realm.[19]

Besides organizing the promiscuous maskers into a parade and creating the Royal Host, Rex invented other new traditions. Starting in 1874, Rex enlivened the day before Mardi Gras, Lundi Gras, by his court's shipboard arrival, in this case on a federal revenue cutter, the *John A. Dix*. By 1876, shops sold Carnival flags, which was fortunate, since St. Rex had ordered that all houses be decorated for Mardi Gras that year. The characters who marched with St. Rex— the lord admiral, the oriental soldiers, the Boeuf Gras (a fat ox symbolizing epicurean pleasure)—became traditional almost as soon as they were invented. And Rex's grandiose claims of ruling the city, made at a time when many parties and factions asserted such claims and hardly a governing institution possessed sufficient legitimacy to function, established him and his krewe as Carnival's sovereign, at least in the eyes of the growing tourist trade.[20]

The creators of Rex and other krewes, the 1870s and 1880s organizers of lavish parades and exclusive balls, inaugurated an ongoing institution. Or, if we adopt the terminology of other historians of nineteenth-century culture, they invented a tradition. Eric Hobsbawm explains, "'Invented tradition' is taken to mean a set of practices, normally governed by overtly or tacitly accepted rules and of a ritual or symbolic nature, which seek to inculcate certain values and norms of behavior by repetition, which automatically implies continuity with the past." He goes on to observe that invented traditions "are responses to novel situations which take the form of reference to old situations, or which establish their own past by quasi-obligatory repetition." This fits Reconstruction and late-nineteenth-century Carnival precisely. Hobsbawm also says that the invention of traditions should "occur more frequently when a rapid transformation of society weakens or destroys the social patterns for which 'old' traditions had been designed. . . ." Emancipation, Confederate defeat, the political empowerment of black men, and economic distress indeed constituted a profound transformation in New Orleans and the South at large. The white elite of New Orleans responded violently to change, but they also responded creatively, by establishing new cultural forms.[21]

Although its greatest significance lay in the invention of new Carnival traditions, the 1872 Rex parade also possessed political overtones. By edict, Rex shut down the Republican state legislature and the Republican governor's office. Throughout Reconstruction, Rex offered himself as a mock ruler at a time when many white New Orleanians denied the legitimacy of their lawful government. Rex even called on U.S. troops to uphold his authority—like some Reconstruction Republican governor. For unknown reasons, troops stationed near New Orleans were willing to dress up as Arabian artillerists and Egyptian soldiers and serve under Rex. Perhaps they enjoyed the disguise; in any case, there was a rumor that their barracks displayed a flag given to Rex's troops by the ladies of New Orleans—ladies unlikely to have honored federal troops in their normal guise. At this time in Louisiana politics, the creation of a mock realm imbued with fanciful legitimacy was implicitly political. But other revelers brought politics into Carnival more explicitly. The combination of Carnival license and street theater proved irresistible to New Orleanians with political points to make.

5

Comus

IN 1873, the Mystic Krewe of Comus presented its first and most elaborate parade of political satire. The krewe mocked radical Republicans as "Missing Links to Darwin's Origins of the Species," thereby deftly standing in opposition to two of the time's most progressive strands of thought. Each member of the krewe marched inside a huge papier-mâché figure with easily recognizable features. Grant, for example, was a tobacco grub, Benjamin Butler—"Beast" or "Spoons" Butler to New Orleanians—was a hyena. The carpetbagger was a fox with human features, "the cunning fox who joins with the Coon." And the black man was portrayed as the Missing Link himself, half-human, half-gorilla, playing a banjo and wearing a pink collar, a "simian Cupid" seeking a Psyche for his "nobler mate." The krewe held up the contemporary political and social order as unnatural.[1]

Local newspapermen delighted in explaining that this was all in keeping with survival of the fittest, and they made pointed remarks as to how the concept might best be applied. The remarks were not difficult to decipher: black people and Republicans were subhuman, and the fittest, the better elements, would not only survive but prevail. Maybe this was a common nineteenth-century phenomenon—Social Darwinism with no accompanying belief in Darwin. The tableaux presented that night ended with the Missing Link crowned king and the king of Comus defying him. The satire was so popular that the next year Momus, a recently organized mystic krewe, copied it and presented "The Coming Races." Two years later a Memphis krewe used a Darwinian theme for the Carnival in that city.[2]

Comus also satirized the Metropolitan Police, even though the Metropolitans marched with them as an advance guard. The Metropolitan Police were racially mixed, state-appointed, and viewed as agents of radical Reconstruction. That night the insulted police refused to force a passage through the crowds at Canal Street for the Mystic Krewe; at that intersection, the crowd jeered at Comus and prevented their march. Manifestly, the crowd rejected Comus's vision of their centrality to Carnival; perhaps they rejected their political vision as well.

Significantly, many of the men who satirized the Metropolitans and tried to damage their reputation by this display in the streets would soon employ more violent means: the next month, well-led mobs besieged police stations throughout New Orleans. The figures of the Metropolitans in the parade functioned as effigies that are burned in mock executions—the ridicule was the prelude to an actual assault. Indeed, the political satire of 1873 was only a first step in the efforts of white New Orleanians to overturn Reconstruction. Carnival was not simply a joke. The men who made up the Carnival krewes also made up the White League, the paramilitary organization that battled the Metropolitan Police in September 1874. A proud captain of the Mystic Krewe later boasted that every member of the clubs traditionally associated with the krewes—Pickwick, Boston, Chalmette, and Louisiana—capable of bearing arms fought with the White League.[3]

The Mystic Krewe of Comus made its reappearance very soon after the war. In reduced circumstances, members celebrated Mardi Gras 1866, when they had to march without the black torch-carriers and the police guard to which they had been accustomed. Whether they felt humbled or outraged, they presented a series of tableaux with a serious and pathetic message. The audience viewed War and his attendants Destruction, Grief, Strife, and Terror; Comus had lost some of its original members to the war. The krewe followed the tableau of War with three others: Peace and her accompanying Industry, Commerce, Science, Mechanism, Agriculture, History, and Art; a vision of the Future, which showed both Peace and Prosperity; and, at the end, the Court of Comus, explicitly bringing humor to the evening's display but also reigning over the earlier visions of War, Peace, and the Future. The young veterans—and Comus was a veterans organization—meant the display as a gesture of reconciliation, but they also defined what they thought the postwar world should be and who they thought should rule. The local newspapers proudly proclaimed that Comus, with this Mardi Gras presentation, expressed the sentiments of the best elements in New Orleans.[4]

Why did Comus return? Arguably, its return was the single most significant event in the shaping of New Orleans Carnival. Its original appearance, if never repeated, would have left it simply another example of the ephemeral antebellum parade. If Comus had failed to reappear during the period immediately following the Civil War—if the people of New Orleans had rejected the notion that organizing an elaborate Carnival parade was a wise use of civic energies and money—it would not have been at all surprising. Yet Comus returned.

The Comus parade and tableaux created a cultural form through which ideas could be asserted. The English folklore parade of 1859 was an early example. During Reconstruction, Comus would take a political stand in support of white supremacy. In 1866, the reorganizers of Comus recognized its expressive potential. And Comus 1866 did have a message, almost a contradictory one: the desirability of peace amid the pain of defeat. Still, it seems unlikely that members of Comus reorganized with a conscious intention of creating a form through which to express what they had learned since Carnival 1861.

The Civil War years were crucial, however, to the reemergence of Comus. The krewe was only one of many fantastic Southern organizations. Others are better known and have a less savory reputation—for example, the Ku Klux Klan, originally formed as a social organization of veterans. In the Klan, former Confederates masked themselves as ghosts. In Comus, they also donned fabulous disguises, although within the context of the old Carnival tradition. One way to express the inward transformation caused by war and defeat was to transform one's outward appearance. More important than the disguises, however, was the organization itself, the camaraderie it offered. The Seventh Louisiana Volunteer Infantry had many soldiers from the Pickwick Club and, thus, from Comus. During the war, these men had grown emotionally dependent on the men they fought with, developing profound loyalties to their fellow soldiers and to their companies, regiments, and armies. As these bonds fragmented after Appomattox, the postwar world must have looked a lonely place indeed. Comus was one of many attempts to re-create the fellowship of the war.[5]

The return of Comus was a momentous event in the history of Carnival in New Orleans. But the Comus parade was just the first of the new, preplanned parades, and it was not the only one to carry some ideological baggage. Reconstruction Carnival saw the advent of numerous marching clubs, of the Twelfth Night Revelers and the Knights of Momus, which initially paraded on New Year's Eve. And after 1873, anti-Republican propaganda continued to be a major theme in organized Carnival until the end of Reconstruction.

The 1873 Comus parade had precedent. Even before Reconstruction, Comus had used its parade as a political theater. In 1860, the Comus parade promoted Unionism. Both in the street and on the stage, the krewe presented "historic sculpture." Before the eyes of their fellow citizens they paraded living statues of great men in American history. There were explorers—Columbus, Cabot, Vespucci, Cartier, de Soto, De La Salle, Hennepin, Hudson, as well as colonists—Bienville, Penn, John Smith, Stuyvesant, and, daringly enough in the context of the times, the Pilgrims, forebears of the Yankees. Fireeaters at the Varieties Theatre commented that "the

Landing at Plymouth Rock was one of the most unfortunate events that ever happened for the country." Indeed, it was hard to see Plymouth Rock celebrated and not think of the arrival of John Brown's ancestors.

Comus also portrayed Washington and other heroes of the Revolution, as well as Andrew Jackson, victor of the battle of New Orleans. They presented Henry Clay, Daniel Webster, and John C. Calhoun, the leading politicians of the previous generation, and the Compromise of 1833, even though some in the audience censured the political connotations. Clay, Webster, and Calhoun were obvious reminders of the virtues of sectional compromise, a weighty subject indeed for a Carnival procession. But the whole parade, really, was a plea for sectional compromise. Comus pointed to past heroes and events shared by all Americans, to the same shared heritage that Abraham Lincoln would evoke, equally fruitlessly, in his first inaugural address. Comus's message was well adapted to a city as diverse as New Orleans, whose citizens were as likely to be from Stuyvesant's New York, Penn's Pennsylvania, or Pilgrim New England as they were from John Smith's Virginia or Bienville's Louisiana. Through Comus spoke the voice of the conservative South, the commercial South, the Unionist South. Comus, after all, was led by cotton factors and commission merchants. In a few months, New Orleans would vote heavily in favor of John Bell and his Constitutional Union Party in the presidential election of 1860. Comus and popular sentiment were in agreement.[6]

But if Comus's 1860 political statement supported the Union, its 1873 parade opposed Reconstruction. And Comus was just one of the krewes that turned the Carnival parade and tableaux into a theater of political protest. The newly organized Twelfth Night Revelers had preceded Comus in January 1873; later parades—most significantly that of Momus in 1877—also mocked the Republican Party and the goals of Reconstruction. Indeed, the 1870s were the most overtly political years in the history of Carnival.

Like Comus, the Twelfth Night Revelers burlesqued the Republican Party. Political conditions in January 1873 were well worth commenting on from any viewpoint. After a remarkably fraudulent election the previous fall, both John D. McEnery, the Democratic candidate for governor, and William Pitt Kellog, the Republican candidate, claimed to have won. Both men took the oath of office that month, and each of them had an assembly calling itself the Louisiana State Legislature that recognized their authority. The state returning board, which had the power to rectify this mess, had itself split into two rival factions. The federal government finally supported Kellog. Carnival took place amid this confusion. When the Twelfth Night Revelers paraded, their presentation, "The World of Audubon," mocked local politicians, with the float "The Crows in Council" meant as a dig at the Republican state legislature.[7]

Even Rex, that mildest of krewes, was unable to stay out of political discussion. Newspaper editors played at taking Rex as one more plausible contender for the disputed governor's office. The editors of the *Republican*, right in the thick of the political wars, described Rex as "a monarch of unknown qualities and antecedents," who issued "divers proclamations of a revolutionary government, smacking somewhat of the McEnery tone." Rex, they complained, ordered "the people of this free State to do and leave undone various matters in a manner that clearly indicates for a time at least the absence of a republican form of government." All of this was very jocular, of course, but, at a time when the democratic nature of Louisiana's government was hotly debated, this was joking with a point. In Louisiana, "the stars and stripes shake wonderingly in the wind under the lee of Rex's more pretentious and orientally gorgeous banner." "A stranger from the provinces," the editors jested, "seeing this mysterious imperial standard lazily floating in the breeze everywhere and across every street in the city, might well be pardoned for believing that a sudden conversion to a joint despotism had settled the long vexed Louisiana question."[8]

The *Republican* editors were not the only ones who contemplated Rex and thought of Louisiana's political situation. On Mardi Gras, Rex arrived at city hall a little before noon. The mayor received him, gave him the key to the city, and presented him with a message that the chamberlain read aloud. The message extolled Rex, the "august and gracious sovereign," as coming from "classic lands where your reign is glorious with the stirring memories of a thousand years, unvexed by revolt, undimmed by the shadow of disloyalty." Thus the mayor distinguished between Rex's never-never-land and the South's recent experience of rebellion and war. We do not know what Rex—or, rather, E. B. Wheelock—made of this pointed speech. The chamberlain read his prepared response, in which Rex promised to return again the next year, and explained that "the exercise of the powers of absolute sovereignty during so many centuries . . . has not dulled the generous enthusiasm of my heart." Then, after drinking champagne with the mayor and breaking the glass on the pavement, Rex had the earl marshall of the empire arrest the mayor and General J. B. Walton, who were conveyed in an open carriage, "that while they graced the triumph of Rex, they might themselves gaze on the universal sentiment of loyalty of the inhabitants." Once again, Carnival figures performed a playful but pointed political act—the mock arrest of rulers when the legitimacy of the state's ruling bodies was being questioned.[9]

No place in the South was more crucial to the Northern decision to implement congressional Reconstruction than the city of New Orleans. Louisiana had been the site of wartime Reconstruction under Lincoln's leadership. In the immediate postwar period, sometimes called "Self-Reconstruction" because white Southerners still made the critical decisions, the laws by which Louisiana regulated black liberties and black labor raised the question of whether or not Southern white people could be trusted to deal in good faith with their former slaves. What shocked the North even more—and decided the question in the negative—was the 1866 New Orleans Riot, which might more appropriately be called the "New Orleans massacre," when a mob attacked a state constitutional convention, killing thirty-seven people, most of them black. After the establishment of congressional Reconstruction, the violence of Louisiana politics disturbed the nation, while its political infighting and corruption fascinated and mystified it. New Orleans sponsored the paramilitary White League; the League and its allies fought another antiblack, anti-Republican battle in 1874—the "White League riot," the "battle of Liberty Place," the "battle of September 14th"—which earned New Orleans a reputation as one of the most violent and restive cities in the South. And yet in 1877, Louisiana was one of the three Southern states key to working out the compromise that effectively ended Reconstruction. Furthermore, Louisiana had exceptionally radical black leaders during Reconstruction, particularly African-Creole leaders who based their demands for political equality on the legacies of both the American and the French revolutions. No Southern city had a greater impact on the course of Reconstruction than New Orleans, Louisiana.[10]

It was also during the 1870s that New Orleanians created Carnival in its modern form. Until Reconstruction, New Orleans had elements of a Carnival tradition, but the celebration remained a folk festival. From those beginnings, from the new cultural needs that war, defeat, and changes in the social order created—and from the political and economic turmoil and racial tension in the city, New Orleans's white elite fashioned its Carnival. This was the period during which Rex and Momus first paraded and the now-traditional, socially exclusive balls were instituted. Men who spent their energies organizing resistance, sometimes armed resistance, to the state and national governments also found time to organize Carnival. New Orleans Mardi Gras in its modern form was thus a child of Reconstruction and counterreaction.

Consider Carnival 1875—the first to be held after the White League riot. That year the krewes withdrew from Carnival as a form of political protest. The White League had been active—murderously active—throughout the state, not just in New Orleans. Federal troops under General Philip H. Sheridan guarded the January 1875 session of the legislature. Sheridan denounced the lawless white supremacists as "banditti." He hoped that either Congress or the president would authorize him to proceed against the leaders of the White League. When rumors of assassination plots reached the general, he responded by saying, "I am not afraid."[11]

At a time when Carnival was political, these events did not pass unnoticed. In 1875, Comus, Rex, and other krewes canceled their Carnival displays. The Conservative Democratic *Bulletin* said that "it would have been like the decoration of a corpse to hold a carnival in this stricken city at this time." And the *Daily Picayune* observed, "The misrepresentations and oppressions" that the people of New Orleans "have suffered have driven all ideas of mirth from their minds, and with one accord they will keep the day as a 'black letter day,' to which the memories of a brilliant past will add a thicker gloom." On January 6, 1875, "joy having fled for a season from our happy city," the lord of misrule ordered the Twelfth Night Revelers to postpone their celebration. The lord censured the "armed hosts," who had become "interpreters of public opinion," and the slander of official orders—referring to Sheridan's condemnation of the White League. The Revelers sent the cake already ordered for their festival to St. Vincent's Orphan Asylum. They told those who ran the orphanage that they hoped "those under [their] charge may enjoy a privilege denied those of older growth."[12]

The krewes canceled their parades, but the masked balls continued. On Mardi Gras itself, people once again "instinctively" assembled on Canal Street, even though they were under "the crushing weight of despotism." The *Bulletin* claimed that only four or five six-year-old boys appeared masked, wearing the traditional dominoes. The *Republican*, on the opposite side of the political fence, saw both the children and a few "lewd women." Jean Marie Guelle, a razor and knife grinder, was bolder than Comus in his defiance of authority. He masqueraded as Sheridan himself, wearing a mocking sign that read, "I am not afraid." More provocatively, he also carried a Springfield rifle marked L.N.G.—Louisiana National Guard—and a cartridge box marked M.B.—Metropolitan Brigade. These were certainly police issue, spoils of the previous September's battle. Governor Kellog had issued a proclamation offering a reward for stolen state arms, including Springfield rifles marked in just that way. Despite the crowd's attempt to stop them, the police arrested Guelle and charged him with possession of stolen property. The police claimed that he had threatened them with the rifle and its fixed bayonet; they also claimed that he was drunk and subject to fits of insanity. The New Orleans *Bulletin* called the affray "almost a riot."[13]

By 1876, political tension in Louisiana had subsided, and New Orleans celebrated Carnival in what was becoming the traditional manner. Even so, conservative political burlesque kept its place in the festivities. The Twelfth Night Revelers returned with a parade followed by a ball at the Varieties and tableaux of the March of Ages. These showed time moving from chaos to the end of time with what were now customary digs at evolution. The tableau entitled "the Present" included "sarcastic allusion to the present age in this state": a "herculean negro," backed by a large cannon, facing the wrong way. It was what the *Bulletin* called "the old political tale." ("The Future" showed Minerva overseeing Amazons—a jab at women's rights.) The lord of misrule distributed programs to the crowd explaining the parade; the *Bulletin* commented, "The general public generally speaking is not up to the classics, and when these pageants are understood they are more appreciated." Clearly, a rift between the folk tradition and the new elite krewes—manifested when Comus's first parade employed allusions to *Paradise Lost*—had solidified.[14]

In 1877 Momus provided the final and most extreme example of political satire in Reconstruction Carnival. Even some conservative New Orleanians regretted this Carnival's satire, because it seemed so unnecessary: the compromise being concocted to settle the disputed Hays-Tilden election was fated to end Reconstruction in Louisiana. The parade of Momus, which presented "Hades," was so ferociously antiadministration in its portrayals of Grant, Frederick Douglass, Sherman, James G. Blaine, Sheridan, and others that Louisiana Republicans suggested its organizers be arrested. The *Republican* exploded in rage, printing criticism after criticism of Momus. "Men from all parts of the country are preparing to pay a visit to this city to witness the next parade of Momus," read one. "They do not often have a chance to sit on a cold curb stone till twelve o'clock at night waiting to see American institutions insulted." Fortunately, they claimed, the displays were so shoddy and cheap that the parade was a failure. Army and navy officers stationed in New Orleans who contributed men and resources to Carnival, particularly the Rex parade, demanded some sort of apology. Otherwise, they refused to participate.[15]

Perhaps the threat was persuasive. In any case, at the request of local army officers, the Krewe of Rex denounced Momus's anti-Republican parade. And Francis T. Nicholls, the Democratic contender for the governorship and probably a member of one of the krewes himself, claimed that the "sentiment of the whole community is opposed to what occurred at the celebration Thursday. It was the act of a few private individuals entirely unauthorized and unknown, and universally condemned and regretted." And the *Times* also reproached Momus. Suddenly, it seems, the best elements of society became anonymous culprits; in fact, the organizers were well-known New Orleanians whose only crime in the eyes of the elite was needlessly turning the attention of the federal government back to New Orleans at a time when conservative victory was all but assured. The Momus reception committee—the "few private individuals"—included some of the most respectable and best-known men of the city, including E. D. White, the future justice of the U.S. Supreme Court. According to rumor, the White League had organized the display. Apparently the Comus parade, with its theme "the Aryan Race," was less strident than its younger counterpart.[16]

Carnival allowed men of violence a means of communicating their view of events. Did Carnival also encourage the violence to which they turned in 1874? As the Civil War had already trained men to violence, blaming Carnival for their willingness to use it is foolish. The krewes, by bringing young men together to plan and celebrate Carnival, helped develop a sense of solidarity among them that made coordinated action easier. Uniting these men, Carnival played its integrative role. However useful Carnival was for mocking Republicans and calling their legitimacy into question, it certainly ran a poor third to politics and violence as the principal method for white supremacists. These Louisianians were remarkably willing to use the foulest means—apparently without any notion that such means compromised their honor or their decency—to overthrow Reconstruction, because they believed that the new regime lacked all legitimacy. To be sure, Carnival ridicule hardly created this belief. But it reflected it and it advertised it just as successfully as it advertised Werlein's pianos.[17]

Comus in 1873, the prohibition of Carnival in 1875, and Momus's presentation of Republicans in hell were only the most blatant examples of political Carnival. Even promiscuous maskers came dressed as carpetbaggers. Yet only one side in the heady political debates took its cause to the streets in motley. Carnival propaganda seems to have been exclusively white supremacist. Republicans might utter a few Carnival platitudes, recognize it as a holiday, and adorn a reviewing platform, but they failed to seize it as an opportunity for relaying their views.

The Republicans simply could not master the cultural forms necessary to communicate to New Orleanians. In the middle of the nineteenth century—a century of progress—and after a unifying war, they did not consider using traditions they deemed parochial. In fact, they sometimes did the opposite, speaking in a Northern, Protestant, modern voice to the citizens of New Orleans. For example, the *Republican* called the Catholic practice of wearing ashes on Ash Wednesday debasing and humiliating. This was an odd insult to offer to the large Catholic population, white and black, of New Orleans. But the *Republican* was the newspaper that also warned Louisianians of a Confederate-Catholic conspiracy to control the political power and religious faith of the freed people.[18]

These reformers regarded Mardi Gras as more than just plain foolishness; it was wastefulness. In 1870, the New Orleans *Republican* condemned the display of the Twelfth Night Revelers. "Had one-half the amount of money expended by the Revelers been devoted to the purchase of bread for the poor, all the bakers in the city would have had a big job." A year later the editors observed that the traditional Carnival in the streets "[was] not in accordance with the genius of the American people." Before the war, as the "Northern element" in the city grew, masquerading had been confined principally to the lower classes; now Comus had revived "the old processional features of the day," but they could expect that to continue only "while the association lasts." The parade of Comus was "the last remnant of the old custom." The *Republican* advised, "Let us enjoy it while we may"—clearly believing that that would not be long. In 1872, the *Republican* did admit that Rex would probably be good for the tourist trade. In general, however, they would prefer New Orleans to become more American.[19]

The vocabulary of Carnival was not one that most Republicans could learn. Some were shrewd enough to see the relationship between Mardi Gras and their political woes. In 1872, the editors of the *Louisianian*, a black Republican paper, at least proposed using Carnival parades for radical political purposes. Unfortunately, they had no real intention of organizing such a parade.[20] What these editors called "Our Mardi Gras Programme" would have been largely an in-house affair—a commentary on the confusion within the fractious Republican Party as much as a challenge to the Democrats. Their parade on paper mocked one faction of Louisiana Republicans and the Democrats with whom they had expediently allied themselves. The *Louisianian* supported Henry Clay Warmoth, Louisiana's carpetbagger governor. His wing of the party was opposed by the Custom House faction, so called because their patronage was centered in federal appointments, of which the most important was collector of the port.[21]

First in "Our Mardi Gras Programme" would come "the soreheads of the Republican Party with their heads bound up in consolatory editorials from the *Times*, vinegar and brown paper emanations from the *Bee*, with a chorus of growls in the way of music." They would be followed by "a model of the *Wilderness* with no Barr to command her, and the Democratic Senators together with the colored Republican Senators practicing before the eyes of the people, social equality." This second representation would have a motto as well—"We're ready to swallow the nigger, if we only get him coated."

At the time, the anti-Warmoth alliance also included black

Republicans under Creole black leadership who were appalled by Warmoth's tendency to appoint conservative white Louisianians to public office, by his refusal to support desegregation, and by the centralization of power in the governor's hands. Furthermore, the white Democrats had allied with the anti-Warmoth forces—both the patronage-fueled Custom House faction and willy-nilly some black radicals. Hence the *Louisianian*'s gibes at the joining of black senators with Democratic ones.

Other proposed floats included "Ray's Body Guard, consisting of the State House Law on crutches, Ray's Railroad drawn by a mule, emblazoned with the figures $546,000 for me"; "a coffin with the dead Levee Shed bill encased therein"; and "the dead Warehouse Bill on a gibbet." The last three referred to the Custom House faction's notorious corruption. For example, the dead Levee Shed bill was yet another anomaly of Louisiana politics. It was a boondoggle proposed by the Custom House faction, and Warmoth had killed it twice. First he had vetoed it. Then, when it was passed despite his veto, he simply refused to let the Treasury issue the bonds.

Another float would represent "United States Marshal Packard, with an enormous key, looking for a hall to hold the Convention in, with half a dozen doors open, not one of which he can procure." The motto for this was: "There are none so blind as those who will not see." The Custom House was to be shown propped up by bayonets, and swarms of idle government workers, from street-sweeps to tax collectors, were to be exhibited; "the dark lantern of the Democracy" was to be carried by "outs of every shade and degree," marked "K.W.C. and 76." (K.W.C. stood for Knights of the White Camellia, Louisiana's own version of the Ku Klux Klan.) There was also to be a representation of "Sambola and the red shirts with knives in their teeth," the accompanying motto being "Let's organize the Senate."

The Custom House faction had used armed troops to keep the Warmoth faction out of the 1871 Republican Convention; Stephen B. Packard, the head of the Custom House faction and a U.S.

Marshall, had had Warmoth, Lt. Governor P. B. S. Pinchback, and members of the state legislature arrested that January. Making bail, Warmoth in turn had used the Metropolitan Police and the state militia to secure the state house. Two rival legislatures met simultaneously. In Reconstruction Louisiana, intraparty conflict was as nasty as interparty conflict. Indeed, President Grant commented on Louisiana politics: "The muddle down there is almost beyond my fathoming."[22]

"Our Mardi Gras Programme" was a rare and probably unique case of the Republicans' using the new theater of Carnival to express their point of view; sadly enough, they directed their satire primarily against other Republicans. The parade appeared only on paper. Even though some Republicans recognized that their enemies manipulated Carnival, they did not try to employ the same tricks, preferring instead to complain about the Carnival representations and misrepresentations that their opponents put forth. During a period of political chicanery and deliberate violence, putting together Carnival parades must have struck them as frivolous and foolish. They should have wondered why their opponents bothered to organize Mardi Gras processions while establishing paramilitary leagues.

Conservative white New Orleanians revived the Carnival tradition, innovated within it, and used it as a theater of protest. In contrast, in Trinidad's postemancipation society, Carnival was taken over by the freed people while the former masters avoided the streets. In much of the New World, Carnival became regarded as a black holiday. But in New Orleans, white conservatives dominated Carnival. They did not relinquish the festivity as a cultural form, as a way of communicating. Neither, it must be added, did the city's black population. But Carnival in its organized form was the product of white reaction.[23]

The New Orleans *Republican* was expressing scorn when it explained that, during Carnival, "the fictitious tyrannies of politics are forgotten in the blazing government of the Lord of Misrule." Just because its editors—or the modern historian—cannot see the Reconstruction experiment in bi-racial democracy as "tyranny" does not mean that there were not many white New Orleanians who sincerely believe it was such. The *Republican* hit upon the fact that for them Carnival functioned as it did in many other societies, as "the blazing government of the Lord of Misrule." Carnival allowed white supremacists both to mock their enemies and to create a fantasy world in which they were absolute. Never before had the cultural form been so valuable. No wonder that during this period of political Carnival a certain segment of the New Orleans white elite formed a loyalty to the festivity that now strains the imagination.[24]

By 1898, it would be possible to joke about the relationship of Carnival, Reconstruction, and white supremacy. The *Royal Herald*, a Carnival paper, gave visitors a political biography of Rex. Rex had first come to the South in 1866 to manage its political affairs. Quoting an 1872 observation, the paper said, "The prince of mischief-makers and jokers, he is credited with having inspired the queer movements and social relations existing in this benighted section. Only a few days have elapsed since his successful attempt at overthrowing the government of Louisiana—one of the most remarkable occurrences on record, in a cheeky point of view." Rex was protean. On the one hand, "the queer movements and social relations" that the lord of misrule inspired included black equality, black suffrage, and the attempt to build a Republican Party in the South—all fiercely fought by conservatives in 1872 and complacently identified as nonsense in 1898. On the other hand, Rex's overthrow of the government of Louisiana was a funhouse mirror of the actual overthrow of Reconstruction in Louisiana and throughout the South.[25]

Postscript. During Carnival 1877, Prosper Jacotot, a French worker living in the United States, was in New Orleans, waiting for a chance to work his way home to France. He was trapped in the city during Carnival. He observed, "The Carnival holidays also close the commercial season. The crops are finished, merchandise shipped to Europe, the heat commences, the city little by little is deserted." It was deserted because of yellow fever as well, a calamity that Jacotot also mentioned. As a Frenchman, Jacotot was proud that New Orleans was "loyal to the traditions of its mother country," and that it celebrated with Parisian costumes and decorations. He admired the tourists who came from all over: St. Louis, Cincinnati, Chicago, New York, the plantation regions of Louisiana and Mississippi, Texas, and Mexico.

Jacotot left us a sketch of Carnival 1877. Rex arrived on "a large steamboat decorated with the colors of all nations." Rex was escorted to city hall, where he received the keys to the city. After that, Rex stayed at the St. Charles Hotel and attended the theater in the evening. The next day, the Rex parade began at noon. Forty-five floats passed the amazed Jacotot. Rex's float, "brilliant with gold and silver," was drawn by four white horses. Rex himself was "costumed as Agamemnon, at his feet were chained the captured kings, surrounded by Greek and Asiatic warriors." Jacotot noted, "These holidays are the occasions for exhibitions of feminine clothes with desperate competition among the elegants." He praised New Orleans Carnival, commenting, "All of this is done in an orderly manner."

Prosper Jacotot had particular reason for praising the civility of Mardi Gras. Louisiana and its racial relationships had shocked him deeply. "The whites inspire the black populace with stark terror. . . ." The method of terror was lynchings and other forms of violence. "One day I saw five negroes hanging from the same tree."

How pleasant Carnival was in contrast. The Frenchman reported that "the New Orleans Bee, in rendering an account the following day, stated without any unusual amusement, that there had been no fights, not one gun shot, not even a small stabbing." Jacotot could only conclude, "It is too bad that it is not Mardi Gras everyday."[26]

6

Northerners

IN 1881, the Royal Host of New Orleans—the Krewe of Rex—along with the state government, the city government, the Louisiana National Guard, and Confederate veterans, invited New York's Seventy-first Infantry, National Guard, to come south for Carnival. John R. Cowan, the Seventy-first's historian, recognized immediately this invitation's symbolic importance. As he expressed it, the invitation was the South's way of saying, "The soldiers of the South are Americans like yourself, they have been and are misrepresented by designing men, and they are tired of misrepresentation." The battalion, which had fought against Louisiana soldiers in the Civil War, accepted the invitation, and began what Cowan called "A New Invasion of the South." This time, however, the Yankees surrendered.[1]

The soldiers stayed aboard their steamship, the *Robert E. Lee,* which was pulled up alongside the levee for repairs. They were feted at the Washington Artillery Armory, where they drank champagne punch under a painting of Jackson and Lee. They enjoyed New Orleans's continental Sabbath, particularly the theatrical performances. They held ceremonies over Confederate graves. They watched the arrival of Rex, listened to the artillery salutes and the cheers, saw the mayor offer the king the keys to the city, and joined the military parade that escorted Rex to the Opera House. There Rex presented them with his royal colors. On Tuesday, the battalion was given special seats from which they admired the parades of Rex and Comus, while the Seventy-first's band was honored as "Court band" to His Majesty Rex. The themes this year were, as usual, mythical: the Rex tableaux presented *The Arabian Nights* while Comus portrayed the Scandinavian myths that Wagner also used. Later, the New Yorkers attended balls. They were treated throughout with courtesy. According to Cowan, the New Yorkers came away thinking, "No one could spend Mardi Gras in New Orleans without believing in the genuineness of the happy disposition of the people."[2]

Indeed, Rex sent them home with a message for the entire North. Praising "the national yearning for more intimate intercourse, which the great city of New York is so actively engaged in satisfying . . . the unexpected display of resources and wealth producing energy in the Southern States attested by the census reports and by the marvelous manifestations of the happy condition of the colored people of the South," Rex told the Seventy-first to bear his colors home with the message that "the King of Carnival has sent his royal command that hereafter all the citizens of this great nation shall be united and constitute one family, bound together by the indissoluble ties of friendship and patriotism."[3]

The invitation to the Seventy-first New York Infantry was part of a larger project of the 1880s and 1890s: the use of Carnival as a means of sectional reconciliation. Tourists, attracted by the parades and balls, were already an important element of Carnival by the 1870s. As early as 1876, white citizens had been taking advantage of Carnival to address Northern visitors to the city. That year, the New Orleans *Bulletin* published a special editorial for visitors, explaining that they were seeing New Orleans in hard times, in part because of Reconstruction. The *Louisianian*, the most perceptive of the Republican papers when it came to Mardi Gras, recognized that conservatives used tourism to rehabilitate the city's national image. After Carnival 1880, the *Louisianian* said that the *Picayune*, a Democratic paper, should be "extremely happy since our Northern visitors have seen the National colours profusely displayed, courtesy shown them, and invitations given them to paid balls." With bitter irony, it described the point of Carnival civilities: "Somehow in this section we need to do all these little things to convince the obstinate Republicans of the North that we are neither sectional nor prescriptive." These new images were intended to supplant those of New Orleanians rioting in 1866, conducting anti-Republican military operations in 1874, and engaging in racist violence throughout Reconstruction and thereafter.[4]

Rex led the way in courting Yankees. For example, during Carnival 1879, Rex dubbed the visiting W. T. Sherman "the duke of Louisiana." Sherman, a former citizen of the state, was nonetheless better known for his March to the Sea. A wartime opponent, the Confederate general John Bell Hood, was named "the duke of Texas" at the same ceremony; he assured Sherman that honors paid to him reflected the feelings of all Louisianians. In the 1880s, the Royal Host carefully added national members to its organization. The honorific appointment of Sherman and other prestigious Yankees, including Ulysses S. Grant, Schuyler Colfax, Chief Justice M. R. Waite, Admiral Robert Wyman, and Captain James B. Eads, signaled the desire of Rex and the business community it represented to be accepted as loyal Americans, Americans who could be trusted, funded, and fundamentally left alone. One newspaper editor explained, "We regard our Rex as simply the grand chamberlain of a new and greater Union that shall command the best affections of its whole people, and hence the more numerous our visitors from the North, the better."[5]

As early as 1877, Rex illustrated that favorite theme of late-nineteenth-century America: the blue and the gray. That year the overall theme of the krewe's spectacle was the "military progress of the world," from African warriors to von Moltke's Prussians. One float attracted considerable attention and approval from the crowds:

"a camp scene, but one of amnesty. Yankee lad and Johnny Reb intermingling peacefully." With the invitation to the Seventy-first New York Infantry, Rex went from incorporating papier-mâché Yankees on their floats to inviting real Yankees to march in the streets of New Orleans.[6]

Reconciliation itself became something of a Carnival tradition in the years before 1900. In 1891, the *Times-Democrat* observed that Carnival had "a military cast." "There is a good representation from the North, West, and South of both Federal and Confederate veterans; and they have fraternized in spite of sectional lines and past 'unpleasantnesses' as only soldiers can." The editor's conclusion was that "nothing tends more to restore a fraternal feeling in this country and bring the people, and particularly the soldiers, closer together than these reciprocal visits." The parades became rituals of reconciliation in which both former Yankees and former rebels entered the city as conquerors, and in which both Yankee and rebel pledged service to the king of Carnival.[7]

Never before had prominent New Orleanians made such high moral claims for Mardi Gras and the guests it brought to the city. Civic leaders presented Carnival as a solution to a national dilemma—how to reunite North and South emotionally now that the legal framework had been established. The tourists who came to see the parades and attend the balls were to be considered representatives of the Northern elite who would preach understanding and reconciliation upon their return. In New Orleans they would leave not only understanding but capital as well, helping rebuild the South. This was the New Orleans version of the New South movement that arose throughout the region during the last third of the nineteenth century.

The claims made for Carnival as a sort of national duty reached their apogee in an article written by the man who was Rex in 1887. George Soule wrote two nearly identical articles in the early twentieth century, but the concerns he expressed were more characteristic of the post-Reconstruction South in which he reigned as king of carnival. "What does Rex stand for?" he asked. The answer

was sectional reconciliation. Rex and its Carnival—Soule was unabashedly proprietary about the old folk festival—brought Northern
visitors to New Orleans. This was tourism with a higher purpose.
Rex encouraged the hobnobbing of visitor and local, Northerner
and Southerner, "that they might exchange thoughts on various
subjects and learn from one another the true political and sociologi-
cal conditions of the country." For Soule, Carnival was educational,
and Rex a great patriotic organization entitled not just to civic but
to national support. He claimed, "In its functions it recognizes the
wisdom of the words of Grant, when he said: 'Let us have peace.'
In the words of McKinley, when he said: 'Let concord, not discord,
prevail.' In the words of Lamar, when he said: 'Let us know one
another better, and we will love one another more.' In the words of
Lincoln, when he said: 'With malice toward none and charity toward
all.'"[8]

New Orleans leaders incorporated a ritual of reconciliation into
a Carnival parading tradition that had been more notable for its
anti-Republican sentiments. That in itself was an innovative use of
an old form. Even more noteworthy was the way the leaders invented a new context for the old form. For various reasons, New
Orleanians identified the important audience for Carnival as no
longer local but national. Carnival became, in part, a show to put
on for visitors. Carnival organizers envisioned these guests convey-
ing the images of Carnival to their friends back home. Their accounts and the accounts of the celebration in the national press
would present New Orleans to the rest of the world. The rituals of
sectional reconciliation, clearly designed for a Northern audience,
were part of a new vision of Carnival as a national event, but they
were only a small part. After Reconstruction, all of Carnival was
imagined to have a national audience—the parades, the balls, the
masking in the streets. Although Carnival never became something
primarily for visitors, New Orleans did succeed in establishing a
national audience for itself.

The Carnival that New Orleans leaders wished to display to
this audience was the new, organized Carnival. The "promiscuous

masking" that for all practical purposes had been Carnival in the streets was dismissed by one guidebook as "a minor accessory" in 1903: "The chief feature of the festive season now centers upon the street pageants, balls and tableaux." In 1893, the *Times-Democrat* carefully explained that, while masking was "common among children of all grades of society," respectable adults masked only if "engaged in the regular parades." The newspaper warned visitors away from the traditional promiscuous maskers. These mummers consisted of social undesirables, with black people in particular enjoying the masquerade. Although the maskers were vulgar, at least in the eyes of the editor of the *Times-Democrat*, "They add picturesqueness and coloring to the great Carnival crowds, and they are tolerated in consequence." The respectable valued the "picturesqueness and coloring" for setting off the pageantry of the parading organizations. In 1910, Soule, admittedly biased as a former Rex himself, wrote in answer to the question, "What is Carnival?": "The New Orleans Mardi Gras Association is an organization that, under the direction of Rex, places on the streets of New Orleans annually on Shrove Tuesday a magnificent pageant. . . ."[9]

In 1882, America's most famous travel writer arrived in New Orleans too late to see Carnival. But that didn't stop Mark Twain from commenting on it: "There is a chief personage—'Rex'; and if I remember rightly, neither this king nor any of his great following of subordinates are known to any outsider. All these people are gentlemen of position and consequence, and it is a proud thing to belong to the organization; so the mystery in which they hide their personality is merely for romance's sake, and not on account of the police." As for Mardi Gras itself (held, Twain claimed, in the spirit of Sir Walter Scott), he argued, "It is a thing that could hardly exist in the practical North. . . . For the soul of it is the romantic, not the funny and the grotesque. Take away the romantic mysteries, the kings and knights and big-sounding titles, and Mardi Gras would die, down there in the South." But he also admitted, perhaps even boasted as a man of Southern birth, that "the city is well outfitted with progressive men—thinking, sagacious, long-headed men."[10]

Twain was no mean critic, and we certainly should take seriously his identification of romance as the core of late-nineteenth-century Mardi Gras. He might, however, have speculated on what those "gentlemen of position and consequence" were up to, particularly since they probably included some of the "thinking, sagacious, long-headed men." In fact, in 1882, the mayor of New Orleans and Rex himself were the same man: Joseph Shakespeare. Civic leadership remained devoted to Carnival in the late nineteenth and early twentieth centuries.[11]

These leaders pointed to sectional reconciliation as one way of justifying all the civic energy that now went into organized Carnival. Nonetheless, the possibility of Northern investment motivated them as well. The rhetoric of the period drew little distinction between trusting former Confederates and investing in their business enterprises. As the fear of Northern animosity and political interference in Southern (white) affairs receded and the city entered the twentieth century, Carnival organizers increasingly justified the pomp, the preparations, the expenditure of time, energy, and talent as a shrewd commercial investment.

They were not subtle. The "selling of New Orleans" proceeded openly. Carnival was used to pitch the city to the tourist, who was sometimes portrayed as a chipper capitalist. One newspaper claimed in 1894, "As a general rule only those in comfortable circumstances visit our city during Mardi Gras." In 1900, one guidebook expressed the hope that its reader, the Carnival visitor, would leave New Orleans with "his heart full of good feeling, and his mouth full of good words." Why? Because "the greatest business projects invariably find their origins in social amenities." The visitor was promised that New Orleans was "on the eve of one of the greatest and most substantial booms in the history of the world's cities."[12]

A boom was needed. Time, history, and its own fecklessness had battered the city. In 1840, New Orleans had been the third largest city in the country. On the eve of the Civil War, it had still been the sixth largest. In 1880, it was the ninth, with a little more than two hundred thousand inhabitants. By 1900, it slipped to twelfth; after twenty years it had only sixty thousand more people.

Population figures and rankings relative to other, mainly Northern, cities were not the whole story. Financially, New Orleans was a mess. The city's debt seemed huge—more than $24 million in 1883. Most of the time, the city could not even pay its employees cash. In 1880, New Orleans had only 915 manufacturing industries. It was still primarily a commercial city, but one that faced increasing competition from other cities better linked to railroads. Even the wharves along the Mississippi were dilapidated and in need of repair.

The late nineteenth and early twentieth centuries saw the development of yet another set of tensions within the city, this time between Italians and everyone else white. New Orleans terminology, as noted earlier, can be extremely slippery. Even the seemingly obvious term "Italian" requires explication. People of Italian "descent" constitute the largest white ethnic group in New Orleans. Their ancestors were almost all Sicilians. Italians began arriving in Louisiana in the French colonial period; they also immigrated during the antebellum era—according to the U.S. census of 1850, New Orleans had more Italians than even New York. But it was in the 1880s that mass immigration of Sicilians to New Orleans began. By 1910, the Sicilian community in New Orleans numbered about 24,000. In addition to the poverty, poor living conditions, and discrimination often faced by immigrants, the Sicilians suffered from popular fear of the "Black Hand."

Besides arresting commercial decline and adjusting to new immigrants, New Orleans faced other challenges. The threat of violence and the reality of fraud still marked municipal elections. In 1888, Mayor Joseph Shakespeare received a letter explaining that "the reputation of our city has been fearful and it has been utterly impossible to interest capital in any enterprise in New Orleans solely on account of the political condition of the community." It was with good cause that the state legislature decided to move the capital upriver to Baton Rouge—away from yellow fever and from

New Orleans's political mobs. Of course, not all violence was politically motivated. Lawlessness was still common, as evidenced by
the 1884 public murder of a man by the judge of the Second
Recorder's Court and the 1891 lynching of helpless Italian prisoners
by a mob led by respectable and prominent reformers—many of
them the sons or associates of the 1874 White Leaguers. The
lynching received a surprising amount of approbation, both in the
city and beyond. One out-of-towner wrote Mayor Shakespeare, "I
admire the sort of judgment day that New Orleans held yesterday.
It will wind up an epoch of misrule." Perry Young, the Carnival
historian, claimed the latter murder for Comus: "The sixty men, for
instance, who, with shouldered arms, and undisguised, marched
from Clay Statue to Parish Prison and exterminated the Mafia gang,
were not the Mistick Krewe of Comus—but put your finger on the
man of them who was not its member."

The city was working toward reducing lawlessness, working
toward paying off the municipal debt, working toward rebuilding
its infrastructure and sanitizing its streets and protecting its citizens.
Furthermore, the 1880s and 1890s saw an expansion in both commerce and commercial facilities. Both machine politicians and business-oriented reformers agreed on the importance of attracting
capital and fostering enterprise. As outsiders already seemed interested in Carnival—perhaps the best-organized civic event New
Orleans could brag of—why not use it as a lure?[13]

The new Carnival was also supposed to reassure Northerners—
both potential tourists and potential investors—of the health of the
city. New Orleans was not a particularly healthy city; there was a
yellow fever epidemic in 1878, and there would be one in 1905.
After the 1878 epidemic, most of the new Carnival societies decided
that the holiday should go unobserved. Rex, however, having already paid for its costumes and decorations, thought otherwise.
That krewe paraded, arguing, "Our friends everywhere would prefer
to see us give evidence of life and energy, than to have us sitting in
sack-cloth and ashes." Rex, the king of Carnival, believed that his
presence would "tend to dispel the gloom caused by the afflictions

of the late epidemic." Rex also argued that the parades would draw tourists, who in turn would "do much to set in motion the wheels of trade."

Ernst von Hesse-Wartegg, a German tourist, reported that "the public took little part" in that year's Carnival; "the breach of etiquette hurt the thousands of families in mourning." The Republican *Louisianian* said that, for celebrating Carnival after such a calamity, "we are about to get supreme contempt as a silly people, or a tender pity as madmen who know no better." This was the Carnival during which Rex made John Bell Hood the duke of Texas—just in time, as by the next Carnival Hood and his wife would be dead of yellow fever. J. Curtis Waldo's guidebook, *History of the Carnival in New Orleans from 1857 to 1882*, assured visitors that "the excellent sanitary regulations which have since been carried out, demonstrate the fact that with proper care a recurrence of the scenes of 1878 need not be feared, and that New Orleans can be made and KEPT AS HEALTHY AS ANY CITY IN THE UNION."[14]

The very streets through which Rex and the mystic krewes paraded had taken on a more commercial appearance. Although the parades ended in the French Quarter, the home of traditional Mardi Gras, the more significant visual spectacle became the floats rolling through the central city. Ever since Rex, Canal Street had been the focal point for organized Carnival. Just before the Civil War, what Bernard Lemann called "the commercial building front" made its appearance in New Orleans. This style—which appeared throughout the United States during the mid-nineteenth century—came to characterize much of the center of the city after the Civil War: imposing, busy facades, generally covered with advertisements. And during the late nineteenth and early twentieth centuries, the size of commercial buildings grew: the ten-story Huyghenian Building dominated the city from 1895 until 1903; the Carondelet Building was an even more imposing thirteen stories; and the twenty-three-story Hibernia Bank, constructed in 1921, was believed to be as tall a structure as could be built on the swampy land of the city. This period created what is now called the CBD—the Central Business

District—out of the old mixed residential-commercial Faubourg St. Mary. There was little that was native to the city in these buildings; New Orleans looked more like other American cities than ever before. The setting for the parades, the commercial buildings in front of which passed the gaudy floats, served to remind visitors that they were in a city devoted as much to enterprise as to pleasure.[15]

Anywhere visitors turned, they might discover the greedy—well, serious—face of enterprise beneath the Carnival mask. For example, if they picked up the so-called Comus edition of the *Daily Picayune* in 1901, expecting a guide to the city's pleasures and Carnival frivolity, they would find pictures of the Comus parade, but also the text of a speech by the New South politician Hoke Smith entitled "The South's Future," and the article "New Orleans Is a Great Commercial City."[16]

The mechanism of combining Carnival with commercial appeals has had a long run. In 1913, the Algiers *Herald* advocated extending Carnival so that tourists would spend more time in the city and "thus see its great opportunities for investment and home-making." In 1916, Mayor Martin Behrman, head of the business-oriented city machine, called upon "every progressive citizen" and the "many welcome visitors" to attend the "Industrial Parade," held the Saturday before Mardi Gras. This parade would show "the world the rapid strides of the metropolis of the South." In the late 1920s, New Orleans Public Service, the streetcar and utilities company that had a long association with Rex, distributed a booster pamphlet entitled *A Special Service Dedicated to the Convenience of Our Carnival Visitors.* In the 1930s, Chris Valley sold "BOOST NEW ORLEANS" tire-covers, which advertised the Sugar Bowl, Mardi Gras, and New Orleans, "WHERE ROMANCE AND COMMERCE MEET." And in 1950, New Orleans Public Service took out an advertisement emphasizing that tourists should remember New Orleans as "a city of progress and opportunity"—and offering to give them information on suitable "factory, warehouse, and branch office locations."[17]

The Seventy-first's John R. Cowan quickly recognized that Carnival and tourism were a business. He called Carnival "a huge business speculation, sustained by leaders of trade, fostered by the wealth and fashion of the city, and invariably successful." Not only did tourists—many of them well-to-do—flood the city but commercial buyers liked to schedule their business trips to coincide with the spectacle. "The thousands of dollars spent by the Royal Host and kindred societies are returned to the merchants by the thousands who throng the streets for days before."[18]

The money spent by "the thousands who throng the streets" proved the most important financial reward of Carnival. If Carnival visitors could not usually be persuaded to part with thousands of dollars for investment, at least they could be enticed to spend a few dollars at local merchants. As early as 1879, the editor of the *Democrat* observed, "The Carnival pays New Orleans, and pays her handsomely, and for this very reason it should be sustained." The owners of what we would now call "the tourist industry"—hotels and railroads in particular—benefited most from the now annual influx of visitors. Indeed, it was during the late nineteenth century that New Orleans began to think in terms of a tourist industry.[19]

The railroads played a significant role in promoting Carnival. They subsidized the Krewe of Rex. They arranged special excursions to New Orleans during Carnival season. They distributed some of the guidebooks for the city and its Carnival. Hotels, too, benefited directly from the annual influx of visitors. By 1884, W. I. Hodgson—under orders from the king of Carnival—had set up a visitor's accommodation bureau to coordinate hotel bookings. Hotels and boardinghouses paid a fee for their listings, and the bureau had agents in places as far afield as Washington, D.C.; St. Paul, Minnesota; Lacrosse, Wisconsin; Corpus Christi, Texas; and New York, New York. Even so, there was not always enough hotel space for the annual influx, and some hotels "roomed" guests in their halls and dining rooms. Viewing stands were built and seats in them sold; one proprietor advertised his stand as "an excellent Stand, substantially constructed."

In 1901, W. G. Bowdoin, a visiting journalist, warned that "the Mardi Gras season affords excuse for the general raising of prices all along the line." Restaurants raised prices; even shoeshine boys charged ten cents instead of five. "One hates to be robbed and yet they go about it so systematically and yet so delicately that it is needful to submit." Or as the New Orleans *Times* society column said, perhaps sardonically, in 1880, when acknowledging that boardinghouses and restaurants charged Carnival visitors more, "The strangers don't seem to mind all this a bit." The columnist later observed, "We fulfilled in a mercenary manner the saying, 'they were strangers and we took them in.'"[20]

Rex was self-conscious about its role in the tourist trade. The reports that the earl marshall (actually H. H. Isaacson) gave to the Krewe of Rex at the turn of the century reveal an organization quite concerned with its relationship to the city's prospects—concerned and occasionally petulant. In 1899, the earl marshall bragged of Carnival's growing reputation and "the enormous amount of money brought to this City through the influence of our Carnival." It is not clear whether "our" refers to the city at large or the Rex organization. Apparently it is the latter, for the earl marshall went on to complain, "The only part of this great benefaction that is surprising to us is, that we of the Rex Organization have to work hard and to use every effort to get sufficient of this money to pay our expenses." In fact, this line of thought led him to an extraordinary demand: "The people of this city should place in our Coffers enough money to pay our requirements without asking a Dollar from its Members."

The Royal Host at this time consisted of 97 "Regular Dukes" and 22 "Railroad Dukes." Appointing railroad dukes was the price paid for the railroad money that Rex received. The Carnival court had 203 members enrolled, which led the earl marshall to hope that in the future it would not be necessary to use substitutes in the parade. He warned, "The substitutes utilized have been from the connections of Members, and of a class acceptable, but the discipline of the Organization cannot be enforced with those who do not feel the obligations necessary to our success."[21]

The earl marshall's complaints about the difficulty of raising money for the annual pageant continued into the twentieth century.

In 1902, claiming that "the financial benefit" of tourists coming to see Rex to "Hotels, Boarding Houses, Merchants, Restaurants, and other lines of Trade and business" was "enormous," he fumed that "the contributions to our organization are meagre indeed." He wanted those who benefited "to swell the membership of the Royal Host and the Carnival Court to five hundred, and save us the mortification of soliciting subscriptions from Restaurants and Bar Rooms."[22]

The oddest commercial success that Rex achieved was selling the parade itself—or at least the floats and costumes in it. They sold the 1899 Rex parade to people in Dallas. The Momus parade that year was bought by "a Texas town, the name of which has not been given out." In 1901, a committee from Saratoga Springs came to New Orleans to buy that year's Rex parade so they could reproduce it at September's Floral Celebration. In 1906, it was Houston that bought the Rex parade to restage in October. New Orleans Carnival had so attracted the attention of the rest of the nation that other communities wished to reproduce it, becoming spectators while staying at home. And one year the New Orleans Shriners bought the Rex parade so they could show a Carnival parade to visiting Shriners that April.[23]

The parades certainly continued to serve their earlier functions. They claimed the city's central space for the white elite; they ritualized the display of wealth and power; they perpetuated the integration of the well-to-do and respectable by offering them a shared, exclusive rite that fed their fantasies of dominion. Carnival lived within its old civic context. But now it had a national context as well. New Orleans leaders had self-consciously claimed a national audience for their organized Carnival if not for the old folk festival. On Lundi Gras, when John Cowan and the others soldiers of New York's Seventy-first Infantry first marched under Rex, they were willing actors in a ritual of sectional reconciliation. On Mardi Gras, when they sat watching Rex and Comus parade, they embodied the new American audience for a New Orleans festive ritual.

7

High Society

AT THE OLD FRENCH OPERA HOUSE in 1891, the Atlanteans, a socially elite krewe that sponsors no parade but holds Carnival balls, staged their premiere tableaux and ball. Their theme was Atlantis, the mythical lost continent from whence they pretended to come. They presented four tableaux in all. The first, "a sight of splendor such as is seldom seen on a stage," featured the warriors of Atlantis. Three chieftains stood toward the front of the stage, one in "a suit of glittering gold," one in a suit of silver, and one "whose costume was black, which served as a background for countless scales of glittering gold." Behind them stood four Scandinavian swordsmen wearing copper, four Grecian archers in brass, four Semitic stone-shooters in silver, four golden Gothic axemen, four spearmen of no particular nationality wearing "armor of Orichalcum," four sailors in white tunics wearing helmets with the wheel and cross that was "the symbol of Poseidon, the God of Atlantis," and four stone-slingers in steel. All of these warriors stood motionless while the audience gazed at them.

The second tableau, "The Sacrifice," showed the altar of Poseidon; the third was Poseidon in his chariot. The final tableau presented the destruction of Atlantis. This was accompanied by light and sound effects—the crash of thunder, the flash of lightning. A flame appeared on the temple's altar. Finally, a torrent of rain and the ocean itself destroyed Atlantis, leaving only one survivor. (Unfortunately, newspaper accounts fail to explain how this effect was achieved.)

After the tableaux, the curtain rose a final time: "It disclosed three arches through which, after a time, the lines of the warriors, followed by the kings and queens and Poseidon, filed." Apparently there was some delay getting the maskers into line. "They marched around to the music of 'Tannhauser's March,' and formed a symbolic figure of a wheel, in the centre of which was a cross." After this, they marched to the box on the left-hand side of the stage, and Poseidon called his queen. "She stepped from her box followed by her maids of honor, and as they took their partners' arms the march was resumed and the remaining warriors selected their partners for the first quadrille." The audience watched the krewe and their court dance the quadrille, then a lancers, and finally a waltz. Then the ball began.[1]

The organization of Carnival in the streets during Reconstruction and the uses to which this new Carnival was soon put were significant developments in the history of Mardi Gras in New Orleans. Equally important was what happened in the late nineteenth century in the ballroom, specifically, in the grand ballrooms where the new organizations invited their honored guests and presented their tableaux. For Carnival was still about the bals masque even as the bals masque began to have less to do with dancing. During the remaining years of the nineteenth century, the Carnival krewes created yet another tradition—the Carnival ball, an institution so implausible that it continues to baffle outsiders and alienate residents.

The rise of the fashionable Carnival ball contributed to new distinctions within New Orleans society. Invitation and admission to these balls became a way for the New Orleans elite to acknowledge their own, established group cohesion and exclude other New Orleanians while inviting the privileged from the rest of the country.

Carnival parades ended in the ballroom. The sponsoring krewe would present a series of tableaux following the theme of the parade they had just given. At the end of the tableaux, they would greet the queen and the maids of honor, who customarily joined them in the first dance. Several dances would belong to the maskers and their partners alone; then the "black-coats"—other men in full dress—would join the dance. Being "called-out" for a dance with the maskers was considered an honor. The general dancing would continue for several hours.

A ballroom is always a kind of theater. The new Carnival balls, however, put theatricality at the center of the bals masque. Indeed, the new balls were held in theaters—principally, the French Opera House. Instead of the dangerous hodgepodge of disguised dancers there was a new hierarchy of participants. Some came to present themselves, others came to observe. The model for this new theater was courtly. The parade of Comus or some other krewe was a king's procession through the city followed by a stately masque. The courts also expanded the role that respectable women could play in Carnival. Still fundamentally relegated to the role of onlookers, women—ladies—could now become queens and maids of Carnival courts.

For some New Orleanians, the new ball became the essence of Carnival. In the 1890s, several new mystic societies were created. The Atlanteans debuted in 1891. The Elves of Oberon and Nereus began holding their balls in the 1890s. Eighteen ninety-seven saw the appearance of two new societies—Consus and the Priests of Mithras. These were notable both for their social exclusiveness and for the fact that they presented only balls. These nonparading organizations contributed nothing to public Carnival—although it is not clear if this was entirely a matter of choice or if the expense of a parade on the lines of Comus or Proteus kept the new krewes from the streets. Their very first year, the Atlanteans announced that, in the future, they would hold a parade on the Monday night before Mardi Gras; however, they failed to organize such a parade. For the Atlanteans and the other new societies, the tableaux and balls were not the conclusion of their parade but the only activities they organized.[2]

The new, nonparading societies were also joined by one old krewe. The Knights of Momus gave up parading in the 1890s and restricted themselves to balls. They returned to parading in 1901, at which time the *Times-Democrat* explained, "The Momus parades were among the best presented here of old, but they were abandoned some time ago, when the interest in the Carnival seemed waning." The decision of the Knights to desert their parading tradition demonstrates the lure of the new private ball.[3]

The balls represented a retreat from public space to semiprivate space. They implied that the people of New Orleans at large could not appreciate the new splendor associated with Carnival. In the late nineteenth century, the art of both parades and the tableaux was held in high regard by local artists and their sponsoring krewes. The retreat into the ballroom also suggested that some of the concern of those staging Carnival events now focused in part on the cohesion of their social sphere. These were rituals meant to exclude the unworthy and to integrate friends and families into a whole. Thus it was not surprising that, as will be discussed later, the new ritual of the court centered around a mock marriage.

Who made up the audience? The balls were by invitation only. In one sense, this was hardly an innovation. Private balls had characterized Carnival. The public balls had long been regarded as, well, too public. But if these new Carnival balls were private balls, they were well-attended private balls. They created a new kind of social space, something neither private nor public, something between the parlor and the streets. Literally held in theaters, the balls created a new kind of theater—the display of the social elite to the social elite.

The mystic societies took pride in their snobbery. After the 1895 ball of the Atlanteans one newspaper boasted, "The balls of the Atlanteans, distinguished at all times for their exclusiveness, have never witnessed a more brilliant assemblage of wealth and culture." In 1894, the barb of the Momus tableaux was the satirical attack on social climbing. In 1895, the *Times-Democrat* boasted that "of late years the Carnival balls have come to be watched with a zealous interest by those who pretend to keep an account of the fashions of the country." Carnival balls now set the fashion, and among the balls, the newspapers claimed, Comus was paramount: "Coming, as its balls do, on the last night of the Carnival season, when everything has reached a crisis and with a policy of exclusiveness which makes it representative of the best element of the country, its guests must be accepted as types of the wealth and fashion of the United States." Notice the logic—exclusivity makes Comus representative. This account further boasted, "At the Comus ball last night were assembled the belles and fashionables of a hundred cities."

Around this time, the krewes probably made the individual decisions to exclude Jews that became an elite social policy, although this discrimination possibly waited until the early twentieth century. Jews had been involved with at least three principal parading krewes—Rex, Momus, and Proteus—that had been formed before the 1890s, but it is not clear that they were ever admitted to the nonparading ones.[4]

The value of the balls was their exclusivity as well as their art. Beyond that, present at the balls, both as part of the show and as part of the audience, were the social elite of "a hundred cities." Even though the balls, unlike the parades, were socially restrictive, their sponsors sought to reach beyond the limits of New Orleans. Some of the out-of-towners were friends, relatives, and business associates of members of the mystic societies. Others, however, were respectable strangers. A guidebook of 1885 advised visitors to get ball invitations from their friends as soon as they came to town: "If the tourist has no friends in the city," however, "it is considered proper to address a note to any of these societies, through the Post Office, asking for invitations." In fact, it was easier for a visitor to New Orleans to attend the fancy Carnival balls than it was for a native. The retreat from the streets was not accompanied by any retreat from the wooing of visitors. That motive for Carnival continued throughout the late nineteenth century. The outsiders to be kept out were those separated by class, not by geographic distance.[5]

The audience for the new tableaux and balls was for the most part, however, composed of people whom the men of the krewes already knew. They were their friends and families; they came from their own social circle. Indeed, in many cases, the audience included members of other krewes, which resulted in both the appreciation of those who share an artistic form and the competition so traditional to Carnival masking. Far more than the parades in the street, the tableaux were a ritual of class solidarity.

So if the first question is "Who were the audience?" and the second is "Who were the performers?" the answer is the performers and the audience were in one sense the same people. In his discussion of "the invention of tradition," Eric Hobsbawm observes that "more commonly [invented traditions] might foster the corporate sense of *superiority* of elites—particularly when these had to be recruited from those who did not already possess it by birth or ascription—rather than by inculcating a sense of obedience in inferiors." This applies exactly to the new ballroom ritual. The participants were demonstrating that they were part of an elite by performing for other members of the elite, who in turn might replicate what they saw.[6]

One battle that took years for the krewes to win was over their insistence on formality at the Carnival balls. Throughout the 1880s, Comus and Proteus put notices in the newspapers explaining that women wearing bonnets or otherwise not formally dressed would "be conducted to the upper tiers" and would not "be allowed on the dancing platform." They also continually reminded men that they had to stay away from "the dancing platform" until the maskers had had their first dances. In 1886, the rules for the Rex ball demanded "FULL EVENING DRESS" for both men and women. "Gentlemen with colored suits or oversuits, and ladies with hats or bonnets WILL UNDER NO CIRCUMSTANCES BE ADMITTED." The new rules were hard to learn.[7]

But in the end people learned them. And the societies learned to enforce them. In 1886, Rex held a post-Carnival, mid-Lent ball—apparently because Mardi Gras had come so early that year. An estimated two thousand people attended. The rigor of the reception committee, when it came to admitting people, drew praise. "Hundreds of persons, ladies and gentlemen, were refused admittance for the reason they were not in full dress. The enforcement of this rule added materially to the elegance of the ball." Earlier Rex balls had been lax; from now on, the new rules would be executed by Rex, Comus, and the other societies.[8]

The fostering of a sense of superiority was also evidenced in the rise of a new, sexually inclusive tradition. Besides the tableaux and a new insistence on formality, the late nineteenth century saw the creation of the Carnival court. The Carnival court added women, young women, to the ceremonies of the krewes but kept them in a thoroughly subservient role. The male krewes appropriated the youth and sexuality of women to adorn their Carnival balls. From the late nineteenth century on, the rituals of Carnival and the ritual of the debut became so intertwined in New Orleans society as to be indistinguishable.[9]

The Krewe of Comus designated their first Carnival court only after the fact. In 1884, Confederate daughters were guests of Comus at the ball—the Misses Lee, Miss Jackson, Miss Hill, and Jefferson Davis's daughters, Mrs. Hays and Miss Varina Davis, familiarly known as "Winnie." There were also Confederate wives—Mrs. Davis and "Mrs. Stonewall Jackson," as she was called. Jefferson Davis himself attended Comus that year, sitting with his two daughters. The Confederate daughters received dozens of flowers; floral arrangements decorated their proscenium box. Comus and his court danced the first quadrille with them. The mystic krewe also gave the women presents by which to remember the occasion. As courts joined the newly emerging Carnival traditions, these women were considered the first Comus queen and maids of honor—the unmarried daughters of Confederate generals, the five Confederate virgins. The Confederate "nobility's" attending these balls lent the events some of the dignity and romance of the Lost Cause.[10]

Unquestionably, the male krewes valued beauty highly in their courts. Furthermore, when newspapers printed accounts of the balls, the comeliness of the courts—and the clothes the queens and maids wore—was always reported in detail. When Proteus picked Miss Joubert as their queen, she was described as "a youthful beauty of the highest Creole type of feminine loveliness." Consus was praised for their selection of Miss Marietta Laroussini as their queen, which was called "a sample instance of the absolute good taste of the court." "This lovely young woman is recognized as one of the great beauties of the season, and it is natural that she should skim off first honors which she is so fitted to wear." But the focus on feminine beauty reached beyond individual women. Writers customarily portrayed the ball itself as a means of displaying feminine beauty. "In other respects, the ball was much the same as other balls," a reporter confessed of the Consus ball, which portrayed the meeting of Henry VIII and Francis I on the field of gold. "New Orleans society was present, as at all representative balls, and New Orleans society always means the presence of many beautiful women gowned with the taste and refinement for which the women of this city are famed."[11]

But there were reasons other than physical beauty for selecting Carnival courts. In 1892, Comus picked the ubiquitous Winnie Davis, "the daughter of the Confederacy," as queen of the ball. Nothing could have made clearer that the honors of the Carnival court were often meant more for the fathers of those chosen than for the women themselves. Winnie Davis was queen of Comus because she represented her father, who represented the Confederacy, which had been transformed into a dream of honor and a memory of youth for middle-aged men. This was recognized at the time. What did Winnie Davis think when she read that Comus's choice was "a gallant and touching tribute to the ulterior recollections of that dead cause, from the ashes of which have sprung, phoenix-like, such blessings of unity and peace"? By this time, she was used to such language and such tributes. True, she was praised as being "stately, dignified, and graceful." But those who so praised her went on to say, "This is the first time in its history that the Krewe of Comus have ever gone outside of the historic shades of its native city to choose a partner for its King, and it must go upon record as the tribute of gallant and patriotic people to the memory of him who was the incarnation of that for which they spilled their blood, saw the houses of their fathers totter into ruins an[d] ashes, and lay upon themselves the Atlantean burden of years of recuperative toil and plodding." Poor Winnie Davis had to spend much of her short life receiving homage meant for her father; for example, in 1886, when she was twenty-two years old, she received a watch inscribed to "The child of the Confederacy." She died in 1898, six years after being crowned queen of Comus.[12]

Consider the announcement of the king and queen of Carnival 1891. The king was James S. Richardson, "the largest cotton planter in the world" and "one of the foremost men of the South." "He is the son of the late Col. Edmund Richardson, and succeeded his father in the management of his vast estate, showing superior business judgment and ability." And the queen? "Miss Bessie Behan, who has been selected as Queen of Carnival, is a charming young debutante, who made her first appearance in society at the handsome ball given at the residence of her father, Gen. W. J. Behan, three weeks ago." Although there was reference to Richardson's father, the source of Richardson's wealth, he was himself an important man. In contrast, Bessie Behan, though charming, was portrayed principally as General Behan's daughter. Behan was a planter who lived outside of New Orleans except during the social season. After Carnival 1891, Bessie Behan studied at the Sorbonne. Later, she came back and worked with charities such as the Community Chest and the Red Cross. She was on the board of directors of the Eye, Ear, Nose, and Throat Hospital, the Catholic Women's Club, and the Beauregard House. These were the kind of civic services that were expected in Rex; bestowing the title king of Carnival on a man was a recognition of his business and civic career. But in 1891, Bessie Behan had no civic achievements to recognize—she had charm and her father's prestige.[13]

One seventy-eight-year-old woman looking back on her 1914 reign as queen of Comus almost sixty years later recalled, "I was born to be a 'Southern Bell' they vowed, and I would become queen of Comus ball someday—which I was in 1914." That fulfilled her "social ambition as a girl." She proudly listed other family members who had also been queens for Comus; her daughter presented her Comus costume—"my gown, mantle, and jewels"—to the Carnival exhibit at the Cabildo. In 1904, an aunt of the queen of Nereus wrote her niece, "It is certainly a great compliment to be selected as queen, especially your first winter, and enough to last the rest of your life." The 1911 queen of Rex, later Mrs. George Hastings, recalled years afterward that her reign was one of the two "pinnacles of her life"—the other was when the Hastings were close friends of President Hoover.[14]

Reigning as queen or attending a queen as a maid was simultaneously a rite of passage, an act of submission, and a mark of honor. Participation in the Carnival courts was the outward and visible sign that a daughter was conforming to the demands that "society" placed upon her. The court image of the woman as debutante, dressed in virginal white, was in sharp contrast with the alternate image of the woman dressed in masculine attire that characterized Carnival on the streets. By the rules of Carnival hierarchy, the most for which a man could strive was to be a Carnival king, and the most for which a woman could hope was to be a Carnival queen. A man became king when he was mature, at the height of his power and ability; the honor crowned his career. A woman became a Carnival queen when she was a girl; queenhood ended her childhood. After she was queen she might go on to become a woman, a wife, a mother.

The court served as a ceremony of integration. The king and queen were mock spouses; the mature man and the young woman played man and wife. The mock court joined the families of the krewes, bringing them together across generations. The central image of the tableaux and balls—the court—represented both authority and family. As they did when parading through the city, the members of the krewes acted out their aristocratic fantasies in their court presentations.

Weddings have resulted. In 1939, Perry Young, a great admirer of Carnival, asked of the debutantes in the Carnival courts, "Do they find unanticipated husbands in the motley?" "Often," was his answer. The kings and queens, the dukes and the maids-in-waiting "have much in common that ordinary folk know naught about and leads to marriage." He refers—in a poetic phrase—to "masks that take a fancy to the way a bud's inclined." His delight in these romances did not stop him from admitting of these royal couples, "Sometimes they have to wait . . . At least two Kings of Carnival have waited for their first bereavements before they made their Queens of Carnival their royal halves." One of these kings was Frank T. Howard, born in 1855, who reigned with Lydia Fairchild in 1895. Howard was also the Rex who presented his queen with so many expensive gifts that the organization thereafter set a limit on how much money kings could spend. This marriage was Howard's second. His first wife, Emma Corey Pike, married Howard in 1880; she died in 1898. Howard married Fairchild in 1899. The *Times-Democrat* observed after the wedding, which took place during the Carnival season, "The romantic interest attached to the union of a former King of the Carnival to his Consort was inspiring generally." A crown made of white and pink carnations hung over them at the church, in case anyone had forgotten that they were Carnival royalty.[15]

Courtship in this other sense was part of a young lady's Carnival. The anticipated groom was to come from her social circle. Carnival was debutante season, when the young ladies were presented to society—that is, to proper families with proper young bachelors seeking proper, ladylike wives. The symbolic integration of society that the court proclaimed was also to lead to the actual integration and reintegration of socially prominent families. The 1904 Rex queen was able to take her Carnival gown, made of Brussels lace, and convert it into bridal veils for herself and her friends.[16]

So the balls ritualized the submission of youth to age, of women to men, of daughters to fathers, of wives to husbands. They also ritualized social demarcations. The balls were presented by the elite for the elite; they reaffirmed hierarchy. Their tableaux were designed to display wealth, education, and taste. Even dancing—that activity that had long been at the center of New Orleans life—became highly organized and highly restrictive, a means of revealing the control of the members of the mystic society. Yet the price one paid for access to the "dancing platform" was putting oneself on display—for the edification and admiration of the audience, true, but for their amusement as well. Recreating fantasies for the public eye, the men of the mystic societies both asserted their social dominance and reduced themselves to the status of entertainers.[17]

At the Atlantis ball of 1891, most of the performers costumed as warriors: copper-clad Scandinavian swordsmen, silver Semitic stone-shooters, and so on. Returning to the first ball of the Atlanteans raises a question: Why Atlantis? Why this particular form of pomp and circumstance? If this question is broadened to include other balls and tableaux, as well as the parades organized by Rex and the mystic societies, it unveils one of the ironies of New Orleans Carnival—that as Carnival krewes achieved their much-desired national audience (as discussed in the previous chapter), they helped create a romantic image of New Orleans that undercut many of their commercial goals.

The late nineteenth century has been cleverly and appropriately called "the Babylonian Period in New Orleans Carnival." Parade and tableaux designers turned, time and time again, to the Orient: for themes, for costumes, for concepts, for spectacle. For example, in 1887, Rex appeared as Saladin. As the sultan, he wore a gold and silver embroidered tunic, silk Turkish trousers and Turkish shoes, and a white, bejeweled turban. He was armed with a golden shield and a jewel-encrusted scimitar. He paraded with a retinue of costumed guards, couriers, sultanas—presumably played by men—and slaves. The *Weekly Pelican* commented, "The oriental gorgeousness, beauty, and barbaric brilliancy of the Royal cavalcade has never been heretofore surpassed."[18]

George Soule, that self-interested justifier of Carnival, said that its parades gave "pleasure to all beholders of all classes." He also argued that the parades had an educational function: "They also serve a grand purpose as an object-teaching school, wherein all beholders are instructed in historical, scientific, geographical, zoological, mythological and ethnological subjects." Indeed, Soule makes the parades sound much like contemporary expositions and world's fairs. Certainly, the parades presented in the years between Reconstruction and World War I covered many subjects, particularly mythological ones. But edification was rarely the immediate consequence of a Carnival display, and instruction was hardly the primary motive of the parade designers. If anything, designers wanted spectators to experience misty raptures and vague sensations of awe and nostalgia rather than learn facts and morals from parading encyclopedias. This was the intention of the Atlantis tableaux— to overwhelm the spectators with foreign grandeurs, with another civilization, to present them with "oriental gorgeousness."

This artistic impulse was hardly limited to the Carnival krewes of New Orleans. In the late nineteenth century Western artists and writers indulged in the exotic, seeking in spectacles and dreams clues to what we would now call the subconscious. And in the midst of this, staid New Orleans businessmen came along and asked not for paintings or sculptures but for whole parades of floats. What did the designers do? The only thing they could—they ran amuck.

The four principal parades in the period between the end of the Civil War and America's entry into World War I were Rex, Comus, Momus, and Proteus. These four krewes used five designers: Charles Briton, Bror Anders Wilstorm, Carlotta Bonnecaze, Jenny Wilde, and Ceneilla Bower Alexander. Briton, a lithographer, and Wilstorm, a painter, were both Swedish. They designed floats for all four parades. Bonnecaze designed floats for Proteus, Wilde for Momus and Comus. Georgia-born Wilde published poetry as well as designing parades. Alexander, who studied at the New York School of Art and was the wife of William Alexander, pastor of the Prytania Street Presbyterian Church, designed for the Rex parade after the turn of the century. She loved esoteric themes and spent much of her time quarreling with float builders over the feasibility of her designs. No matter who designed the floats, they were always built by George Soule, whose firm controlled the parade business in New Orleans. The floats were papier-mâché creations, built atop wagons. The theaters and the opera house supplied the craftsmen who painted transparencies and backdrops.[19]

The themes that designers and krewes chose were foreign and fanciful. For example, in 1882, men belonging to the New Orleans Cotton Exchange organized a new krewe, Proteus. For its first parade the theme was "Ancient Egyptian Theology." That same year, Momus presented *The Ramayana*, a work they described to their Western audience as "the Iliad of the East." The scenes they chose included the Temple of Indra, the nuptials of Rama, the abduction of Sita, the combat of Rama and Ravana, and Sita's descent into the earth. A small book was published commemorating the parade and tableaux.[20]

Other Eastern spectacles followed. Comus presented "Nippon, the Land of the Rising Sun" in 1892, "A Leaf from the Mahabarata," in 1903, and "Izdubar" in 1904. Rex offered "the Arabian Nights" and "the Semitic Races"; Momus "the Moors in Spain," another "Mahabarata," "Vathek, Ninth Caliph of the Abassides," and "Leaves from Oriental Literature"; and Proteus "Chinese Myths," "the Hindoo Heavens," "Tales of the Genji," and "the Shah Nameh."

The East was not the only source of parade themes. In their search for edifying spectacles, parade designers turned to history as well—Proteus drew on the history of France, Comus on the history of Ireland, ending it cautiously with the eve of the battle of the Boyne—and to classical literature. Comus presented Ovid's *Metamorphoses* and Proteus illustrated the *Aeneid*.

Rex offered some fine abstractions befitting late-nineteenth-century symbolist art and literature. These included parades dedi-

cated to "Visions," "Fantasies," and the "Symbolism of Colors."
(White was purity; rose, martyrdom; pale green, baptism; purple,
justice; gold, power; yellow, jealousy; scarlet, glory; green, faith; red,
charity; pale yellow, joy; pale blue, good deeds; grey, grief; orange,
marriage; and silver, chastity.)[21]

Finally, on Mardi Gras 1890, in a fine display of self-referen-
tiality, Comus presented its own history for its parade and tableaux.
"The Palingenesis of the Misticke Krewe" devoted floats to each
parade from 1857 to 1884—Paradise Lost, Greek mythology, English holidays, the history of America, the Missing Links—a kind of
greatest hits of Comus. The reason for this odd theme was Comus's
long absence from the Carnival scene; hard times had shut down
the parade for a number of years and Comus had to struggle to
assert their Carnival supremacy over the newer Krewe of Proteus.
The 1890 parade was intended to remind the onlookers of Comus's
past glories and its key role in organizing Carnival.[22]

The city developed a Carnival aesthetic that blended popular
Carnival tradition with the artistic currents of the late nineteenth
century. The latter contributed largely to Carnival's orientalism.
Carnival with its costumes, processions, tableaux, and bals masque
played to the late-nineteenth-century love of fantasy, of exoticism.
T. C. DeLeon, a contemporary historian of Carnival in Mobile and
New Orleans, went so far as to distinguish between the proper
aesthetic of Mardi Gras day—the Rex parade in New Orleans—and
Mardi Gras night—Comus: "Mingling the grotesque with the gorgeous" was the principle behind the daytime processions. Nighttime
demanded "the harmonized unity of the more dignified themes of
the Mystics proper." The role of the day parades was to amuse the
onlookers; the role of the nighttime parades was to instruct them.
Also, torchlight and evening darkness were kinder than sunlight to
the papier-mâché and painted transparencies. In 1891, the *Times-
Democrat* advocated moving the Rex parade to the evening as well.
"Tableaux of such a description are not so well fitted for exhibition
in the fierce light of the 'garish' noon, as by the feeble rays of the
illuminating torch," the editor said. "The sun's splendor is apt to take

the 'shine' out of the brightest artificial scintillations, and to expose, without mercy or without the possibility of concealment, any weakness or flaws that may exist in the coloring or the mechanical construction."[23]

What seems to have been overlooked is that the series of images these parades and tableaux created for the visitor undercut— or overpowered—the images of New Orleans as a bustling, businesslike city. If Mardi Gras was New Orleans, and Mardi Gras was "oriental," then it would be difficult to persuade outsiders that New Orleans was also progressive and businesslike. Even George Soule had to admit that people had objections to Carnival because it not only enticed New Orleans's young men to squander their money but also "gives the thinking and the investment class of the country the opinion (of us) that we worship folly and pleasure at the expense of business and progress." For the goal of sectional reconciliation, being viewed as quaint—and harmless—served as well as being viewed as businesslike. For the goal of Northern investment, however, quaintness was hardly a desirable image to project.[24]

Orientalism is a term now applied to the ways in which Westerners—read masculine, hardheaded imperialists—perceive other peoples, casting them and their cultures as feminine, exotic, irrational. This, of course, fits neatly with the way that New Orleans has been perceived for the past century. Yet if New Orleans is perceived as exotic, it is because in many ways the city has invited orientalism. The identification of New Orleans with the high romance of Carnival backfired. And this was only one of the ways in which the city marketed itself as a place of romance and not a place of business. George Soule, the local booster and businessman who profited from building the fantastic designs of symbolist artists even while protesting that Carnival should attract investment, makes a good symbol himself, a symbol of the way the civic leaders undercut the city's national image.[25]

Fortunately, some of the pomposity of the new tableaux was noted at the time. In 1896, the *Times-Democrat* complained that "of late the Carnival has run too much to abstruse, mythological, and historical subjects . . . There has been too much stateliness, too much formality, too much earnestness about the Carnival affairs of recent years." The nonmystic krewe the Phorty Phunny Phellows shared this opinion, for their 1896 parade parodied the tableaux of other krewes. Their burlesque drew the *Times-Democrat's* praise: "The essential Carnival grotesquerie has been subordinated to the desire to be magnificent and original." The Phorty Phunny Phellows returned humor to Carnival, in contrast to the mystic societies, where "the maskers have almost got to that stage where they take themselves seriously, forgetting that the origin of the Carnival committed it to a spirit of the most absolute abandonment to pleasure." The Atlanteans—whose later tableaux portrayed Lafcadio Hearn's *The Bird Wife*, Shakespeare's *Tempest*, and the *Garden of Irem*—deserve inclusion among those indicted. They too confused Carnival with Art.[26]

An antebellum parade of the Mystic Krewe of Comus.

The invitation to the 1866 Comus ball, the first after the Civil War. Note the emphasis on death and destruction.

The 1873 Comus tableau, "Missing Links to Darwin's Origins of the Species," the krewe's most ferocious piece of anti-Reconstruction theater. The half-simian Missing Link is crowning himself king, as the Carpetbagger Fox prostrates himself.

The 1879 arrival of Rex on Lundi Gras.

1887: The Independent Order of the Moon illustrates the reconciliation of the Blue and the Gray.

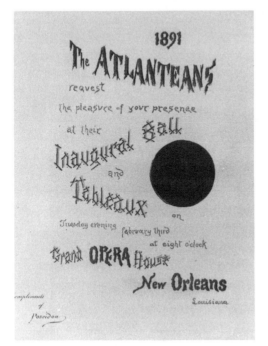

The invitation to the first ball of the Atlanteans.

The 1920s: women, automobiles, and public dance come to the streets for Mardi Gras.

A turn-of-the-century parade.

A Mardi Gras icon: the female pirate, circa 1930.

(facing page, top) An early parade of the Zulu Social Aid and Pleasure Club.

1946: the king of Zulu arrives at the New Basin Canal, and the parade begins to form behind the brass band.

(facing page, bottom) In this segregated parade, white schoolchildren blackface to portray African-Americans.

1949: Louis Armstrong (center) reigns as king of the Zulus.

8

Mardi Gras Indians

ACCORDING to the *Times-Democrat*, "a small size race riot" took place at Burgundy and Mandeville on Mardi Gras day 1908. A group of Mardi Gras Indians—black New Orleanians masking as Indians—"attacked and beat up some young white boys." Two white men passing by in a buggy intervened. The Indians turned on them, hitting one in the head with a brick. After this intervention failed, "many white citizens rushed to the scene, pursuing the blacks in all directions." The police came and arrested all the Indians, including the man believed to have thrown the brick; he was found hiding under a bed.[1]

Carnival assertion was carried to its blatant extreme by the Mardi Gras Indians. These black people costumed as Indians, paraded through the streets singing, and pitted themselves violently against other Indian tribes. What made the 1908 incident distinctive was that the violence was between black people and white people rather than between rival Indian tribes. By the second half of the twentieth century, however, the contest became one of song, dance, and spectacle, with different Indian groups vying with one another. Such aesthetic competition has long been commonplace in Caribbean festivals, from the rival displays of the Red and Blue Set-Girls in eighteenth-century Jamaica to the well-organized costume competitions in post–World War II Trinidad. New Orleans Indians fit easily into this tradition, as well as into local and international traditions of Carnival violence.[2]

. The Mardi Gras Indians date back at least to the late nineteenth century. Unfortunately, nobody recorded the first appearance of a black tribe on Mardi Gras day or when other black people began to copy this tribe. There are at least two traditions explaining the origins of the tribes. One holds that Brother Tilleman, chief of the first Yellow Pocahontas and then the Creole Wild West, organized the first Indian tribe in the mid-1890s. That date is almost certainly too late. More likely is the account which holds that the first tribe, the Creole Wild West, appeared in the 1880s, led by Chief Becate. Tradition has it that Chief Becate was of mixed African and Indian descent—hence his decision to masquerade as an Indian. The practice spread, however, to New Orleans black men and women who claimed no Indian blood. A contemporary Mardi Gras Indian concedes, "People ask me why do we dress like Indians and I wonder myself. I never have seen a real Indian my color. Maybe they have them, but I never have seen them." Michael P. Smith plausibly links the emergence of the Indians to the Buffalo Bill Wild West Show, which wintered in New Orleans in 1884–1885; he points out that some of the Indians in the show paraded on Mardi Gras 1885.[3]

One of the earliest accounts of a Mardi Gras Indian parade appeared in 1899. According to this story, forty to fifty bewigged and painted Indians paraded, "jabbering and waving their tomahawks," behind their chief. "Their costumes and make-ups were above the ordinary, and in addition to mock weapons, a few of them carried old swords that would have proved terrible weapons in a fracas." Some kind of fracas did occur on Camp Street near Lafayette Square, but the account does not reveal what happened, except to say that "for a time there was cursing and uplifted clubs." The Indians could have encountered another tribe, but it seems unlikely that this would have escaped comment. In any case, the police broke up the crowd, "and the Indians went up the street jabbering as before, and walking with that peculiar swing that is characteristic not of the Indian but of the negro buck." In 1902, according to the *Times-Democrat*, the Indians went out in "bands of from twenty to thirty," "singing war songs and doing the war dance." The paper noted that "the negroes are the only ones who came out as Indians, and they made good savages."[4]

The tradition of black people masking Indian is widespread in Caribbean Carnival. There are such "Indians" in Trinidad, Bahia, and Cuba. Christmas maskers in Jamaica, St. Kitts, and the Dominican Republic include Wild Indians. Gombey dancers in Bermuda also dress as Indians. Michael P. Smith's conclusion is the most judicious: "It is not my understanding, as others suggest, that the Mardi Gras Indians are actually an extension of analogous traditions such as Haiti's or Trinidad's. I suspect a separate, parallel development with some cross-fertilization, based on West African models. The Mardi Gras Indian tradition of New Orleans is more likely a sibling rather than a child of the pan-Caribbean tradition." Although it is useful to conceive of New Orleans and the Gulf Coast as part of a cultural area that also includes the Caribbean, Carnival traditions there were not imported directly from the islands. There certainly has been cultural exchange between salt-water port cities such as Port-of-Spain and New Orleans, but since the late-eighteenth-century emigration from Saint Domingue to New Orleans and the early-nineteenth-century migration from Cuba to the city there has been no large-scale influx of islanders to New Orleans. The Mardi Gras Indians are a "Creole" product, indigenous to Louisiana.[5]

With the Mardi Gras Indians, the working-class black people of New Orleans too "invented a tradition." Like other late-nineteenth-century innovators, the Indians claimed historical continuity for their cultural practices. Some asserted that they were in fact descended from Native Americans (many doubtless were), and that the Indian traditions were just that—authentic Native American traditions. Clearly, the costuming, the parades, even the violence allowed these men to assert themselves, both collectively and individually. Considering that the tribes were composed of black men living in a violent, racially segregated city—black men apparently drawn from the poorest communities in New Orleans—the lure of masking Indian is easy to understand. Carnival provided them with the opportunity for self-expression.

But the timing of the Indians' emergence was also significant. The tribes arose in the 1880s. Thus, they appeared after some twenty years of hopes and expectations raised and shattered. Although a tradition of protest against racism continued (Homer Plessy, of Plessy v. Fergusson, was a New Orleans Creole), the days of black political participation were ending—the days of mass political rallies, black voting, black electioneering. It was dangerous for a black person to assert himself in the political realm. The creation of the tribes, then, should be seen as a safer way—in historical jargon, it would be called, ironically enough, "prepolitical"—to engage in public assertion. Masking Indian was a form of black protest in a Jim Crow New Orleans. It contrasted significantly with black New Orleanians' day-to-day compliance with the city's norms. People had to put on one mask to take off another.

The parade of the tribes claimed ritual space. "Big chiefs"—the leaders of the tribes—boasted that they would take their tribes all over the city, uptown and downtown too. Everyone would get a chance to see that they were the best-costumed and the bravest, ready to go anywhere no matter what their traditional enemies thought. The claim to space might be made by aesthetic spectacle—with superior singing, dancing, and costuming establishing the right to the street—by threats conveyed by gesture, song, and weapons, or by actual violence. The streets that the Indians contested were those of black New Orleans. They rarely ventured onto streets in the center city; they did not rival Rex. Instead, each tribe asserted its primacy within its own neighborhoods. Black Carnival remained something almost hidden from white observers.

The Indians also developed within the context of black population growth and black ethnic rivalry. The black population of New

Orleans had been roughly twenty-five thousand in 1860; by 1880 it was almost sixty thousand. This population increase was caused largely by migration from the country to the city. After emancipation, freed people flocked to New Orleans. Some of them would have been Francophone, but many of them spoke English. Within the black community at large there was a rivalry between African-Creoles and African-Americans. Among the Indians, the strongest rivalries were between Creole Downtown and American Uptown.[6]

Trinidad offers a comparison. It too had a nineteenth-century tradition of Wild Indians, originally modeled on South American tribes. Like the Mardi Gras Indians in New Orleans, the Trinidad Indians fought one another in the streets, spoke a strange, invented language, and developed characteristic dances. Students of New Orleans have frequently pointed to them as possible prototypes of the Mardi Gras Indians.

An equally useful comparison is Trinidad's nineteenth-century stickfighting bands. While in bondage, black Trinidadians established a Christmas tradition of mock duels, using wooden swords, song, and dance. After emancipation, this stick-play became a part of Carnival. Stickfighting groups—in New Orleans they would be "gangs" or "tribes"—led by kings went out looking for other groups on Carnival Sunday. The historian Bridget Brereton describes the bands: "They boasted their skill and bravery, verbal wit, talent in song, dance and drumming, their indifference to the law, their sexual prowess, their familiarity with jail, and sometimes their contempt for the Church." Like the Indians, they sang songs of brag and engaged in battle with their counterparts. This ritualized violence occurred amid new migration to the cities, high unemployment, and rivalries among people of African ancestry, particularly between the older native community, which spoke French and a French patois, and the newer Anglophone migrants, who came principally from Barbados. In 1881, a police effort to put down stickfighting led to the Canboulay Riot. The stickfighters' competition immediately became a challenge to police authority. By the middle of the decade, the government of Trinidad had outlawed stickfighting, banned skin drums, delayed the start of Carnival until Monday morning, and kept a warship posted off the coast every Carnival. And in Trinidad, Carnival competition shifted to the arena of costume, dance, music, and spectacle—the calypsos.[7]

Alice Zeno, interviewed in 1958, testified that in the 1880s and 1890s the Mardi Gras Indians dressed "like real Indians, not like now." Presumably she meant that the original Indians dressed much like the Choctaws who visited New Orleans in the late nineteenth century. The historian Jerah Johnson argues that New Orleans retained a Native American presence far longer than most cities on the eastern seaboard, and that the Indians gradually disappeared by merging into the African-American community. Zeno reported that female Mardi Gras Indians wore "guinea blue dress[es] with . . . stripes . . . red and green . . . and then the little, short, short waist." They wore beads, carried baskets, and danced in the streets, "dance[ed] like real Indians." Zeno's comments pointed to one set of changes within the Indian tradition. Costumes grew more elaborate, particularly as competition shifted from violence to display. Today the blue dresses would not be recognized as Mardi Gras Indian costumes. The Indians came to dress in costumes that looked less like Choctaw Indians and more like the Hollywood version of Plains Indians. The change can be accounted for by the ubiquity of that Hollywood image in popular culture. When New Orleans black people, even those of Indian ancestry, wanted to know what an Indian looked like, this was the image available to them. Black New Orleanians who wanted to mask Indian might consult pictures in magazines or books at their local libraries for decorations or scenes to reproduce on their costumes.

Maurice Martinez argues, however, that elements of the modern Indian costumes were derived from the Natchez Indians, not from Hollywood imagery; he cites the feather crown as an example, concluding, "These descriptions surely demonstrate that there were abundant Louisiana Indian costumes and customs." He argues, "No doubt, these customs were passed down to their children, many of whom were half black." Perhaps both Hollywood images and remembered Louisiana traditions fed the creation of the modern New Orleans Black Indian. It must be borne in mind, however, that there are key differences between the costumes of uptown and downtown tribes.[8]

A 1925 account in the *Item* said, "As early as sun up, bands of negroes made their appearance on the streets. Their costumes were of deer skin packed with beads and hieroglyphic designs." In 1932, the *Times-Picayune* described the costumes, drawing racist conclusions: "True to his aboriginal ancestry, the civilized negro of the South assumes the habiliments of a savage on the day of general masking." "The civilized negro" "comes forth early Tuesday morning arrayed in a magnificent Indian costume, with a huge feather headpiece and bead-strung leather garments." These costumes were far more costly and beautiful than the one described by Alice Zeno; indeed, the newspaper marveled that "the suits and headpieces are not carelessly put together from odds and ends, but equal the beauty of the costumes of the great American Indian chiefs"—something worth commenting on, "especially in view of the fact that the average negro is in impoverished circumstances."[9]

The 1932 *Times-Picayune* also noted that "the negroes leave their settlements early and are the first maskers on the streets, their war whoops sending blood-curdling shivers down the spines of children who arise soon after dawn to peer through bedroom windows for a glimpse of the 'Indians.'" Customarily, Mardi Gras day began early for the Indians. "My gang got ready by the light of the moon," is a traditional boast. They would meet at the house of the big chief, who organized them and sent them onto the streets by singing the chief's song: "My Indian Red." This was the traditional start of the Indians' parade.[10]

What follows is a description of what might be termed an "ideal type" of an Indian parade. Unfortunately, accounts of the Indians prior to the 1970s are sketchy; exactly at what point in the twentieth century certain elements became part of the Indian ritual remains unknown. The number of tribes and their size certainly varied over the century. "Parade" itself is a misleading term for what the

Indians did on Mardi Gras day. They marched, but with considerable distance between individuals. The parade was led by the spy boy or, if there was more than one, the first spy. His job was twofold—to lead the Indians on the route the chief revealed only to him, and to watch out for other tribes. The flag boy followed the spy; his job was to communicate the spy's signals to the rest of the tribe. Both for this purpose and to identity the tribe, he carried "a rectangular piece of cloth, approximately three to three and one-half feet long, and one and a half to two feet wide"—a flag. The flag matched his costume and had the name of the tribe or its symbol emblazoned on it. If the tribe had enough members, the first flag boy was followed by a second spy, who in turn was followed by a second flag boy. The chiefs, including the big chief, came next. They carried "totem poles"—decorated lances. The scouts marched alongside the chiefs, acting as bodyguards. "Indians," tribe members of no particular rank, also marched with the chiefs. Finally, there was the wild man, or witch doctor. If Carnival gave license to all Indians, it gave double to the wild man. His job was to act "wild" and clear the streets for the Indians.

The women who paraded with a tribe were called "queens." The 1908 incident revealed a role accorded to women in the gangs not commonly known. The members of the Indian gang who were arrested were Samuel Kindle, Olivia Dorsier, Mary Jones, Emma Butler, Wallace Thomas, Paul Marshall, and Joseph Jones. According to the *Times-Democrat*, which presumably got the information from the police report, Mary Jones was "the leader of this obstreperous band of negroes." I know of nowhere else where leadership of Mardi Gras Indians was attributed to women, although in the 1920s and 1930s the Wild Squat Toulas had a spy girl, Amelia Lambert, Big Chief Daniel Lambert's sister.[11]

At prearranged stations the group stopped for refreshment. Along the way, the tribe might encounter another tribe—in the early twentieth century, a signal for combat, now a signal for competitive singing, dancing, and display. Fighting was a central component of the Indian experience. Chief Tuddy Montana, a descendent of Chief Becate, said, "They used to carry hatchets, razor sharp, and real shotguns." When rival tribes met, one might demand ritualistic obeisance from the other, which meant "bowing" or "kneeling." The alternative to bowing was fighting. For example, in 1900 the Red, White, and Blues challenged the Chickasaws at the corner of Perdido and Franklin; John Henry Lewis shot Lawrence Clementine in the abdomen.

In case the more or less random itinerary of the day did not lead to an encounter with a particular tribe, the day ended on "the battlefield," the place where all the tribes came together to meet those they had not run into on the streets. (The battlefield, no longer existent, was not far from Louis Armstrong's old neighborhood.) These fights were ways of deciding which tribe had the most prowess. They were also means of settling "grudges" held throughout the year, perhaps since the last Carnival. The zone that Carnival created, in which things not ordinarily allowed were allowed, was in this case a zone in which vengeance and violence could operate. Chief Tuddy contrasted earlier Indians with those of the post–World War II era: "Today people run to the Indians. During them days, people would run away from the Indians." When Sugar Boy Crawford wrote and sang the Carnival song "Jock-A-Mo," better known as "Iko Iko," he celebrated Indian traditions. But Crawford confessed, "I never was interested in being an Indian, because to tell you the truth I was afraid of them."[12]

In their fine history of New Orleans music since World War II, *Up from the Cradle of Jazz*, Jason Berry, Jonathan Foose, and Tad Jones argue that "it must be stressed that the Indians, at heart, were not a violent tradition." But the competitiveness inherent in the early tradition, the pride in the ability and readiness to use violence, and the very songs that are central to the heritage of the Indians suggest otherwise. The recent understandable admiration for the Mardi Gras Indians' costumes, music, and folk culture sometimes obscures the fact that people, no matter how colorful their garb, going out to seek violent confrontation is a sad spectacle. Masking Indian permitted the self-avowal of people who did not have much opportunity for it in their daily lives. But the violent assertion was directed against others who were equally downtrodden. Whatever the symbolic rebellion against white institutions that was embodied in assuming the identities of free and proud braves, in fact it was black bodies that received the blows the Mardi Gras Indians inflicted on one another.[13]

Indian songs were a repository of the Indians' past. But they were elliptic. Stories were only hinted at, alluded to—"Cory he died on the battlefield"; "Brother John is gone." Scholars have tried to identify who Cory and Brother John or some other figure were, but in the songs they remained shadowy heroes. The songs were improvised on the spot. A leader sang whatever he pleased and was usually answered by a repetitious, insistent chorus. He chose his words from a stock repertory of phrases, and the couplets passed effortlessly from song to song. The chief was expected to be able to respond with song to any situation that arose on the street—a role somewhat akin to that of the calypso singer in Trinidad's Carnival. The singing and the drumming that undergirded the chief's performance had been passed down from performances such as those of the king of the wake and the dancing at Congo Square; the Indians in turn kept this African musical tradition alive and available for New Orleans jazz and rhythm and blues musicians.[14]

In *The Signifying Monkey*, Henry Louis Gates, Jr., argues that "free from white people's gaze, black people created their own unique vernacular structures and relished in the double play that these forms bore to white forms." The earlier king of the wake had been part of "a unique vernacular structure," but he probably was not intended as a commentary on white forms. The king of Zulu and the Zulu parade certainly were examples of Gates's "double play"— African-American forms performing in dialogue with, and "signifying on," white parade traditions. The Indians existed in the middle, between the Congo-dance and the Zulu parade. Black people masquerading as Amerindians—and, in the more extreme cases, claiming identity with Amerindians—gains meaning primarily from the history of race relations in America, both relations between black people and white people and relations between Indians and white people. Furthermore, the specific model may have been Buffalo Bill's Wild West Show, in itself a white representation of race in America. But unlike Zulu, the Indians' parade made no reference to white models.

Gates also shows that "repetition and revision are fundamental to black artistic forms, from painting and sculpture to music and language use." "Signifyin(g)," he explains, "*is* repetition and revision, or repetition with a signal difference." Presumably, Gates would not be surprised to learn that "repetition and revision" lie at the core of the Mardi Gras Indian aesthetic. (That they may lie at the core of all New Orleans Mardi Gras aesthetics, including those of white New Orleanians, suggests that much more thought needs to be given to the African origins of New Orleans culture.) Visually, the Indians' costumes are remarkably similar from year to year—yet each year's costumes must be different from the previous year's. Musically, the same songs celebrating the same legends are performed, but each performance demands an element of improvisation, and a good singer should be able to adapt the traditional text to fit the situation around him. A good singer must know the lyrics and know how to revise them. Despite the allure of the costumes and the music, no other Carnival tradition in New Orleans is as rooted in language as that of the Indians, no other tradition so celebrates the word. If all Carnival is about play, black Carnival is about word-play.[15]

Much of the singing was ritual boasting of strength, bravery, and skill, with lines that might have been heard in New Orleans in the days of riverboat men: "I walk through fire, I swam through mud; snatch the feathers from an eagle, drink panther blood." Costumes were also cause for bragging: "The only thing make the white folks mad/People we got some clothes they wish they had." A chief bragged of his lack of respectability and conventionality—"I'm a low down Eagle, got dirty ways." Some bragging *might* refer to competitive spectacle: "Meet the gang on Mardi Gras day; make your whole damn gang look shitty." Some recurrent phrases reassured or instructed the rest of the tribe. "Say trouble come, Nobody run, I got the pistol, Shoot the Gatling gun." Other phrases admonished rival tribes: "If them Arrows ain't ready, I'm gonna turn 'em back."

Other lines, with references to old-time Indian ways, made the threat of violence more direct; for example, one traditional song was "Get the Hell out the Way." "I carry my hatchet right in yore head" was another possible line, as was "If you don't bow down, I hurt your head." In another song, the singer bragged, "I got four little sisters when you cross my train/I got four li'l bullets with a ball and chain." The singer "signified-on" other tribes.[16]

The rhetoric of violence was pervasive; the songs were litanies of threats. This was true even of songs that are held to indicate peaceful intentions, such as "Shallow Water, Oh Mama." One version of this song warned, "If you hurt these flags, then they'll hurt your spy"; "I tell head spy boy, to kill you dead"; "Don't you hurt my chief and don't you touch my spy; cause if you do that's the day you die." Without these threats, "Shallow Water," a signal that the tribe wished to avoid fighting, might have been interpreted as a sign that the tribe was afraid to fight. This would have been as humiliating as losing a fight or bowing to another tribe. The basis for peace between the tribes seems to have been mutual deterrence.

Denying the violence behind these songs or in the Indian parades of the early twentieth century is difficult. By the mid-twentieth century, the Indians did relegate force to a minor role in their competition. The Indian traditions are now among Carnival's most lovely, although the competition among tribes remains. If spies from rival tribes spot each other and their chiefs decide to contest supremacy, the two spies will face off on opposite sides of the street, waiting for their entire tribes to line up behind them. Then each Indian will cross the street, encountering, one by one, each Indian of the opposite tribe—boasting, showing off his costume, dancing a mock fight, singing traditional songs.[17]

Although proclaimed a thing of the past, violence still hangs over the Indians. In theory, no Indian goes looking for trouble. But each Indian has to feel prepared to deal with trouble. Monk

Boudreaux, chief of the Golden Eagles, explained that "I don't mask to go out there and have trouble. I mask to have fun." But having fun does not mean being defenseless. "If somebody starts something," this chief warned, "it's him that's gonna get hurt, not me, 'cause there's a whole bunch of people just waiting to defend me." Even though the Indians themselves no longer carry weapons, they are still accompanied by bodyguards who do. The anthropologist David Draper saw one mother following her daughter, an Indian queen, carrying the daughter's pistol in her purse. During Mardi Gras 1979, the police arrested a man accompanying one Indian tribe for carrying a concealed weapon—a sixteen-gauge shotgun encased in a velvet wrapping decorated with rhinestones.[18]

The ultimate meaning of the Indians goes beyond their contests in the streets of New Orleans. Masquerading cannot get any more serious than it does among certain Indians, for some of them testify that, by donning Indian garments and singing Indian chants, they become Indians. The song "My Indian Red," sung by the chief as the Indians start their parade, is regarded as a "sacred song"—as, in fact, an authentic Indian prayer. In his rendition of "My Big Chief Got the Golden Crown," one Indian sang, "I'm a Injun boy, got an Injun mind." In 1977, Monk Boudreaux tried to explain the transformation. "When I put on my costume, I feel like an Indian." Feeling like an Indian entailed a mental transformation: "Sometimes when I'm singing, I'll be thinking about things I don't know where they come from." The transformation expressed itself in the Indian songs, for which Boudreaux became a vehicle. "I'll be standing in front of people and I won't see their faces, because I'll be concentrating on what's coming out of me. The songs will just be popping out of my mouth. I'll be singing songs I never even heard before." And the transformation could be observed by others. "My voice and manners will be different." Boudreaux did not claim that all Indians had a similar experience, but he was "sure the guys that get into it and stay with it feel the same way."

What Boudreaux describes is reminiscent of spiritual possession, and it is not surprising that the Indians have their roots in the same families and neighborhoods where the spiritual churches are strong. Celebrants in Carnivals elsewhere undergo similar transformations; a Trinidadian masker playing Lucifer observed, "When the moment comes for me to take up that mask, and I take up that mask and put it on, I become a different being entirely. I never feel as if I'm human at all." Spirit possession also characterizes the religion variously termed "voodoo," "vodun," and "vodou"; and vodou raras participate in Carnival in the streets of Port-au-Prince. In New Orleans, for some participants masking Indian is not just a means of claiming public space for ritual; it is a means of recasting interior space as well.[19]

※

The fight between the Mardi Gras Indians and the white boys and men that took place at Mandeville and Burgundy was a small part of the long development of the Indian tradition, which provides one context for the incident. In 1908, the *Times-Democrat* suggested another context for this fight: "a small size race riot." Many readers of the *Times-Democrat* would have viewed this brawl as an incident of black defiance. After the turn-of-the-century, many New Orleanians believed that Mardi Gras permitted such defiance and encouraged the breakdown of Jim Crow law and order. It is noteworthy that in the 1908 affair the police arrested only black people.

The last major race riot in New Orleans had occurred eight years earlier. It had been sparked when a black man, Robert Charles, fired on a police officer. In the days following the initial confrontation, many people, black and white, were wounded or killed, and white men went on a rampage against the city's black community. Charles himself hid in a house. Discovered, he held off a mob with sniper fire until the building was set on fire. Flushed into the open, he was shot down and his body mutilated after death.[20]

After 1900 and the Robert Charles riot, white New Orleanians sensed that the city's black people were more assertive than ever before. In 1909, the *Times-Democrat* complained that black people no longer viewed the old-line parades in residential areas but came to the business district. "The objectionable feature was the manner in which the negroes elbowed and shoved their way through the crowds to get in the front row. . . . Complaints were many, especially from women with children, who were powerless to hold their places. . . . The change in demeanor of the negro crowds was strongly remarked by nearly everyone." Carnival had long been a time when the city's black population could assert itself. But many black Carnival traditions and activities had taken place largely within the black community. Even the Mardi Gras Indians stuck largely to black neighborhoods. Respectable New Orleanians after 1900 worried because some black people were venturing into white areas of the city, particularly the business district, to take part in a civic festivity. The black population took advantage of Carnival to violate the Jim Crow code and culture of New Orleans.[21]

Beyond new black assertiveness, some turn-of-the-century New Orleanians believed that Carnival threatened racial segregation. The crowds on the streets were racially mixed. In those few days, when so much "inappropriate" behavior became permissible, some New Orleanians, both black and white, failed to conform to the legally and culturally mandated segregation. We sometimes forget when remembering the Jim Crow South that segregation ordinances were designed to keep white people from associating with black people as well as to keep black people from associating with white people.

That Carnival helped break down segregation did not necessarily mean that it helped break down racism. Just as in antebellum New Orleans, the Carnival license to express oneself on the streets clearly extended to racist behavior. In 1902, George Purcell and Thomas Mahan, two white masqueraders, came into Allen's Barroom at Poydras and Rampart. Black maskers also patronized the bar. Purcell announced that "it was time to kill a negro," drew a revolver, and fired into the group of black people. He killed Joe McClair. Had the segregation laws of the state been obeyed, Purcell would never have been close enough to McClair to have killed him.[22]

Once again, the *Times-Democrat* spoke for respectable white citizens concerned with racial decorum. In its Ash Wednesday editorials in 1911, the newspaper generally praised the way the police had enforced the law and handled the crowds on Mardi Gras: "The police administration yesterday was entirely satisfactory, except in one respect, which has attained importance of recent years." The one respect was racial: "The negro question has been a little troublesome; and it is a very delicate and difficult one to handle satisfactorily." Even the police inspector admitted that it was difficult for them to separate the races during Carnival. "The laws of Louisiana provide for race segregation in the cars, theaters, and public places," the editor explained. "This is difficult if not impossible as to the Carnival, and there was practically no separation yesterday." The editor said that black people, particularly those from the countryside in the city for Carnival, offended white people by their crowding and pushing; he also thought that black behavior was steadily growing more presumptuous. The police would have to devise some means of restraining black people "for the preservation of the Carnival and to prevent trouble."

Yet Carnival itself was part of the problem, and the editor acknowledged as much. "It is, of course, impossible to separate the races in a public festival of this kind, for the streets are public and open to all; but the exercise of a little discretion and judgment, such as the police otherwise show on Mardi Gras, would tend to prevent unpleasant conditions, certain sooner or later to mar the success of Carnival, if not to produce unpleasant racial friction." The murder of Joe McClair might be viewed as an example of "unpleasant racial friction."[23]

The renewed concern with disorder in the streets was partially a result of the segregation laws themselves. When segregation was largely the result of convention, occasional lapses were less threatening than they were after it became legally mandated. What had previously been distasteful to some Louisianians was now criminal. Furthermore, the racial ideology that had called forth Jim Crow encouraged white people to view black people as more dangerous than they had at any time since Reconstruction. Now white supremacists continually harped on black viciousness to justify both disenfranchisement and segregation.[24]

By the late twentieth century, white New Orleans would use Mardi Gras as a symbol of the city's racial harmony. Earlier, however, the space it gave black New Orleanians for assertion worried some white people. In the years before American entry into the First World War, perceptions of black disorder—and disorder in general—rose. During the first two decades of the twentieth century, respectable, white New Orleanians once again pronounced Carnival dangerous, just as they had during the 1850s. Now, however, it was too integral to the city—to the self-definition of its elite and to its commercial prospects—for any to call for its abolition. Nonetheless, though committed to the continuance of the festival, many New Orleanians feared its potential for disorder; more particularly, they feared that Carnival encouraged black assertiveness, the breakdown of Jim Crow, and violence between white and black. The violence was close to the surface—hence the rapid escalation of the fight between the Indians and the white boys and men that took place at the intersection of Burgundy and Mandeville on Mardi Gras 1908. In the 1900s, the respectable fear was close to the surface too—hence the decision on the part of the *Times-Democrat* to alarm its readers by calling that fight "a small size race riot."

Postscript. On the afternoon of Mardi Gras 1927, Patrolman Frank Nelce saw a car driving against traffic on Tulane Avenue. He flagged it down in front of the First Precinct and arrested the driver, Charles Baptiste, a black man. Nelce stepped onto the running board to tell Baptiste to drive his car to the station; when he stepped back off, "Baptiste drew a revolver and fired four shots at the policeman." Baptiste missed the patrolman, but apparently shot one of his own friends in the stomach. (This part of the story is puzzling. How did Baptiste shoot a man sitting in his car? Did someone else shoot his friend? Or did his three companions leave the automobile after Nelce stopped Baptiste?) This happened on a crowded street, filled with Carnival maskers. Some maskers ran toward the car. Baptiste tried to escape on foot. A clown tackled him. Baptiste and the clown—a white man—wrestled on the ground. Another white man came to the clown's assistance. "Soon a dozen others had joined the two men in handling the negro." The small crowd around Baptiste beat him; in fact, the *Times-Picayune* reporter said Baptiste "was in danger of being beaten to death by his captors." Fortunately, Patrolman Nelce forced his way into the circle around Baptiste and rescued him. Patrolmen from the nearby station "ran across the street and soon had the crowd in order." But once inside the station, Baptiste made another break, trying to grab an officer's revolver. The police subdued him but there was a "near riot as civilians and more police hurried toward the sound of the shooting."[25]

9

Mardi Gras Queens

The Dancer and the Fat Man. On Mardi Gras 1928, a crowd gathered around a woman on Canal Street dancing the Black Bottom. A friend of the dancer's played the ukulele while the crowd "stamped their feet." An admiring fat man "flung her a handful of coins." If he thought the dancer would appreciate his largess, he was wrong. She gathered the coins together and threw them back at him. "Anybody can tell you're not used to Carnival!" she cried. "On Mardi Gras we dance 'cause we want to."[1]

Who was the dancer? Was she white? The reporter thought so. If she had been black, the designation "negro" would have been used in the story—and her language probably would have been reproduced with an abundance of "darkey" pronunciation. Still, many people legally "black" in New Orleans were "white" in appearance and speech. So the dancer's race is unrecoverable. Whatever her racial categorization, however, the dance she was doing was "black"; the Black Bottom, as the name suggests, originated in African-American culture. By 1928 this dance bordered on acceptability, but nonetheless was viewed as sexually provocative. It was probably the sexual provocation to which the fat man responded. As was customary during Mardi Gras, the dancer asserted herself through performance, demanding that people stop and look at her. And she staged her performance on the city's central public space, Canal Street.

Who was the fat man? The dancer immediately characterized him as an outsider, someone who didn't know what Carnival was about. His act offended her. The fat man implicitly treated her dance as commercial—a show for his titillation, done in hopes of financial reward. His gesture reduced her performance. Beyond this, the dancer was offended because the fat man acted as if her sexual display was primarily for his benefit and the benefit of other men in the crowd. His response made her sexuality a product of greed.

The fat man's distasteful reaction—his misreading of the dancer's performance—was understandable. Some expressions of sexuality were commercialized. Erotic dance could be profitable. That same Mardi Gras two police detectives paid ten cents to go to a show at a house on North Rampart Street. The dance they watched was nothing special, but during that "decent" show, the master of ceremonies announced a second attraction. For twenty-five cents more members of the audience could go to the rear and see "a real hot dance." The detectives did so, evaluated the dance, and arrested nineteen-year-old Ruby Cook. Cook performed her "hoochy-koochy" dance wearing only "some pretty pink tights and a brassiere." The fat man's response to the Black Bottom dancer made her another Ruby Cook.[2]

Indeed, tossing the dancer money represented bidding for her favors. Traditionally, Carnival was associated with prostitutes. In the years before the First World War, when prostitution, though confined to certain districts, was nonetheless legal in New Orleans, Storyville was an enticing lure for tourists. Some visitors traveled to the city because of its reputation as a haven for sin. New Orleanians devised a different kind of advertising for these visitors than they did for the tourists who came in hopes of attending the Comus ball (although perhaps some of them were the same people). For example, in 1895, twenty-thousand redlight district directories were circulated. In 1906, the *Sunday Sun*, a "sporting" paper, printed a special Carnival edition for visitors. Block's Store offered to sell them Mardi

Gras masks and costumes and whips. The proprietors predicted "a fine Carnival business." Lulu White advertised her octoroons at Mahogany Hall; and "the establishments kept by Miss Ivy Abronds of Bienville and Robertson streets" were "filled with a bunch of swell little ones for Mardi Gras." As the *Sunday Sun* put it, "Mardi Gras is now upon us and everybody will lay aside business cares for a few days and give way to fun, frolic, and sport. . . ." Carnival was a busy season for the brothels.

The association of New Orleans with prostitution paralleled the city's association with Carnival—it became a way by which the city gained a national reputation as a zone in which license was permitted and encouraged. Perhaps the most famous event in underworld Carnival was the masquerade ball given by "Two Well-Known Gentlemen." At these "French balls" women of the redlight district vied for the title "Queen of Carnival." An 1891 guidebook assured women tourists that "ladies attending the ball are not required to unmask." Girls at Tom Anderson's wore masks on Mardi Gras, at least in the mid-1920s. And time-out-of-mind, prostitutes spent Mardi Gras boldly riding in carriages while dressed as men.[3]

Perhaps this was the Carnival that the fat man had in mind. In any case, his gesture commercialized the dance and transformed the dancer into a whore. Her response, "on Mardi Gras we dance 'cause we want to," hardly denied that some women in New Orleans might occasionally have to prostitute the dance. She asserted, however, that on Mardi Gras things were different—that women could express themselves in ways forbidden them the rest of the year, that any display of sexuality was a matter of choice not commercialization, and that whatever identity one had to live with daily, on Mardi Gras one constructed one's own. With words and action, the Black Bottom dancer claimed Mardi Gras as a time and a space for women's performance, assertion, and enjoyment. Anyone who misunderstood this Mardi Gras right—and this Mardi Gras rite—she proclaimed "not used to Carnival."

The 1920s brought vigor back to Carnival in the streets. New Orleanians returned dance to the center of Mardi Gras. Their dancing was not confined to the ballrooms and nightclubs; indeed, dancing in the streets became a common Mardi Gras activity. On the afternoon of Mardi Gras itself, the Lions Club sponsored street dancing on Canal Street. They further encouraged dancing by sponsoring a Charleston contest. One year the Lions Club had the public dancing but could not hold the Charleston contest—the portion of Canal Street where the dancing was staged was jammed and the Charleston contest "made physically impossible by the seething crowds which forty policemen and a patrol of Boy Scouts were powerless to control." Some maskers rode in trucks complete with bands, so they could stop and dance wherever and whenever they felt like it. Sometimes they danced in the streets, sometimes on the lawns in front of people's houses. In the latter case, if the house was owned by friends or sympathetic strangers, those inside might serve the dancers refreshments—an odd echo of traditions associated with Christmas mumming.[4]

All kinds of people engaged in street dancing, although it appears that it was particularly indulged in by the young. For example, in 1921, "Six girls in yama-yama costumes created a sensation by dancing a wild dance in the street just in front of the Boston Club to the accompaniment of a jazz orchestra they brought with them. At the conclusion, they turned handsprings. . . ." Who they were the reporter did not know—children of the proper Boston Club members? But in 1921, it was reported that South Rampart Street, "alive with colored maskers," was also the scene of street dancing. Many maskers carried musical instruments—banjos, guitars, mandolins. These bands would play on the street and dancing would begin. In 1926, the Clara Street Jelly Roll Club, a black social club, showed their expertise in "the latest Charleston steps" by dancing through the city. In 1927, a business district merchants association held Black Bottom contests for both races.[5]

Public dancing returned Carnival spectacle to the individual. It was a way for small groups to resist the separation of Mardi Gras into paraders and observers, actors and audience, spectacle and spectators, which the development of commercial Carnival, with its focus on well-organized parades, tended to foster. Dancing in the streets reclaimed Mardi Gras as a holiday in which everyone could participate. As the Black Bottom dancer learned—if she didn't know already—public dancing also directed attention to the human body and the sexual possibilities of Carnival.

Female assertion, women dressing as men, men dressing as women, the display of sexuality, and even prostitution have long characterized Carnivals—and not just those in New Orleans. In Renaissance Venice, for example, prostitutes dressed as men roamed the streets during Mardi Gras. In Yoruba ritual, women cross-dressed during certain festivals. In New Orleans, the respectable had long complained that women, particularly prostitutes, helped create Carnival disorder. In 1860, the *Bee* protested that far too many maskers were "of the most degraded classes of both sexes, who seized with avidity upon a pretext for strolling about the city, playing poor antics, drinking in coffee-houses, and conducting themselves in a riotous manner to the disturbance of all decent citizens."

The most notorious yet long-lived Carnival tradition was that of cross-dressing. Women—always assumed by the respectable to be prostitutes—dressed in men's clothing on Mardi Gras. In 1857, two women "were arrested for being dressed in masculine apparel, and suffering themselves to be carried away beyond the boundaries of even Mardi Gras propriety and license." One traveler noted on Mardi Gras 1869 that "the innocent amusements of the day were marred and degraded by carriages being allowed to drive about filled with abandoned girls dressed up in men's clothes, with eyeglasses and false mustaches." In 1872, "feminine-looking individuals" dressed as men rode in carriages in the Rex parade. In 1875, some women grew bolder. At a barrelhouse on the levee, "five or six rude women who were dressed in men's clothing" started brawling. A policeman entered the house and was immediately "knocked down and robbed of his revolver"—whether by the women or by others in the house it is hard to say. Whoever robbed him fled into the night, "leaving behind them their fine Mardi Gras clothes." This kind of Mardi Gras celebrating continued into the twentieth century.[6]

It has been argued that the function of this cross-dressing was provocative—that it served to entice customers. The chorus of male disapproval, however, suggests that something more than titillation was going on. What the respectable found most disconcerting was not the sexual allure of these women in men's clothing but their assertiveness. They dressed like men, they smoked cigars, they rode up and down the streets in carriages. They assumed for themselves privileges generally denied their gender and class. In her essay "Women on Top," Natalie Zemon Davis argues that transvestism—like Carnival itself—can be a criticism of the existing social order. Certainly the "abandoned girls" and "degraded" women of New Orleans who garbed themselves as men on Mardi Gras affronted the sensibilities of respectable New Orleanians. They exhibited "masculine" boldness; they laid claim to male sexual freedom. More important, they used the license of the day to assert an identity other than that of prostitute: "On Mardi Gras we dance 'cause we want to."[7]

The masquerade they assumed was that of men, but it was more than that. They modeled themselves on their customers. Not only that, they mocked their customers. Their parody of virile swagger and masculine licentiousness was as pointed as black burlesque of white officialdom.

As the 1857 arrests showed, women were sometimes punished for their Carnival daring. Those who cross-dressed or in other ways challenged the sexual order might find themselves in jail. In 1855, the First District Court fined Elizabeth Cahans twenty-five dollars "for using obscene language and acting in a most scandalous manner in Perdido Street, on Mardi Gras." Twenty-five dollars was a heavy fine; Pierre Dufour, a masker on horseback who rode down a woman and child that same day, received only a five-dollar fine.[8]

In 1870, the association of cross-dressing with prostitutes and the license that society gave to abusing women who dressed as men caused a minor furor when Officer Mullahy arrested Mary Walker while she was visiting the city. Walker, a Civil War surgeon, was known for her advocacy of men's attire for women. As she stopped on a street in New Orleans, a gathering of men mocked and insulted her because of her clothing. When a policeman arrived, he shocked Walker by arresting not the men but her. As Mullahy twisted her arm and literally dragged her to jail, he asked her, "Did you ever sleep with a man?" Possibly this was an indirect accusation of lesbianism, but more likely Mullahy assumed that this woman in men's clothing was a prostitute. Once Walker was brought to the police court, the recorder recognized her and released her. Eleven years later, one of the marching organizations chose to ridicule feminism by parading with a caricature of Walker as chief of police.[9]

But the more significant punishment for women who behaved boldly on Mardi Gras was not legal but social. The price paid for taking advantage of Carnival license, even if just to don a mask and walk down the street, was the presumption that one was a prostitute. Only "degraded women," those of the lower orders, could be found on the streets. Or so many New Orleanians assumed. "Masking in the street is common among children of all grades of society," warned the *Times-Democrat* in 1893, "but as for grown-up street maskers, excepting those engaged in the regular parades, few if any of them are of a class among whom one would care to mingle socially."[10]

Women challenged this social prohibition against their participating in Carnival. By the eve of the First World War, increasing numbers of women ventured onto the streets on Mardi Gras day. Generally, their costumes were considered modest—for example, in 1906 long linen robes were popular—but some women used the masquerade as an opportunity for sexual display. And sexual display continued to be associated with prostitutes. In 1911, one New Orleanian complained about "the stream of scum that was turned loose in the redlight district and permitted to flaunt itself, vulgarly clad, on Canal and St. Charles streets, in a most indecent manner, giving exhibitions of bodily contortions before blushing, respectable women and innocent children that lined these streets to view the Carnival parade."

But other women ventured onto the streets as well. According to a 1908 account, "Some few women were seen as ballet girls and in other attire designed to display the feminine form divine." In 1912, one man complained that "observing the dress of some female maskers, likewise the dress of some females who were not masked, the question comes to my mind: which was the more grotesque or immodest?" Their skirts were high and their dresses tight. In 1914, a "party of winsome girls" paraded the streets "with their petite figures encased in tights." A young man pinched one of them; she screamed; he fell flat. "Some representative of a fast disappearing generation had landed a well-aimed blow on his jaw." As feminine display increased, it was in itself regarded as both a form of disorder in the streets and a possible incitement to further disorder.[11]

During the "jazz age" even more women masqueraded. In 1920, one reporter had the unquantified impression that there were more women masking than men. What the women maskers asserted was their sexuality. The woman "with [an] almost perfect figure" who masked as a ballerina created "a near sensation on Canal Street." Surely she knew this; surely this gave her a sense of both freedom and power.[12]

There had been ballerina costumes before World War I, although I have not seen any account of the maskers garnering the kind of attention that the 1920 ballerina did. The war did not create the trend toward more feminine display; it was already under way. But after the war revealing costumes seem to have become more common. Furthermore, in the jazz age, they became more accepted. Newspapers employed the same figure over and over again to illustrate their Carnival editions. This female masker was a pirate, always dressed in a black hat, flowing shirt, black boots reaching to mid-calf, and abbreviated shorts. Always, there was a lot of leg displayed in these drawings. The spirit of Mardi Gras, henceforth, would be acknowledged to include female sexuality—although this female pirate also exudes a wholesome "girl-next-door" quality, making her sexual allure seem respectable in itself; she is clearly a good girl pretending to be a pirate.

In the 1920s, women masqueraders also continued to don masculine attire. But this too elicited far less condemnation than it used to. After World War I, military uniforms became a popular female costume. In 1920, the *Times-Picayune* observed, "A 'Battalion of Death' in full uniform might have been recruited in short order in the streets of New Orleans Tuesday." The streets had been filled with women in U.S. army uniforms. "There were trim feminine soldiers in Sam Browne belts and boots; others not so well set-up and some badly in need of a rigorous course of exercise." Naval uniforms were seen less often; indeed, "if they did appear, they usually were not the real article, but adapted affairs." Presumably, the uniforms were coming from the closets of relatives who had served in the First World War.[13]

Even cigarette-smoking, while still mildly censured and gently ridiculed, was hardly condemned—certainly not the way nine-teenth-century cigar-smoking had been. "Tobacco has taken rank with trousers as masculine appurtenances in which it is the annual Mardi Gras delight of the feminine population to indulge." Women costumed in feminine attire also took up public smoking. "Men looked somewhat shocked, and women smiled at the sight of a somberly clad 'widow' smoking a cigarette through her mask. A block away, a Spanish lady raised slender, heavily ringed fingers to her lips for an occasional puff, and laughed lightly as she passed a 'mammy' inhaling the aroma from a pipe as black as her face."[14]

Beyond the new assertiveness of women—women dressed as men, women flaunting their sexuality—there was another common custom of Carnival inversion. Men masked as women. Usually male cross-dressing was treated as simply hilarious. In 1920, the *States* wrote that "a quartette of hairy-armed men made a great impression as female impersonators . . . The two blondes were especially well made up, while one of the number, the tallest, had a slit skirt on that reached above the knee, pink silk stockings, and everything else of women's wear." The tall cross-dresser was funny not only because he dressed as a woman but because he wore a costume that would have been considered immodest on a woman. Indeed, this man, knowingly or not, was asserting women's sexuality at the same time that he was burlesquing it.[15]

The most scandalous feminine costumes of the early twentieth century (besides those the Ruby Cooks performed in) were worn by men. Such elaborate attire may have been the work of men who wished to assert their own femininity. If so, their daring passed unremarked by many. Others wanted to assert the notion of *human* sexuality. In any case, men costumed in ways that cut deeper and upset people more than the traditional figure of the large burly man in women's clothes who accompanied pantomimes. One year a policeman accosted "what appeared to be a chubby-faced girl of about eighteen" who was accompanied by a "man about town." "Look here, miss, you must get out of that and go back to your home," he said. "We don't want any such costumes as you have parading the city." The costume included both tights and stockings; the face was "gorgeously painted." The "girl" had to remove her hat and show the officer that she was a boy. Another Mardi Gras it was "the boldness of a fair one . . . attired in what, but for its exceedingly abbreviated condition, might have been regarded as a fit costume for a bathing beach," that shocked the respectable on St. Charles Avenue. "Her white shoulders gleamed in the sunlight and her shapely limbs were liberally displayed." And once again, the Carnival joke was that this exceedingly sexy woman was a man. In both cases, the figure is initially regarded as female, alluring, and therefore lawless. The revelation that the figure is in fact male brings relief—the figure is transformed into one of humor. The threatened arrest becomes unnecessary; the sexual provocation can be treated as if it never took place. The man disguised as a woman poses less, not more, of a threat than a woman asserting her sexuality would have.[16]

Carnival cross-dressing was routinely discussed in the newspapers, with no hint that it was anything other than Carnival fun. The newspapers pointed to gender confusion with glee. A stock Carnival story emerged, one of how some man, usually a rube, followed a woman down the street, only to discover that "she" was a "he." Yet at other times such gender confusion was thought dangerous and the proper subject of legal intervention. There was, for example, the story of Leonard Dogimont's Lundi Gras.

Forty-seven-year-old Leonard Dogimont spent the Monday before Mardi Gras 1924 carousing in the French Quarter—as a reporter put it, he "staged a carnival all his own." Roaming the Quarter's circuit of illegal cabarets (it was the era of Prohibition) he met Mabel. They decided "to make a night of it." "It was a cock-tail here and a gin fizz there and a light beer to wash 'em down." Between bars he was robbed by "two unmasked white men with drawn revolvers"; they took his last three dollars and two medals. Dogimont and Mabel went to the local police station. The police escorted them through "the haunts of the underworld" until they found the two robbers eating at a Dumaine Street restaurant. After their return to the station, the police not only booked the two robbers but also pulled off Mabel's wig. "A tug at her wig convinced them as well as Dogimont that the 'queen' was—well, if not a 'king'—he was at least a joker." Mabel was twenty-year-old George Leroy. They arrested him, too. "He was charged with associating with thieves and appearing on the highways in disguise."[17]

Mighty Apollo. In 1983, the Mystic Krewe of Apollo held its ball where the most prestigious heterosexual organizations traditionally held theirs, the Municipal Auditorium. The ball opened with the New Orleans Gay Man's Chorus singing the "Star-Spangled Banner" and "Mighty Apollo." The former king and queen took the traditional route through the ballroom, as did the four debutantes who followed them, three dressed in white, one in a gorilla suit. Then the krewe's captain, "attired in pink and black and attended by a bevy of scantily clad pages," made his appearance. Mystic Apollo staged a lavish series of tableaux on the theme "Genesis Revisited." After the captain, but before the king and queen, a red and yellow firebird, a green merman, a three-headed monster, a centaur, and a spiderwoman all graced the stage of the auditorium.[18]

The gay community in New Orleans has been long-established. The city's lax moral code, its situation as a port and its association with customary port vices, its openness to nonconformists, its regional and national reputation as a sin city—a reputation both deplored and carefully nurtured—and its exoticism have all combined to make it irresistible to America's gay bohemia. Lucy

J. Fair points out that "New Orleans has long ranked as a major gay center and mecca for homosexuals from all the American South."[19]

The employment opportunities available in this city of sin have traditionally included roles for gay men and women, whether in Storyville or on Bourbon Street. The allure of interracial sex, long associated with New Orleans, has often been the allure of homosexual sex, from enslaved "fancy boys" to lovers ensconced as butlers and valets to tricks picked up on the street. Furthermore, New Orleans commercialized transvestism. Female impersonators have been part of Bourbon Street's offerings for many years. And transvestism went beyond Bourbon Street. For example, after Prohibition, black female impersonators became part of the club scene. Bobby Marchan, the rhythm and blues performer who sang on many Huey "Piano" Smith records, frequently performed in drag. The gay performing community—particularly transvestites—is a rich resource for Carnival design, costuming, and display.[20]

As noted earlier, the tradition of cross-dressing has long existed in European Carnival. Lucy J. Fair introduces the article "Mardi Gras and Masked Balls" in *The Encyclopedia of Homosexuality* by noting that "carnivalesque observances of this kind have long homosexual associations." In New Orleans, gays have traditionally regarded Carnival as their own holiday—just as do uptown elites or working-class black people. That it was during the 1970s and 1980s that gay Carnival attracted public gaze and gained a kind of respectability should not obscure the longevity of gay Carnival. Calvin Trillin called attention to it in the *New Yorker* in 1968: "Among homosexuals, Mardi Gras is the Harvard-Yale game." "Gay people, in turn, have added their own special flavor to Mardi Gras," a gay writer said. "While Straight America comes to be something that they are not (at least not on the surface) Gay America comes to be something that they are but cannot often be the rest of the year."[21]

Carnival licenses the flamboyance associated with French Quarter commercialized gay life. During Carnival, the female impersonators working at nightclubs on Bourbon Street and elsewhere can take to the streets openly—as can any other man, gay or straight, who feels like cross-dressing. A 1978 article in the leading gay newspaper advised novice masqueraders, "You may even be a closet female impersonator, seeking release and what better time to 'come out' than Mardi Gras? When you look just like any other person at Carnival . . . Crazy!" The same article contained practical advice: "If you are planning to do your face as a woman, don't shave for at least three days, and you will have a closer shave and smoother skin"; and "Want a Cleavage? Try an ace bandage wrapped across the back, under arms and under the chest for uplift. Or you can use masking tape as long as you can go through the pain of taking it off."[22]

A highlight of Mardi Gras itself has long been the Gay beauty pageant at the corner of St. Ann and Bourbon. The Clover Grill began sponsoring the Bourbon Street pageant in the late 1950s; later sponsorship was passed to Cafe Lafitte in Exile. In 1979 the categories of costumes judged were Best Male Costume, Best Female Costume, and Best Group Costumes, with a special award for men with beautiful bodies—the Macho Man award. The crown, however, was the Grande Prize, won by extravagant presentations such as that of the Texas motorcycle club, which staged Cleopatra's entrance into Rome.[23]

Describing the gay krewe as "a support group," George Jesse said, "I think it's a form of peer acceptance, a form of creative expression, a form of thumbing your nose at the rest of society." Perhaps the first gay krewe to give a Carnival ball was the Krewe of Yuga, formed in 1959, and the subject of a now legendary Jefferson Parish police raid in the early 1960s. Krewes that followed included Amon Ra, Apollo, Armenius, Celestial Knights, Dionysius, Memphis, Olympus, and Petronius. By the late 1960s these organizations were holding their Carnival functions openly—or as *Impact: New Orleans' Gay News* said, "A number of groups were ready to officially charter a krewe, rent an auditorium, pass out tickets, and show the rest of New Orleans how a ball SHOULD be run."[24]

Gay Carnival balls both mocked traditional Carnival and appropriated it. Just as Zulu originally served as a commentary on white Carnival, gay krewes were initially formed to mock straight Carnival. "We're not serious about our ball," said Apollo's founder. "It's a farce. The whole thing is a farce. We take off on the regular straight balls." But as Fair observes, "The gay krewes now closely copy, and often equal in size and wealth, the straight krewes they once parodied." And in 1983 a gay critic observed, "Apollo attracts people who are maybe a little more serious about drag or traditional Carnival."[25]

In fact, there was also a gay version of a familiar claim, gay answers to an old question: Who defines Carnival? Some gays demanded acknowledgment of gay Carnival as equal to—or better than—traditional Carnival. In 1979, *Impact* claimed that "the gay balls of New Orleans are even more elite than those given in straight society. It is not unusual to see a member of Comus go begging for a ticket to a gay tableau. Compared to straight krewes which often have upwards of two hundred members, gay carnival organizations are small (under 50 members) and limit the number of guests to less than a thousand. The preparations are more arduous, the costumes more fanciful and refined and the tableaux more imaginative. . . ." In short, gay Carnival was better.[26]

What was going on? This was a New Orleans response to national movements for gay pride and gay rights. At a time when gays were coming out of the closet, gay Carnival could come out too. Carnival had always offered the chance for creative individual and group presentation; gays in New Orleans took advantage of this as had many other groups. This also reveals, once again, the curious New Orleans expression of national trends; of course in New Orleans gay rights would be manifested in Carnival.

The gay rights movement in New Orleans also took more traditional political forms. In 1977 the Gertrude Stein Society, a gay literary group, transformed itself into the Gertrude Stein Democratic Club; it in turn was followed by the New Orleans Regional Chapter of the Louisiana Gay Political Action Committee. According to Fair's estimate, "NORCO has succeeded in electing a number of city council members and state legislators sympathetic to gay rights and in influencing gay rights ordinances and legislation."[27]

Even as gay Carnival balls emerged to compete with traditional straight balls, even as gay krewes appropriated Carnival forms for their own purposes, straight New Orleans proved willing to offer them the same recognition and admiration it offered any group with mastery of gaudy display. Even the mainstream—and stodgy—*Times-Picayune/States-Item* joined the gay and alternative newspapers in covering gay Carnival. And *Dixie*, the photographic supplement read every Sunday along with the funny papers, devoted an illustrated article to gay Carnival balls. As more gay balls went public, their audiences became more mixed between homosexuals and heterosexuals, arousing fears that gay Carnival might be reduced to just another form of entertainment for straights. Lucy J. Fair has commented on the general phenomenon of New Orleans's ability to absorb—to creolize—gay culture. "But gay parades and public drag contests, designed to pique, instead delighted the local population who simply coopted them and turned them into new civic festivals. 'Southern Decadence,' for example, a drag parade that originated in 1974 as a protest march, is today the center of the New Orleans Labor Day celebration." A note of resentment crept into the observations of Charlene Schneider when she spoke of Mardi Gras 1979, the year that a police strike shut down much of organized Carnival and kept most tourists home. Schneider said, "The Bourbon Awards were held—with probably a lot more success—since for once gay people were the majority, not having to play second to the hordes of straights that usually attend."[28]

If the gay community in New Orleans made the customary claims of Carnival proprietorship, Carnival could also divide New Orleans gays along lines similar to the 1960s split over Zulu in the black community. For example, in 1978, using the forum created by *Impact*, some gays accused their fellows of immaturity and lack of political consciousness. According to this critique, Carnival distracted gays from their political struggle; Carnival reenforced homophobic stereotypes. And that same year, *Impact* ran a column saying that Mardi Gras should not become an excuse to abuse sex and alcohol: "It may be too heavy to hear about it, but there IS more to being homosexual than drink and sex." Its author advised the gays of New Orleans to "get off a bar stool for once and get on a church pew." The gay community felt the tension between revelers and the respectable. There has also been a split between the "uptown crowd" and the "Quarter crowd," which is more flamboyant. "You're not going to find a lot of Uptown people who are serious drag queens," George Jesse observed in 1983. "I mean, it's a little strange to walk out on State Street in high heels, whereas on Bourbon Street it's an everyday happening."[29]

This conflict produced an anguished response from *Impact* writer Jim West. He mourned the fact that New Orleans gays would divide over the question "What face should we show Mr. and Mrs. Straight America?" Rephrasing the question, he asked, "Do we convince them that we are the same as they are, that we put our pants on one leg at a time just as they do?" If that strategy was best, "What about those gay men and women (subminorities in both cases) who don't wear pants at all, but prefer dresses?" West raised one more question, the most troubling of all, and it was his answer to the respectable critics within the gay community: "Is it consistent, or even logical, for us to insist upon our right to be who we are to the rest of the world, and, at the same time, deny that same right to some of our own people?"[30]

Thus the New Orleans gay community, debating on how to celebrate Carnival, reproduced the old dichotomy between reformers and revelers. And thus New Orleans—which really is a part of the United States—produced its version of the national gay rights movement. But the relationship between the gay assertion appropriate to the political arena and gay cultural assertion as might be displayed at a Carnival ball or on the streets of New Orleans Mardi Gras remained troublesome. Speaking of a particularly elaborate ball, one New Orleans gay man carefully pointed out, "We didn't do it to make a point that we're gay. We do it because it's fun, and that's what Mardi Gras is all about."[31]

10

Louis Armstrong's Mardi Gras

LOUIS ARMSTRONG, New Orleans's most famous native son, felt bitter toward his hometown, although he was a man who rarely let this bitterness show. Growing up poor, the son of a prostitute, incarcerated in an orphans' home because of an exuberant and dangerous prank involving his mother's boyfriend's pistol, he learned to play cornet and left New Orleans for Chicago as a very young man. He never lived in New Orleans again. But he would return when he was asked to be king of Zulu, the city's oldest black krewe. Mardi Gras was part of his identity.

Zulu called him in 1949. Even the patronizing accounts in the national press make clear Armstrong's enthusiasm for the role. After all, being king of Zulu was a boyhood dream. He had played in Zulu parades as a teenager; he had had a hit record with "The King of the Zulus" back in 1926; and when he visited New Orleans in 1930, Eureka—Zulu's band—met him at the train depot and brought him to town. In the past, Armstrong acted as if he didn't distinguish between Carnival royalty and "real" royalty. In the 1930s, at London's Palladium, Louis introduced one song by gesturing toward the Royal Box and telling the king, "This one's for you, Rex."

On Mardi Gras 1949, Armstrong seated himself on the throne of the Zulu float, saying, "Man, this is rich." When a scuffle broke out between a bystander and the mayor of Zululand, Armstrong commented, "My, my, just like old times." He enjoyed lunch at the black funeral home that sponsored the parade; they served champagne and turkey and ham sandwiches with pickles and olives. Armstrong returned to the float with three bottles of champagne and announced, "This king stuff is fine, real fine." When Armstrong failed to appear at the Zulu ball after the parade, a duke explained, "Man, that old Satchmo done drunk up all the champagne in this town."

Armstrong's reputation demanded an interview between the musician and the mayor. Chep Morrison invited Armstrong to the mayor's office at city hall—quite a rise for the man whose earlier contacts with governmental agencies had revolved around the court system, the orphans' home, and Parish Prison. Morrison and Armstrong even engaged in some banter. "Satchmo, I read in *Time* where you said—all you wanted was to be the King of the Zulus and you were ready to die." "Yes, mayor, I do remember saying those words—but it ain't no use of the Lord taking me *literally*." Even though the mayor had invited him to city hall, Armstrong had to stay in a Jim Crow hotel.[1]

Armstrong's reign reveals much about the man, the city he came from, and the times in which he lived. In order to receive the long-desired honor from the community of his childhood, he had to swallow local racial mores. The city that honored him with a visit to the mayor also demanded that he observe the law and the humiliating ritual of Jim Crow.

Ordinarily, Armstrong was not a man to defy Jim Crow. Early in his life he had concluded that the best a black man could do was find a white protector; as he put it, some white man who would place his hand on his shoulder and say, "That's my nigger." Armstrong wasn't heroic, but he wasn't stupid. His very reluctance to challenge segregation was probably based on his observation of just who had—has—power in American society. One time a fellow musician dropped by his dressing room and asked, "Hi Pops, what's new?" Armstrong answered, "White folks still in the lead." But New Orleans, like Central High in Little Rock, provoked Armstrong to make one of his rare public statements against segregation.[2]

In the 1950s, Armstrong and his manager tried to bring his racially mixed All-Stars to play a concert in New Orleans, only to be informed that it would violate Louisiana law. Armstrong uncharacteristically blew his top: "I don't care if I never see the city again. Honestly, they treat me better all over the world than they do in my home town." He went on to give his opinion of the segregation laws, which he believed unconstitutional. "Ain't it stupid. Jazz was born there, and I remember when it wasn't no crime for cats of any color to get together and blow." His conclusion: "I ain't going back to New Orleans and let them white folks be whipping me on my head."[3]

Armstrong shook the dust—or the mud—of the city of New Orleans from his sandals. "I don't go to New Orleans anymore," he told the *Louisiana Weekly*, New Orleans's black newspaper. He did not keep his promise. Later on, during the 1960s, Armstrong returned to the city of his birth. But no other return he made to New Orleans was as satisfying, as triumphant, as the time he came back to reign as king of the Zulus. This was recognition from his old Perdido Street neighborhood, from the men and women whose African–New Orleans street culture created jazz and created Louis Armstrong himself.

To understand fully how Zulu could call Armstrong home, we need to look at another, earlier Carnival that Armstrong described in *Satchmo: My Life in New Orleans*. This account suggests something of the freedom Carnival represented for Armstrong and other black people in New Orleans. We also need to consider the influence of black Carnival, its parading traditions, and the celebration in the streets on the formation of jazz.[4]

⊗

In 1918, a teenaged Louis Armstrong stopped at Henry Matranga's to buy a bottle of beer. He had hardly greeted the white proprietor when Captain Jackson, "the meanest guy on the police force," came in with a squad of policemen. There had been a holdup a few blocks away; Jackson simply arrested the nearest assembly of disreputable black men, including Armstrong, and took them to Parish Prison. Nobody booked Armstrong; he and the others were held in the yard with convicts waiting to be sent upriver to Angola. Armstrong identified the men in the yard as Downtown Creole, practically a different people. He knew them by names like Dirty Dog and Steel Arm Johnny. No innocent himself—he always liked those he called "good old hustlers"—he would be a pimp for a bucktoothed woman named Irene, he would marry a prostitute, and he had watched men shoot other men. But he felt he had no one in Parish Prison who would protect him. He was scared and he was kept scared. The captain of the yard, Sore Dick, poked him with a broom, tripped him, and then insisted he sweep the yard: the ritual all newcomers to the prison observed. It isn't clear how many days Armstrong stayed in the prison yard, but he had to depend on the Italian saloonkeeper Matranga to arrange the release of all the men falsely arrested in his bar. No wonder Armstrong came to believe that the only way a black man could survive in America was to have a white patron.

On Mardi Gras they set him free. "It's funny how life can be such a drag one minute and a solid sender the next." He came out in time to see the Zulu Aid and Pleasure Club parade. The Zulus were the black working man's own organization. In 1959, the trombonist Sunny Henry reminisced that "the Zulus were here when I first came here, but they was a tough gang." Many of them were longshoremen; many came from Perdido Street, Armstrong's own neighborhood. White people thought them ludicrous and charming, respectable black people were embarrassed by them. But Zulu— black men in blackface—ridiculed white stereotypes and gave black New Orleans its own royalty. Indeed, the king of the Zulus traditionally boasts, "There has never been and will never be another king like me." The king of the wake reappeared as the king of the Zulus.

The Krewe of Zulu had its origins in a Carnival marching club called the Tramps. The Tramps paraded dressed in white shirts, ragged trousers, and straw hats. King Willie Stark wore a lard-can crown and carried a scepter made of a stalk of cane. Around 1909, some of the Tramps attended a stage show at the Elysian Theater that featured an African skit entitled "There Has Never Been and Will Never Be Another King Like Me." This inspired them to rename their organization after the Zulus. The king continued to sport the lard-can crown. In 1912, King Peter Williams wore a white, starched suit, a tie that was a loaf of Italian bread, and an onion stickpin. The first Zulu queens were men in drag.

In his way, Zulu did everything that Rex did. If Rex traveled by water, coming up the Mississippi with an escort from the U.S. Navy, Zulu came down the New Basin Canal on a tugboat. If Rex held a scepter, Zulu held a ham bone. If Rex had the city police marching before him, Zulu had the Zulu police—wearing police uniforms until the municipal authorities objected. All that Zulu did caricatured Rex; a black lord of misrule upsetting the reign of the white lord, a mocker of a mocker. Zulu was perhaps the best example of what Henry Louis Gates, Jr., has called the "double play" of black "vernacular structures"—a black Carnival parade that commented on white Carnival parades.

In 1918, as in years past, everyone in Zulu masqueraded as a well-known local figure, satire similar to that Comus had used against Republican authorities. The man who excited Armstrong's admiration most was Papa Gar, the captain of the Zulu police force. Papa Gar had the audacity to strut through the streets costumed as Captain Jackson, the meanest man on the force, and the man who had just mishandled Armstrong. Zulu was signifying on Captain Jackson. Armstrong could do nothing about the injustice he had suffered, but the Zulu Aid and Pleasure Club could and did speak for him.

Armstrong stepped out of Parish Prison, then, to find black values reaffirmed and the pretensions of white society revealed. "It had been my life-long dream to be the King of the Zulus," he said, "as it was the dream of every kid in my neighborhood." Armstrong remembered his glee at Papa Gar's impersonation more than thirty years later. The power of Carnival in the black community lay partly in the opportunity it provided for satire of the white community.

Armstrong would also remember the "good jumping music of the brass bands" that marched with Zulu that day. He had been a marching band musician himself, and would be again. The marching band, intimately related to Carnival, was also intimately connected to the development of jazz.[5]

Mardi Gras did not "create" jazz. It did, however, reflect the reasons New Orleans would become the birthplace of jazz; the Mardi Gras spirit was a precondition of jazz. The links between Carnival and music are strong. Their strength is even more apparent when Carnival is considered merely one specimen of New Orleans's cultural scene. Parades and balls alike provided employment for musicians and would-be musicians. The demand for musicians seemed insatiable, and included white and black alike. No parade was complete without at least one band, and the more lavish parades, such as those of Comus or Rex, would have a band before every float. Playing parades was an essential part of being a musician in New Orleans. The drummer Ram Hall said that when he began playing, his three ambitions were to play a picnic, a funeral, and a Mardi Gras parade. Small groups were also in need of bands; for example, in turn-of-the-century New Orleans, white maskers hired black bands to ride with them in spring wagons, providing music for their dancing.[6]

And balls meant dancing and dancing meant music. And music, until the advent of the radio and the record player, meant musicians. In 1925, the *Times-Picayune* revealed that, according to local music companies, the only reliable copy of "If Ever I Cease to Love"—a song long out-of-print—was in the hands of "Prof. John P. Robicheaux, leader of the Lyric theater orchestra, and well known negro violinist and composer." Robicheaux was one of the key figures in the development of New Orleans music. Indeed, "More than one band leader, called upon to lead the Rex parade, and knowing that he must play the piece when Rex from his float, greets his queen on the balcony of the Boston Club, has sought out Robicheaux." Carnival, by providing the audience, the money, and the forum in which to develop music and musicians, helped create the New Orleans musical tradition. There would, most likely, be jazz without Mardi Gras, but at the very least, Carnival provides an example of the culture that developed jazz.[7]

At the turn of the century, when young Armstrong first started listening to parade bands, a musician could work many jobs on Mardi Gras. Jack Laine, a white musician, remembered playing six jobs in one day, including advertisements for the Merry Widows Social Club Ball—and the ball itself—music for the viewing of maskers at Frenchman and Decatur, and a day and a night parade on St. Charles Avenue, presumably those of Rex and Comus.[8]

Parades marched to the tune of brass bands. For Rex and the mystic krewes, this meant white brass bands. For black organizations such as Zulu and some white marching clubs, it meant black bands. The period after Reconstruction saw the formation of many such musical organizations in New Orleans. The early brass bands were made up of "reading" musicians; that is, musicians with some formal training who could read the sheet music for the frequently elaborate marches and dirges. Although they played some music indigenous to New Orleans, they also mastered the Sousa marches and Broadway tunes common to the nationwide marching band repertoire. Around the turn of the century, however, "routiner" or "head" music and "ear" musicians began to appear at parades. This was music more exclusively rooted in black traditions, played by men who often could not read music but who instead improvised. In short, jazz began to be heard in New Orleans parades.[9]

Parades drew out another New Orleans black institution—the second line. The second line were the people who followed the band, marching alongside their favorite musicians. A parade in New Orleans was not complete until the arrival of the second line. Indeed, one distinctive drumming style is known as the "second-line beat," and "Second Line" is the name of one of the songs most associated with Carnival.

Second-liners do not merely watch the parade, or even walk

calmly beside it. Rather, they act as part of the parade. They strut, they dance, they encourage—or discourage—the musicians, they twirl umbrellas. In other words, they assert themselves. In the second-line tradition, a parade is an opportunity for all to display themselves. The second line has been much celebrated—and justly so—as a New Orleans tradition that helps break down the distance between performer and audience, that takes spectators from the periphery and puts them into the center of the show. This should not hide the fact that relationships between the second line and the parade bands occasionally have been difficult. Even though the "parade aesthetic" involves mutual display and assertion, musicians and second-liners sometimes find themselves in competition.

Occasionally, the second-liners' desire to assert themselves led them to try to dominate the band and the parade. The musician Sunny Henry explained in 1950 that "sometimes they rule the band—they wants to rule the band—tell them what to do, tell them what to play." Second-liners sometimes prevented the bands from marching by dancing in front of them. More often, second-liners competed with one another. The display of personality and style was crucial. Second-liners implicitly challenged one another by dancing and strutting. Thus, second-lining was a less elaborate, less planned version of the confrontation that characterized the Indians' parade. Discussing second-liners, Percy Humphrey said, "They want to show the public how much they can dance."[10]

As with the Indians, competition among second-liners could become violent. In 1959, John Casimir remembered that "they'd fight and everything." He thought that there was less violence by the 1950s than there had been in his early days as a parade musician. "Got civilized, that's what, got civilized." When he was younger, people in the second line would hit each other with "bricks and sticks and everything . . . Sometimes used knives, cut you and shoot you too; take an old broom handle, beat you all up." Even the festive umbrella, long associated with good times in New Orleans, might be used as a weapon. One category of weapon that did not, at least according to the memories of some musicians, make an appearance in the early days was firearms. Unlike Casimir, Sunny Henry remembered, "No guns—I've never seen anybody shoot."[11]

The violence was not only between individuals. As a group of second-liners followed a parade, they sometimes crossed neighborhood boundaries. Conflicts between groups of second-liners were sometimes over turf. Casimir said that it "used to be uptown fellow couldn't come downtown," that fighting would break out when people came into an unfamiliar—and unwelcoming—neighborhood.[12]

If conflict with the second line could mark—and sometimes mar—parades with black bands, tensions were increased when a black second line followed a white band. One musician remembered the confrontations between the second line and the white musicians in the band he played with before 1915: "I remember the time when Didi Stevens—see they had ten men for a Carnival parade band and Didi Stevens would make those niggers dance just by playing the march, did[n't] need the band. Oh did you know at that time there was a fellow with a billiard cue that used to beat those niggers back?" He said black people would rush Jack Laine's Reliance Band—they would be beaten back with clubs—but that if a marching band was not hot, "none of the niggers wanted to get around those guys because they was nothing to it, just a march."[13]

The drummer Monk Hazel remembered playing his first Carnival parade, probably Rex, in the early twentieth century. He was on the outside of the marching band. At one corner, "a little jig kid" about fifteen years old hit him in the foot with a torpedo stick—a stick with a metal ending in which caps, or "torpedoes," could be placed. "That was a favorite sport around Mardi Gras time." Hazel did not see his tormentor but an older musician, Ragbaby, did. After marching all the way to Canal Street, the parade circled back so they passed that corner again. This time, Ragbaby made Hazel get in the middle, handed his drum to Hazel's father, and used the bass drum beater to strike the black teenager.[14]

In all fairness to Ragbaby, black bands used the same procedure. The relatively genteel and predominantly Creole Onward

Brass Band had trouble dealing with second-liners and sometimes recruited the uptown tough Black Benny to march with them. A drummer, Benny wielded an extra heavy beater and was not reluctant to use it on the second line. The obstreperous second line was what gave the grand marshal of a parade a more than ornamental role. When asked, "What makes a good grand marshal?" Casimir explained, "Make the second line get on back. . . . Get on the side, he'd tell them; they'd get on the side too."[15]

When second-line unruliness grew so great that the grand marshal could not keep it under control, the police might intervene. Sometimes police on horseback would rush the second line, keeping it out of the path of the parade. At this point, the second line was engaged in a contest not only against the band or the marching organization but against white officialdom. The second line was "bad," an adjective sometimes used to express approval, especially in a situation in which second-liners communicate their personal style despite those who seek to hamper them.[16]

An important, although less threatening, component of the second line was children. At the turn of the century, following a parade, Carnival or otherwise, was a source of great delight for children. More important, parades and the exposure to music and musicians fed their dreams of becoming musicians themselves. In this way, parades functioned to recruit New Orleans boys into marching bands and a life of music in general. Barney Bigard, who played with Armstrong's All-Stars and the Duke Ellington Orchestra, remembered the process well. "That's really my first interest in music: as a kid watching the brass bands. We'd hear the parade coming down the street, and well, that was the end of the game. We would try to follow the band as far as our folks would let us." Danny Barker—whose musician grandfather forbade his second-lining—still could watch jazz bands on the streets advertising dances when he was young. Both "the vibration the jazz created" and "how these musicians were greeted, applauded, the reception they were given" struck him as wonderful things.[17]

Children would follow parades playing tin flutes or homemade instruments such as cane flutes. They would bang on tin plates with spoons or play washboards. George Lewis, later an internationally known clarinetist, would jump the fence and chase after parades even when he had "scarlatina fever and was peeling like potatoes." Or instead of following a parade, children would lead it. They would run ahead and dance on the street corner until the band caught up with them, at which time they would run another block ahead.[18]

After a child decided to become a musician, the streets became his school. Although many black families managed to collect small sums of money to pay for some formal musical training, the source of inspiration and ideas was the music that could be heard on the streets. And when a musician reached a certain level of proficiency—and, perhaps more important, the stamina to march all day long—street parades would usually be his first paying job. As Percy Humphrey said, "Many [or] most jazz greats started on the street parade."[19]

Furthermore, the streets, the parades, the second line all shaped the music he played. New Orleans drummers learned the rudiments of military drumming to play in parades, but the drumming also influenced the way they played dance music and later jazz. Horn players learned to blow full force—the only way the horns could be heard as the band paraded. March times permeate New Orleans music. In fact, when traditional military 4/4 time with its accents on the first and third beats met the African-American tradition with its accents on the back-beats, an unpredictable suppleness emerged in parade music, syncopations appeared, and the bands began to swing. Finally, the influence of the audience—the second line—shaped the repertoire and the styles of turn-of-the-century musicians.[20]

The streets were a forum for competition among musicians, not just second-liners. Crowd approval determined questions such as "Which band was the best," "Which musician in a band was the best," "Who was the best trumpet player in town." Parades could turn into "bucking contests." These contests were serious affairs. If they involved marching bands, the two bands might march in-between each other, with each striving to play better—and each playing a different tune. If the bands were riding in wagons, sometimes the crowd would chain the wagon wheels together so that the contest would go on until one band was thoroughly licked. And the crowd picked the winner. Barney Bigard claimed, "Whichever band had the nastiest lyrics would win. Like Ory had a tune to which he would sing 'If you don't like the way I play, then kiss my funky ass.' That went over big with all the whores and they would gather around the wagon."[21]

Lee Collins identified success in street competition as the key to prestige for a New Orleans musician. "In those days, everybody second lined and picked out their man, who they liked . . . who they'd like to be, and then you got famous by that. It's a funny thing. You played in an orchestra, people didn't pay no attention to you, but as soon as you hit the street, everybody had their eyes on you"—particularly if you were a cornet player. Cornet players were to New Orleans brass bands what saxophone players were to the jazz age and electric guitar players were to rock; the cornet was the sexy, hot, attention-grabbing instrument. Collins himself defeated cornetist Kid Rena in a near mythic bucking contest in the 1930s.[22]

Collins won that particular contest by playing the latest Louis Armstrong hot solos just as Armstrong played them on the record, whereas Kid Rena played more old-fashioned jazz. Kid Ory won the second-liners over with his version of "Funky Butt," a "ratty" song. So bucking contests were not simply about the relative skill of a band. They were also about the style a band played in. Indeed, the streets, perhaps more so than the clubs, were where the battle between traditional music and jazz music took place. It was the second line who insisted that jazz be played in the streets; it was the force of popular approval and disapproval that transformed the music of the brass bands.

Traditional musicians praised the old standard repertoire and lamented its decline. Peter Bocage told an interviewer in 1959 that brass bands had not always played so much jazz. "The people wanted marches . . . and the band sounds so much nicer when you're playing good, standard music." John Joseph explained, "That's what killed all them big bands, when they started playing jazz in the street, that kilt them kind of bands, you know, nice band—reading music." John Casimir, who favored the change and benefited from it, agreed. What kind of music did the band play on Carnival? "All ragtime. . . . They don't care about no marches. They want to jump." And what did the second line want to hear during Carnival? "Oh, they liked them 'Whooping blues.'"[23]

Punch Miller claimed, improbably, to remember precisely when brass bands started playing blues in the street. In the early 1920s, he played in a band with Armstrong, Kid Rena, Henry Martin, and Black Benny Williams. This group, which was known as the Zulu band, was a particularly hot brass band. The principal musicians could not read music but they could "come down the street and tear the street up." Marching with Zulu, this time for a funeral, not a Mardi Gras parade, Martin, the snare drummer, decided to play some uptempo blues—the first time, according to Miller, this music had been played as parade music. After that, all bands had to follow suit or lose their popularity.[24]

The blues was "ratty" music, low class. This competition between cultures—the older, traditional, music-reading culture and the newer, illiterate, improvising culture—contained elements of class conflict. As Louis Armstrong said, "Jazz and I grew up side by side when we were poor." The new music represented an assertion of the value of the culture of the less formally educated, black working class—the same people whom Armstrong identified as the core of Zulu.[25]

This assertion of value among those thought of as valueless was not directly aimed against white New Orleanians. Rather, this cultural competition was between middle-class black people and working-class black people. Occasionally, it has been described as a conflict between African-Americans and African-Creoles; however, not all Creoles were respectable, nor were all Americans working class. And not all Creoles refused to play jazz, as the example of Sidney Bechet makes clear.

In 1958, Dick Allen of the Hogan Jazz Archive asked the musician John Joseph about playing at balls for the Francis Amis, a prestigious black Creole organization. Allen asked, "Could you play 'Careless Love'?" Joseph assured him, "Sure, they liked the blues, all that kind of stuff." Allen pressed the issue further. "Funky Butt—would you play Funky Butt?" Joseph first responded, "No, they never played that," but then his memory cleared. "They played it but they didn't sing it." The lyrics that pleased the second line on the streets would not suit the respectable in their ballrooms. On the other hand, a good tune is a good tune.[26]

The black middle class had respectability, education, and wealth—*comparative* wealth—on their side. But in the streets, where these cultures competed, none of that much mattered. The working-class black people, Creole and American, had numbers and a willingness to assert their preference even over the preference of the band, which might in fact favor traditional music. They had the second line. And on the streets, the second line's preference counted most.

The same battle was fought on the white side of the color line. Steve Brown remembered that playing "ragtime"—by which New Orleans musicians meant something closer to jazz than Scott Joplin music—was the province of lower-class white people. "The people that were wealthy . . . taught their sons legitimately." It was poorer white people who picked up on the street music. According to Brown, it was also poorer white musicians who incorporated the ideas of black musicians into their own playing. "We took ideas from out in through that country as well as through the darkies that we heard play around here too, you know what I mean, we took the ideas, the white people did—that's the poor white trash as we called ourselves in those days."[27]

The white men who helped create jazz were those willing at least to absorb black ideas. It is not surprising that so many of the early white jazz musicians were Irish and Italian—white people who lived near the racial boundaries both geographically and economically. For example, in Willie Parker's St. Claude Avenue neighborhood, "colored and white lived neighbors, next door like this." The jazz musician and historian Danny Barker noted that the eastern half of the "French" Quarter had a large Italian population: "In the hundreds of tenements in the rear of the front-street buildings there were people of all nationalities, living side by side in these rooms which were surrounded by patios, and there was a whole lot of integrating going on. The poor Italian immigrants, newly arrived from their native land, knew this and did not mind living next to Negroes or people of other races." Barker also realized that these immigrants became assimilated. "Soon, however, they learned the southern system of discrimination."[28]

Working-class white people or white musicians were not somehow immune to "the southern system of discrimination." But interest in working-class black music—jazz—was stronger among poorer white people, and their desire to learn this new music was part of the process by which New Orleans became identified with jazz. Indeed, jazz created an interracial musical vocabulary among New Orleanians; it sometimes even led to interracial association. As a young man, Lee Collins played in a racially mixed band. "That's why I say that ole New Orleans had mixed bands, I think before any city, before they ever thought of that." Monk Hazel also testified that in the old days white and black musicians jammed together. "Jigs—we used to sit in with them and record with them; course you'd get where nobody could see you, you know." One time in New York, the white drummer was playing a recording session at Victor, when the black musician Red Allen arrived to make a record with Ethel Waters. The New Orleans black musician had only to listen to Hazel's drumming to recognize a fellow New Orleanian; he came in and said, "[As] soon as I heard the beat I knew it had to be somebody from down home." They recruited Hazel to play on the Ethel Waters record—they wanted that New Orleans beat, that parade drumming.[29]

Mardi Gras itself helped break down lines between the races— usually to have them firmly in place again by Ash Wednesday. For example, the desire of white clubs for parade music and of black musicians for paying jobs brought black people into neighborhoods in which they ordinarily were not permitted. Punch Miller recalled going to the Irish Channel to sign his yearly contract to play for the Buzzards. Toughs stopped him, asking, "Nigger, where you going walking?" They warned him, "You ain't got any business through here." Miller tried to explain, "Well, I come to see the man about signing the contract for the Buzzards. I play for the Buzzards every year." The white men brought Miller across the street to the saloon that "the man" owned. Miller had to remind the man who he was. "He said, 'Oh, yeah, yeah. What's happening?' I said, 'Well, I'm trying to get home. The white boys want to whip me up there.'" The saloonkeeper vouched for him, going out on the street and telling the toughs, "Goddam, y'all leave that fellow alone; that fellow plays music for me every year."[30]

Carnival also played its part in the spread of the new music of New Orleans. Hearing the music played on the streets, visitors took home an interest in the city's music. Sometimes they tried to bring home the music itself. Jack Laine, a white band organizer, was hired to play the St. Louis Exposition of 1904. He explained, "Well, you see, during Carnival time, they used to come down here from St. Louis and all around—all around up north, you know, that's how the bands got up north, they come down here you know, and listened to the bands—different bands playing in these parades, you see, this of course, this manager or the leader, you know, and give an engagement right away." Because only white bands played the most famous parades, this process favored white musicians. Nick LaRocca, the leader of the Original Dixieland Jazz Band, took his first job to go north immediately after a Carnival parade; on the next day, Mardi Gras itself, he missed the parade he had booked and was already heading north.[31]

In the streets, jazz won. And it won in the national cockpit as well. As the music traveled upriver and cross-country, New Orleans became the jazz mecca. New Orleans Public Service, tourist commissions, and the Chamber of Commerce may have hoped to lure visitors to New Orleans with Carnival, business progressivism, and investment opportunities. They wanted the city associated with white business values. Instead, Carnival hand-in-hand with jazz brought the people to New Orleans. The city's regional, national, even international image was that of hedonism and disreputable music. (It's well to remember that in the early years almost nobody championed jazz as an art form.) The city was associated with black, lower-class, leisure values. Louis Armstrong became the king of jazz and the king of the Zulus. So the second line won the battle over the city's image as well—much to the distress of the respectable, black and white.

Let's not forget that in winning this cultural clash, the creators of New Orleans music—first jazz, and later rhythm and blues—contributed something worth far more to the culture of the world than the best business investment imaginable. The people whom the respectable tried to keep at the margins of the city culturally as well as economically and politically refused their assigned roles and brought their creativity to the center of New Orleans culture. And in doing so, they transformed all music. The rhythm and blues singer Ernie K-Doe was not literally accurate when he said, "I'm not sure, but I'm almost positive, that all music came from New Orleans," but in some ways he had a point.

Consider the New Orleans musical tradition and the Mardi Gras legacy: that serious things are best dealt with in good-natured disguise. New Orleans music is always good-humored, frequently comic, danceable, a polyrhythmatic beat at its core. In that context, though, are expressed all kinds of things, including thoughts and feelings about love, death, and eternity that in other traditions would find form in opera, ballads, and so on. Certain characteristic jazz songs—the "Saints" is the most famous—are not only rooted in black church music but are simply sped-up hymns. The rollicking and funny "Junco Partner" is a saga of imprisonment, heroin addiction, and death. "Stagolee" is about murder and hellfire. The humor of the tradition has never been based on looking away from grim realities. The music born of neighborhoods like Armstrong's Perdido Street and of the second line had to express both the pain and the violence of New Orleans as well as its richness, humor, and tradition.

Postscript. In 1969, Proteus asked the Onward Brass Band to march in their parade. Paul Barbarin, a jazz drummer, composer of standards such as "Bourbon Street Parade," and the leader of the Onward, accepted their offer with pride but also viewed the invitation as a challenge. A preeminent marching group, the black Onward Brass Band had to shine in this prestigious white parade. What nobody realized was the difference that had developed between the white and black marching band traditions. The white parades moved to a military cadence. The Onward was, as Danny Barker described it, "a two-beat, swinging, jazz brass band." The Onward Brass Band began to lag behind the rest of the parade. Barbarin, who was already feeling ill, explained to the parade marshal, "If you're out there swingin' with two-beat, the cadence is too slow to keep up the pace those military marchin' cats set. They take long steps, while we're bouncin' and takin' short steps." The marshal told them to either speed up their marching or fall out of the parade. Barbarin, tense, decided that rather than fall out of the parade—as Barker observes, "It had taken too many years to get into the parade; they couldn't let themselves be thrown out now!"—the Onward would change its beat. He told the drummers to play the military beat, while the rest of the instrumentalists kept quiet, at least until the Onward and the rest of the parade behind them had caught up with the portion of the parade that had gone before. Barbarin himself, however, did quit the parade. When it was over, a policeman told the rest of the Onward Brass Band that Paul Barbarin had died of an aneurysm. Barker remembered, "They stood silent for a while, then one of them said, 'It meant so much for him to march in that parade.'"[32]

11

New Orleanians

DURING THE 1930s, New Orleanians organized a number of new Carnival parades. One group, however, had a parade organized for them—white school children. In 1934 and for several years thereafter, King NOR paraded. Opinion was divided as to the success of this krewe. In 1939, the Carnival historian Perry Young dismissed NOR parades as ugly and unoriginal: "They had just as well be built in Los Angeles or Terre Haute." "Children are always wonderful to look on, and most wonderful when they're dressed-up," he acknowledged, "but there ends the wonder of the NOR parades." The city attempted to give the parade some of the mystique of the old-line adult krewes. In 1935 there were stories of "Little King Nor" leaving "his mythical kingdom and speeding toward his earthly domain"— modeled on traditional Rex stories, but without the humor. To little avail. At least one white girl dismissed the children's parade as boring: "It definitely lacked the pomp and circumstance of the other 'real' parades."[1]

More significant complaints focused on the notion of organizing a children's parade that excluded so many of the city's children. Black children could not participate in King NOR's parade. The organizers of NOR showed so little judgment in choosing themes that they drew attention to segregation. The very first parade, a large affair with fifty-six floats, presented themes in Louisiana history. The parade had no black children, but it did not ignore the role of black people in Louisiana history. This in itself produced an ironic idiocy. As the black *Louisiana Weekly* pointed out, because no black children were allowed in the parade, white children had to blackface "in order to represent Negro life during the early days of Louisiana's rise to statehood." The newspaper suggested that in the future black children be permitted to join the parade and represent black figures. But it remained segregated. In 1939, the parade's theme was "Peoples of New Orleans," a celebration of the city's and the country's ethnicity that, though it included Greenlanders, Persians, and Siamese, overlooked the presence of black New Orleanians entirely. Apparently the organizers had recognized the good sense of the *Louisiana Weekly*'s advice and taken it to heart: they scheduled no more parades in which black schoolchildren could play an obvious role, even if it meant distorting the reality of New Orleans's history and population.[2]

⊗

What was at stake in 1934 was the way Carnival represented the people of New Orleans. Many New Orleanians who had previously enjoyed Carnival as a spectacle or participated in street masking as individuals or in small groups no longer regarded that as sufficient. More people wanted to march in organized parades. Although none of these new parades challenged the centrality of Rex or the mystic krewes to Carnival, they did reveal a growing unwillingness on the part of New Orleanians to be relegated to the role of audience. These new krewes claimed the city's performance space for new classes of New Orleanians. Insofar as Carnival symbolized New Orleans, these new parades broadened the category of people who might present themselves as the city to the city. Although these krewes succeeded in integrating more people into parading Carnival, they denied black New Orleanians any additional claims to the city's public space, excluding them from the new parades that supposedly represented all New Orleanians. And in that regard, they truly did convey much of the ethos of Jim Crow New Orleans.

America's entry into the First World War had brought Carnival parades to a halt. High society agreed to curtail its Carnival balls, and the krewes agreed to cancel parades. Even promiscuous masking was outlawed, "because Mayor Behrman held it might give the nation's enemies an opportunity to work mischief while disguised." The federal government shut down Storyville. Finally, the Eighteenth Amendment outlawed alcoholic beverages, a traditional accompaniment to Mardi Gras revelry.[3]

After the war, the krewes were slow to resume their parades. The first postbellum Carnival, that of 1919, occurred too soon for any of the lavish floats to be designed and built, and many in the city felt it more fitting to let that Carnival, so close in time to the bloodshed of the war and the solemnity of peace, pass without formal celebration. The next year the city—and the rest of the nation from whence so many Carnival visitors came—still could not muster the mental or physical resources for a magnificent public Carnival. Momus, for example, held its ball but no parade. And even the ball was a simpler thing—no tableaux and no ornate costumes. The maskers came dressed as Pierrots.

Likewise, Comus and Proteus offered no parades, leaving only Rex among the white, elite krewes. Rex canceled his traditional Monday arrival on the Royal Yacht but did present a parade on Mardi Gras. There were even two visiting luminaries—General John J. Pershing, who agreed to review Rex and to be made "Duke of Victory," and Maurice Maeterlinck. But despite Rex's best efforts, many viewed Mardi Gras 1920 as a failure. With only one parade, there were few visitors from out of town. The weather was cold, wet, and nasty. With Prohibition in force, there was no booze to enliven the crowd. Too few maskers appeared on the streets. The *Times-Picayune* headline the next day summed it up: "NEW ORLEANS REVELS FOR A DAY, BUT OLD CARNIVAL SPIRIT FAILS." Other newspapers—the *States*, the *Item*, the old Creole *Bee*— were more optimistic about Carnival's future. But the *Times-Picayune* predicted that the change would be permanent, that old Carnival would never come back to the city. "Progress"—the quotation marks were used by the *Times-Picayune* itself—had bypassed Mardi Gras. An old prediction and an old explanation. The writer had either forgotten or never realized that organized Carnival had arisen after the Civil War and during Reconstruction. He thought that the Great War had chastened the city so it had grown past ever celebrating so childishly or so exuberantly again. "It is hardly to be expected that the tone and temper of the 'days before the war' will ever be renewed."[4]

The old-line krewes revived their parades. In 1921, Rex alone paraded; the next year both Rex and Proteus held their parades; and a year after that Momus too joined the others. Comus waited until 1925 to return to the streets. The 1922 Proteus parade prompted the editor of the *Item* to announce the complete revival of Carnival: "The night parade of Monday definitely answered the hotly discussed question of the past five years—Will the Carnival come back? The answer is: The Carnival is back, with all its old-time gorgeousness, its abandon to the joys and inconsequentialities of days gone past. New Orleans needs the Carnival and the Carnival needs New Orleans." The *Times-Picayune*, which had been pessimistic as the decade began, waited until Momus's return to celebrate: "With each succeeding Mardi Gras, the old feeling has strengthened, the population has responded more freely to old enthusiasms, and year by year the old organizations, and some new ones, have proven that the Carnival spirit is in the very blood of the South."

Indeed, that editor contrived to turn Carnival into a symbol not only of the South ("For Southern it is, and ever has been—at Nice, at Venice, at Rome as well as at New Orleans") but of the age. "Celebration of the annual festivity that has helped to spread and popularize the name New Orleans, since the world war has been the correct measure of our national recovery from the saddening effects of that conflict," he explained. "During the first year or two thereafter, the scenes of gaiety were somewhat forced, and there were those who predicted that never again would it be possible to regain the full spirit of the occasion. They maintained that the semi-medieval note observable in a true Carnival abandon had been snuffed out by the realism of the great scientific war, that New Orleans could not 'come back.'" But New Orleans had "come back," with "true Carnival abandon."

Then came the Depression. Whereas many had thought it seemly to cancel Carnival during World War I, the Depression called forth no such response. In fact, when cancellation was suggested, the editors of the *Times-Picayune* argued with typical New Orleans logic that the Depression made Carnival a virtual duty. First, Carnival provided employment—there were floats and tableaux to be built, electrical illuminations to be hung, tourists to be served. "In brief, the Carnival expenditure will benefit, directly and surely, the community and its people—notably including the unemployed for whom jobs are being so earnestly sought." Second, it would increase spending and thus benefit industry. Third, and most important, "The genial spirit, enjoyment and good feeling generated by this brief play-time of ours have themselves a psychological value as solvent of the depressed and fearful state of mind which retards the nation's recovery." This was written in 1931, but it looks ahead to Roosevelt's dictum "The only thing we have to fear is fear itself."[5]

Nonetheless, certain krewes gave up parading because of a lack of money. Momus was the most prominent krewe to cancel parades during the 1930s; it skipped 1933, 1934, 1935, and 1936. This was particularly unfortunate, for Momus was the most satirical of the old-line krewes, and there was much to satirize in those years. But new parades appeared. For example, local businessmen organized a krewe for themselves in 1937, naming it Hermes, after the god they regarded as "the patron of travel and commerce." Apparently they had forgotten that he was also the god of thieves. Hermes paraded on Friday night and held a ball "designed particularly for the entertainment of visitors." The krewe invited out-of-towners to its balls, people who had "hitherto foregone intimate contact with such events." An innovation in the ball itself was the brevity of time between the tableaux and when guests of the krewe could start dancing—an hour. Hermes, then, was a parade founded by businessmen who felt that Carnival needed to be more entertaining for visitors to the city and that the exclusivity of the numerous organizations that sponsored balls needed to be countered. Hermes explicitly catered to tourists. Rex had done the same thing in its earliest years, although it had grown remote by the twentieth century. And twenty years later, businessmen would organize Bacchus in part for similar reasons.[6]

Black participation in organized Carnival did increase in the middle of the century. There emerged at that time a second black krewe in addition to the Krewe of Zulu—the Jolly Boys. They began parading in 1933. They seem to have been more decorous than Zulu. In 1941, King Jolly 8th was Daniel Alexander, head cook at the Harlem Grill. The parade marched from the Rhythm Club at Jackson and South Derbigny; the king greeted his queen at the Willis Funeral Home. The New Orleans *Item and Tribune* made the point that the Original Jolly Boys and Girls Social, Aid, and Pleasure Club was distinct from Zulu: "Unlike the Zulus, this Negro group patterns its floats and costumes after those of the white groups and instead of including the downtown commercial district in its parade route traverses only those sections of the city with large Negro populations." In the style of their krewe, the Jolly Boys asserted that black krewes could master white Carnival forms. The public space they claimed, however, was in the black neighborhoods.[7]

The interwar period also saw New Orleans women organizing a Carnival krewe. The Krewe of Venus had its first parade in 1941. "We thought it was time for the women to have the fun of parading too," the captain of Venus announced. "The men had had control too long." The krewe did not copy the costumes of the male krewes, wearing instead "beautiful women's costumes." Even so, the fact that the krewe was all women offended many; people in the crowd threw tomatoes and eggs at them. And the traditional association of women maskers with prostitutes continued. One founding member recalled, "Oh yes, they called us names. You know, ladies of the evening." The theme of the parade, however, was "Goddesses."[8]

Both Hermes and Venus, like the mystic krewes that preceded them, were white-only. This restriction also marked the krewe that best represented the new openness of the era: the Elks Krewe of Orleanians. Just as the NOR parade confined itself to white children, the Krewe of Orleanians excluded black people in all but menial roles. It did so even though Chris Valley, its founder, self-consciously saw himself as the organizer of a parade that all New Orleans could join. The democratic nature of the Krewe of Orleanians made its ritual enactment of racial segregation more pointed: only black people were banned from the parade.

The story of the founding of the Krewe of Orleanians seems a perfect Depression parable. Had it been made into a movie, Frank Capra might have directed it. Mardi Gras 1933 was a miserable, rainy day. Rex himself decided not to parade. The captain explained, "If I send them out in this wet and cold and these men develop five or six pneumonia cases, I should never forgive myself. One human life or even the life of one mule is worth more than a parade. These men, many of them, are not young." But Chris Valley and the other riders from the Elks Lodge who had invested time, money, and energy in readying a truck float for Mardi Gras day were younger, more vigorous men. They hit the streets. Their "five piece band blew its tonsils out playing 'Way Down Yonder in New Orleans.'" But when they tried to drive their truck onto Canal Street, the police refused them entry; no truck floats were permitted to parade on the city's main thoroughfare. That central public space was reserved by the old-line parading organizations—even in their absence. Chris Valley pondered the spectacle of police turning back the individual trucks—motorized equivalents of the old promiscuous maskers—on a day when the prestigious Rex parade failed to make an appearance. Surely these tenacious revelers, the backbone of Carnival, should be encouraged. Why should only the elite krewes be allowed the glory? The situation inspired Valley with true 1930s populism: "Then the idea hit me! The big idea! Why not assemble all these little Carnival trucks into one big parade. Then the police wouldn't run us off the streets."

The Elks had organized Carnival parades before (they had staged the Krewe of Chance parade on the Saturday before Mardi Gras in 1928) but never one on this principle. In the next two years, Valley and his Elks brothers put together a parade made up of individual truck floats. "We had 56 entries the first year, and after traveling about ten blocks we were scattered in about 56 directions." The title he gave the organization reflected both the contribution of the Elks and the democratic inclusiveness of the parade: "Elks Krewe of Orleanians."[9]

The new participatory parade hearkened back to the early days of Rex, when anyone could costume and march behind the king of Carnival. And, indeed, the city administration suggested that the Krewe of Orleanians keep the long parade from breaking up as it made its way through the streets by marching behind the Rex parade. The krewe has done so since 1938. Following Rex clearly established the parade as a subordinate one. Unlike Bacchus, a krewe founded in the 1960s, Chris Valley's Orleanians did not challenge the established krewes for Carnival dominance. Orleanians accepted their place in the Carnival hierarchy. The Krewe of Orleanians claimed the same performance space that Rex and Comus would use on Mardi Gras, but it acknowledged the primacy of their claim.[10]

Like Rex sixty-odd years earlier, the new inclusive parade placed some restrictions on its participants—in fact, one identical restriction: "NO COMMERCIAL ENTRIES, but only groups out for a good time." Groups riding in trucks had to register in advance with the Elks, describing their costumes and decorations. "The parade has been a tremendous success, and we insist that all participants be colorfully costumed, and masked, or [wear] sufficient make-up so as to conceal your identity. Your float must also be fully decorated." Krewe members, as well as the drivers they hired, who were usually black, were not to drink before or during the parade. "Don't drink under any circumstances. This is mentioned mainly for the negro drivers, because we have noticed in past years that they spend some of their time around the negro bar-rooms in the vicinity of the 'den' on Franklin Street." There was another major restriction on who could don a mask, board a truck, and join the Krewe of Orleanians: "The Benevolent and Protective Order of Elks being a strictly white organization—it will be understood that only those of the Caucasian (white) race are eligible for this Elks parade." The emphasis on a white-only parade went hand in hand with Valley's insistence on masking; white people still worried that there might be black faces concealed behind those masks. In fact, the one person on a truck float specifically exempt from masking was the hired driver. He could drive the float, but he must not appear to be part of the masquerade.[11]

The participation of one particular group of New Orleanians made the prohibition against black people even clearer. The 1930s parades turned out to be great triumphs for the Filipino community. In the first parade, the Caballeros de Dimas Along, a Filipino organization that dressed in Filipino regalia, entered their float as a conscious bid for civic recognition at a time when New Orleanians derisively referred to Filipinos as "Manilamen." The float, built along the lines of floats in Manila, represented the Philippines as a beautiful woman, held by chains while Uncle Sam pondered whether or not to grant her independence. It won first prize, and the Caballeros continued to take first prize for the next two years. The Elks Krewe of Orleanians had given them a chance for both ethnic assertion and political statement. The krewe accepted the Filipinos as "Caucasian"; thus they were permitted to parade when black New Orleanians were not.[12]

The Krewe of Orleanians was not what it claimed to be: the krewe of all New Orleanians. Beyond that, this new krewe staged a very old tradition, appropriating the public space of the city for white people only. It did, however, claim that space for a broader array of white New Orleanians than the old-line krewes had. But the Krewe of Orleanians, which succeeded in drawing on deep reservoirs of popular creativity, denied itself access to the imaginations of roughly half the city. The parade itself suffered because of the discrimination against black people—as did, ultimately, Carnival and the city of New Orleans.

In 1941, the *Times-Picayune* called the parade of the Krewe of Orleanians "perhaps the most perfect expression of the Mardi Gras spirit, combining the democracy of street maskers with the planning and organization of bigger clubs." Valley remained the man behind the Elks Krewe of Orleanians for thirty years—and rode before it as Mr. Elk in every parade. When Valley retired in 1965, Congressman F. Edward Hebert wrote to him, "I think you have made, without a doubt, the greatest contribution to Carnival and the New Orleans Mardi Gras in its entire history." An old friend wrote—in words Valley proudly made public—"The REX of today is now in second place, because nothing hereabouts can outdo the Orleanians under your direction through all these years." Walter Lebreton went on to say, "You shouldn't have to follow REX—he should follow you, because you provide more of the true, popular carnival show and spirit than the few oldtime floats of REX."[13]

The Krewe of Orleanians was indeed a fine addition to New Orleans Carnival traditions. Valley deserved much of the praise lavished on him. Nonetheless, his parade also revealed that "the Mardi Gras spirit" in New Orleans and "democracy" in America were still segregationist. By 1965, the year that Valley retired, the Krewe of Orleanians faced a country in which segregation had been outlawed in schools and public places, where both parochial and public schools in New Orleans were being integrated. The registration form to be filled out by groups wishing to join the 1965 parade still contained the warning: "The Benevolent and Protective Order of Elks being a strictly white organization, participation is restricted to those of the Caucasian (white) race." The paragraph continued: "Schools especially are cautioned to clear this angle before attempting to register." And the final sanction: "Anyone attempting to ignore this important ruling of our committee, will be barred from future parades." Thus the Elks Krewe of Orleanians continued doing its part to keep black people from the performance space of New Orleans Carnival.[14]

Postscript. By 1946, the mystic krewes had developed a visible role for black men accompanying the parades: they hired them to carry the torches that illuminated the night parades. These flambeau carriers became viewed as an integral part of the parade, yet it would be accurate to say they marched with the parade, not in it. As the costumes and floats of the krewes became more sedate, the flambeau carriers represented the old-fashioned, wilder carnivalesque. Given the racism of New Orleans culture, it was perhaps inevitable that this Carnival abandon was synonymous with blackness.

The original flambeaux were paper lanterns with candles in them. They were hung from poles and carried to illuminate the parade. Carrying the flambeaux became a competitive art in itself. Flambeau carriers developed a walk that combined strutting and dancing. They created a black parade alongside the white parade; they became licensed second-liners. To white eyes, this grotesque element set off the dignity of the formal parade. Indeed, it became necessary for the formal parade. To black eyes, the flambeau carriers embodied the individual assertion and competition that characterized Carnival.[15]

White people also thought that carrying flambeaux represented a way for black people to participate in Carnival. Although the role was clearly subordinate, the antics of the carriers suggested to white people that they were happy with their place. Flambeau carriers were at the margin: they represented both black incorporation into white Carnival and the limits of that incorporation. In doing so, they demonstrated—to white eyes—that a racially segregated society was still an inclusive one.

In the immediate aftermath of the Second World War, black people made it known that a racially segregated society was not a just society. This assertion affected even white Carnival. The conflict began as a simple wage dispute. Amid the postwar wave of wage disputes and strikes, the krewes that paraded at night discovered that they had an unusual problem. The black flambeau carriers struck for higher wages. Momus had to parade with far fewer flambeaux than traditionally accompanied them, and they had to hire white men to carry them. Then Hermes paraded with flares instead of flambeaux. On Friday night, the night of the Hermes parade, three krewe captains, identified by neither name nor krewe, made an appeal to New Orleans as a whole and to its black people specifically. They denounced the wages the carriers demanded as "exorbitant." The carriers wanted $5.00 per parade. The captains were offering $2.50 per parade for marching with the flambeaux—50¢ more than the old, prewar rate. (In fact, all the krewes agreed upon the appropriate scale, as though the night parades were a Carnival cartel.) They pointed out "that the entire cost of Carnival is borne by private individuals for the benefit of the city as a whole." They sounded like other antilabor spokesmen of the Truman era, as if the National Association of Manufacturers had entered this labor dispute.

Then, in one of the more obtuse and insulting gestures in the history of Carnival, the captains called upon recently returned black servicemen, veterans of the Second World War, to volunteer to carry the flambeaux. Otherwise, the "resumption of the Carnival festivities" would be "marred" and "thousands of visitors and service men and women here to enjoy the gaieties" would be "disappointed." The captains tried to portray flambeau-carrying as a civic, even patriotic duty, and one that could be done only by black men. They had no idea what service in World War II had meant for African-Americans. The black ex-servicemen were to report to the den of the Krewe of Proteus. On Monday night, the Proteus parade too rolled without its usual complement of black flambeau carriers. The next day the *Times-Picayune* reported that "the kerosene-burning flambeaux were missing from the spectacle as the krewe could not obtain bearers, but torches in profusion lighted the way brilliantly."[16]

The next day, Mardi Gras, saw another new development. By 1946 the Krewe of Zulu had realized that its audience was racially mixed, and that they were watched by the entire city. (Indeed, with the reign of Louis Armstrong in 1949, they would be watched by the entire nation.) That rainy 1933 Carnival when Chris Valley and other independent truck floats outshone Rex also gave black New Orleanians a sense of pride. Zulu was the only organized krewe to hold its parade. "Is not the fact to be appreciated that while other carnival clubs are offering excuses for not appearing on the streets, the lowly Zulu organization composed of poorly paid, undernourished and even unemployed men who ventured forth into the inclement weather, are now enjoying the reward of sticktoitiveness?" After the Second World War, Zulu had a new assertiveness. In 1946, for the first time, the krewe decided to venture out of the black neighborhoods in which it had been sequestered and parade on St. Charles Avenue and Canal—the precincts of the old-line parades— as well. They specifically addressed both black and white New Orleanians and brought a black parade into the city's central public space, a space previously limited to white parades. Zulu also erected a viewing stand at Rampart and Poydras, "for white persons who desire to watch the Zulu parade." A white audience for this black burlesque, however, would change the way it looked to portions of the black community.[17]

12

Zulu

IN LATE 1960, after the Louisiana legislature attempted to block the desegregation of New Orleans public schools, ten black social clubs, including the Young Men 22 Club, the Bon Temps, and the Townsmen, hardly political organizations in the usual sense, decided to boycott Carnival 1961. Their message may have been more powerful because these were the social clubs whose annual parades helped sustain both the brass bands and the African–New Orleanian festive tradition. They called upon their fellow black citizens to shun Carnival, to stay off the streets, to refuse to celebrate when celebration was a mockery. If Carnival represented a joyous city with separate but equal inhabitants, it must be rejected. That would show the discontent of the city's black citizens.[1]

The decision of black leaders to organize a boycott of Carnival led them into conflict with the mainstay of black Carnival, the Krewe of Zulu. They went to Zulu and asked that the krewe observe the boycott. If Zulu insisted on parading, could they at least change the theme of the parade to something more seemly? "The Progress of Blacks in the American Way of Life" was one suggestion made to the krewe. But as the headlines in the white *Times-Picayune* explained, "King Zulu Club is Standing Pat."[2]

The pressure on Zulu to cancel their parade increased. Dr. Leonard Burns, director of the United Clubs, denigrated the Zulu parade, saying its best supporters were white merchants who profited from refreshment stops. The students and alumni of St. Augustine joined the demand that Zulu stay off the streets; they called the parade a "drunken spectacle and mockery of respectable New Orleans citizens." Henry Johnson, the designated king of Zulu, abdicated. His boss, Angelo Spinato of the Southern Produce Company, concerned about the boycott, told him to resign either his job or his crown. Then the queen withdrew for health reasons and for the best interests of the bar she operated. After Zulu decided to march despite the protest, the Knights of Peter Clavier, a social organization, asked the krewe to reconsider.[3]

Zulu made its decision under the watchful eyes of Mayor Chep Morrison and Police Superintendent Joe Giarrusso, both of whom attended the meeting at which the vote took place. Burns claimed that this decisive pressure forced Zulu to march; at an earlier meeting the krewe had voted to cancel the parade. Zulu responded that the mayor and the superintendent had attended the meeting merely to make arrangements for police protection if the decision was made to hold the parade. But Burns held that "our mayor is primarily responsible for this disgraceful and embarrassing epic in our lives and that the entire Negro community condemns such actions."[4]

But the white community praised Zulu. When the krewe decided to parade in spite of the boycott, the editors of the *Times-Picayune* wrote, "We don't believe the great majority of Negro citizens favor its cancellation for any reasons; and thousands on thousands of whites would assuredly be disappointed to miss it." The Zulu parade, they claimed, "has always been a fine thing, incidentally, for race relations, and if anything might be needed now more than ever." The parade's influence on racial harmony, however, was a subsidiary point. "But the main thing is: This is Mardi Gras! This is one day we can 'forget all that'—meaning tensions, such as they are, for which 95 per cent or more of our combined citizenship have been in no way responsible."

This was an argument more likely to outrage supporters of the boycott than to soothe them. The editors were praising Mardi Gras as a retreat from social issues and suggesting that the issues were, if not trivial, irrelevant. Neither the overwhelming majority of white New Orleanians nor the overwhelming majority of black New Orleanians, they said, were interested in raising the level of racial tension. After Carnival was over, Royal B. Stein wrote to the editor of the *States-Item* about the Zulu controversy. He too approved of the krewe's decision to defy the boycott and march: "The Zulu parade is as much a part of Mardi Gras as any of the other parades and is enjoyed by the public, both white and black, and the visitors." He blamed "outside pressure" for black New Orleanians' decision to boycott Carnival. "By doing this, I don't think they are doing themselves any good, but to the contrary it is keeping the colored people from having a good time."[5]

When Zulu actually took to the streets, they marched with the protection of two dogs from the police department's K-9 corps. On the urging of the Negro Tavern Owners Association, many saloon-keepers decided not to set up the customary stands used for toasting the king of Zulu as he passed by. The krewe had no queen in 1961 and they kept the identity of the king secret. This was a sad comedown from the days of Armstrong's childhood, when every black child in his neighborhood wanted to become the Zulu king, or from his own reign, when one of black America's most famous sons could make the traditional boast, "There has never been and will never be another king like me," and national news magazines covered the parade.[6]

The boycott itself was a mixed success. The leadership wanted to unite New Orleans black people in a campaign for civil rights. Yet almost immediately it had divided the black community by creating the furor over the Zulu parade. A lot of black New Orleanians loved Carnival and were reluctant to give it up. The fact that Zulu embarrassed other black people misled them into attacking it. The reformers were ashamed of an institution that other black people viewed with pride. The rowdiness of Zulu, the blackfacing and grass skirts, the competitive boasting of the king and the Big Shot of Africa—the traditional rival to the king of Zulu—all represented a chance for assertion that was central to black Carnival in a racist society.

Black participation in Carnival did diminish that year, but white New Orleanians hardly seemed to recognize this as a sign that injustice existed in their city. Some, much like Royal B. Stein, shrugged the whole affair off in time-honored fashion as something put together by outsiders. The boycott aroused fears of racial violence; some white people could imagine black savagery more easily than they could black protest. The White Citizens' Council spread rumors that black people were buying icepicks and lye to use as weapons on Mardi Gras itself.[7]

There was no black conspiracy to turn Carnival into a bloodbath. To the surprise of some white people, Mardi Gras passed peacefully. Noticeably fewer black people participated that year—although King Zulu did march and thus earn public praise from the South Louisiana Citizens' Council. The council president, Joseph E. Viguerie, and its executive director, Jackson G. Ricau, also professed to regret the lack of black enthusiasm on this otherwise splendid Carnival. "One somber note was reflected in the absence on the streets of many of our Negro population. This is to be regretted inasmuch as the white people have traditionally considered the colored as a welcome part of Mardi Gras," they said, adding, "We feel that the Negroes hurt themselves by staying away, and that this was their own choosing and was in no way instigated or even suggested by any segment of the white population." This was genteel racism. However, the local Citizens' Council of Gentilly did not understand the larger organization's logic. Their chairman, L. P. Davis, Jr., put out a cheery statement explaining that the NAACP's "efforts to sabotage the Carnival season" did "a great service to the city of New Orleans." Why? "Their boycott removed a vast majority of Negroes from the Carnival scene, resulting in a very gay, enjoyable, and troublefree festivity."[8]

This sentiment was not unique to the council. A reporter

overheard a conversation between two older white men as they walked home Mardi Gras night. "Good Mardi Gras, huh?" one asked. The other was more hesitant, "I don't know—a little dull." "Yeah," the first one replied, "but at least we kept most of the niggers out."[9]

※

Whether or not it had to happen in 1961, the conflict between Zulu and civil rights activists was inevitable. They represented two different ideas of black culture and, to a certain extent, two different black communities, two different approaches to life. It is not hard to portray members of Zulu as Uncle Toms, woefully unattuned to the civil rights revolution going on around them, content to act out a charade that defamed all black people as comic savages. In this reading, the anti-Zulu leaders become the forces of virtue and progress. It is also possible to portray the Krewe of Zulu as representatives of working-class black culture who were rightly resisting the attempts of the respectable black middle class, sometimes identified as the Creole middle class, to push them around. In this reading, we question exactly why the civil rights community changed a boycott designed to express discontent with racial mores into a condemnation of other black people.

Neither reading is entirely satisfactory. The conflict seems to have been between revelers and reformers. The social clubs that supported the initial 1961 boycott, however, were revelers themselves. As the decade wore on, the respectable increasingly joined those who hoped to reform or remove Zulu. Although it wouldn't do to exaggerate the similarities, the Zulu debate is reminiscent of the way Louisiana Republicans spent as much time squabbling with one another as they did united against the white supremacist threat. The controversy over Zulu also represents the difficulties that the civil rights movement faced organizing a black community as divided as that of New Orleans.

Troublesome relations with the respectable were hardly new for the Krewe of Zulu. Alex T. Raphael, Jr., longtime historian of the club, remembered, "For many years we were regarded as heathens by other Negroes." In 1931, the organization complained that, although the *Louisiana Weekly*, New Orleans's black newspaper, did cover the parade that year, it usually preferred to ignore the krewe's activities; they hoped a change in editors would improve their coverage. In 1940, the Zulus paraded with the less than uplifting motif of hunting and capturing the great pink elephant. And in 1942, they staged a "Zulu Carnival Pageant and Voodoo Ritual," "for the first time open to the public"—tickets one dollar. Advertisements described the ritual as "Weird," "Exotic," and "Primitive."[10]

Despite the complaints of Zulu, the *Louisiana Weekly* offered full coverage of the club during Carnival. But Zulu's suspicions were not groundless. In 1938, the *Weekly* called for the city's black citizens to "make a Contribution in 1939." The editors admitted that Zulu was now a traditional part of Mardi Gras, but that fact hardly gratified them. "It is not at all pleasing that the thousands of white and Negro visitors who crowd the city at that festival period should be led to believe by the white press that King Zulu is monarch of all Negroes on that day, and that he represents the darker elements of the city in his grotesque mimicry of the whites' observance." What they wanted was a parade as beautiful as that of Rex or Momus, put together by the best black social clubs. They also printed an article by a white man calling for an end to Zulu and for a parade that would "portray Negro achievement and the inherent Negro wit and humor." Nine years later, Dr. W. L. Russell, president of the Mobile Colored Carnival Association, called Zulus "undignified"; the Zulus "put on a burlesque of which we colored people in Mobile are truly ashamed." Johnnie J. Smith, king of Zulu, responded, "Nuts to those Mobile peoples."[11]

Initially, Zulu represented a "prepolitical" form of protest. But now the black community had become "political." They objected to the mockery of Zulu—and perhaps that salt had lost its savor. Even if Zulu did ridicule white stereotypes of black people, it also reenforced them. White people certainly took pleasure in the parade, and, judging from the white newspaper columnists, they also enjoyed the Amos and Andy shenanigans its leadership arranged for public—white—consumption.[12]

But the Zulu controversy was not that simple. The black community in New Orleans had been divided since the days of slavery. Black Creoles sometimes had a hard time making common cause with African-Americans. There were cultural divisions between the two communities. Although "Creole" did not necessarily designate racial mixture or class status, it was often taken to do so. Even some black New Orleanians confused Creole identity with matters of class and of skin color. This was the city where it was widely believed among African-Americans that black Creoles employed the paper-bag test to determine with whom they would socialize; if an individual's skin was darker than the color made by an electric light shining through a brown paper bag, that person was not let in the door. When Walter White of the NAACP visited New Orleans in 1938, the division between the two communities shocked him enough that he criticized it publicly. It was probably in reaction to their sense that the Creole black community regarded African-Americans as inferior that Zulu members insisted their king always be "dark-complected." "No mulatto man can be King." Yet the Creole community provided much of the leadership in the New Orleans civil rights movement.[13]

The greater division was that between the city's black middle class and its working class. Behind some of the protest against Zulu could be heard the old demand of reformers for respectability. When Dr. Burns said, "The Zulu parade is a symbol of everything contrary to the hopes, aspirations, and desires of responsible Negro citizens," he censured those he must have considered irresponsible Negro citizens. When reformers put an advertisement in the paper that repudiated the Zulu parade, "in which Negroes are paid by white merchants to wander through the city drinking to excess, dressed as uncivilized savages, and throwing coconuts like monkeys," they must have thought that the point they made about black dignity would be clear to all. But what some black people heard was the familiar lament of the black middle class that their working-class brothers were shaming them.[14]

Zulu was not without defenses or defenders. Zulu leaders argued variously that their opponents did not understand Mardi Gras, that they were middle-class snobs who celebrated Mardi Gras privately and selfishly, and that Zulu was the creation of the black working class. Indeed, in attempting to unite the black community in the drive for civil rights, the reformers succeeded also in confirming some of the bitterness that the working class felt toward the elite. A writer for the *Louisiana Weekly* brought the bitterness into the open in a piece headlined, "Charges 'Intelligentsia' Aims to Destroy Zulu Parade." Unlike the reformers, the writer was proud of Zulu. "The Zulu Parade represents one of the two major contributions Negroes have made to the outdoor Mardi Gras celebrations." He cited the Mardi Gras Indians as the other. Who made these two contributions? The working class—"laborers, riverfront workers, vegetable peddlers, etc." Respectable black people, he charged—"the Negroes who were of the 'silk stocking type'"—restricted their festivities to "their own private balls and parties—all indoors, and gave nothing to the public." These respectable black people were the very individuals who now, having given nothing, wanted to destroy the Krewe of Zulu, which had been created by those they looked down on.[15]

Police protection—the spectacle of the krewe marching alongside the same kind of dog that was turned on civil rights protesters—was no answer to the challenge raised to Zulu. Black New Orleanians continued to question the propriety of Zulu and Zulu continued to search for legitimacy in the civil rights era. In 1962, Zulu stayed south of Canal Street, out of the area traditionally identified as Creole. The *Louisiana Weekly* asserted that the krewe sought to avoid conflict by changing its parade route. Students at St. Augustine, the premier Catholic boys school of the Creole community, once again had organized an anti-Zulu petition drive.[16]

But Alex Raphael, Jr., the parade chairman, denied that the new route had anything to do with the petition. "Lots of people wanted to see the parade." In fact, he thought that "the crowds on the street were more enthusiastic than ever, and it is evident that they didn't pay any attention to a radio message which urged people to 'turn their heads' when the parade passed." He also tried to address the broader question: Why were some black New Orleanians so upset with the krewe? He suggested that they read too much into the yearly parade. "There is no time that the Zulu Club ever said its parade represented Negroes. We created a character which had some features from Africa, grass skirts from Hawaii, moss from Louisiana, and coconuts from South America. We created him years ago, named him 'Zulu' and don't say he's anybody in particular." His conclusion: "So, there's no reason for Negroes to beat their chests and say 'That's me.'" The members of the krewe simply sought to have a good time on Mardi Gras, "a day of fun and make believe." Shrewdly, Raphael pointed out that Zulu had a constitutional right to parade.[17]

The *Weekly* editorialized on the issue. They could not deny Zulu's constitutional right to march—what black person interested in civil rights would be so foolish as to question the right of a black organization to assemble and march? But that right did not prevent New Orleanians from seeking other means of reforming Zulu. They might infiltrate the krewe and reform it from within. Or they might organize another, better parade. The latter "should be quite simple since so many profess to be 'disgusted' at the Zulu Club." Financing, therefore, should be only a minor problem, and as for music, "there are nearly a dozen excellent negro high school bands idle on Mardi Gras Day." Indeed, St. Augustine's band must have struck people as an excellent prospect. Of course, the city of New Orleans was hardly giving away parade permits to organizations interested in promoting black dignity. A minor aspect of the Zulu controversy is that Zulu was the one black organization that already possessed a parade permit; and the reformers wanted it.[18]

Alex Raphael's protest that unhappy black New Orleanians read too much into Zulu—"there's no reason for Negroes to beat their chests and say 'That's me'"—sounded plausible. But Raphael was using everyday reasoning ostensibly to analyze but effectively to obscure carnivalesque logic. It is hard not to find some mockery in Zulu's insistence on continuing their traditional parade despite the protest of some in the black community. By presenting King Zulu and the big shot of Africa, and all the other traditional characters with their pseudo-African costumes and their verbal sparring, Zulu reaffirmed both the origins of black Carnival in the black working class and the burlesque nature of Carnival itself. Perhaps the target of Zulu's gibes had become a black middle class the krewe regarded as too serious. Perhaps they were saying, "That's you."

The 1961 protest had not been an overwhelming success. Nonetheless, black leaders renewed the call for a Carnival boycott. Carnival was too potent a symbol of New Orleans to be ignored. In 1963, a black newspaper columnist complained, "This city has just too many parades and not enough pickets." In "these times of national social unrest," it was "just plain nonsense" for black Americans to hold celebrations and parades except for a worthwhile cause. In the fall of 1963, several black organizations joined and asked for a "blackout" of the next spring's Mardi Gras. They included the NAACP, the Ministerial Alliance, the Consumer League, and the United Clubs. Their spokesperson was Dr. Leonard Burns. He presented the boycott as partly an economic measure, one that is reminiscent of the Montgomery bus boycott. "The total blackout," Burns explained, "is designed to curb the spending of money with local merchants who refuse to give Negroes employment or opportunities." But it was clearly a symbolic gesture as well. The United Clubs attorney, Revivus Ortique, said, "The carnival season is no time for citizens to attend balls dressed in finery and drink their cares away in nighttime revelry and the next day they will face segregated policies. Unity for the cause of freedom and employment in this city is important, more important now than ever, since adults here are being jailed when they seek their constitutional rights."[19]

Yet 1964 was, for reasons not clear, the year that Zulu decided to celebrate their fiftieth anniversary. The krewe was determined to parade. In their usual fund-raising letters, sent to white businessmen, they argued, "Any organization or business that [has] continued to operate for 50 years is entitled to a 'big blow out.'" (Zulu's fund-raising, particularly its appeals to taverns, has attracted a certain amount of scorn; it should be remembered that at the turn of the century Rex collected money from railroads, hotels, and barrooms.)[20]

One of the "leaders" of the blackout was Ernest Morial, president of the New Orleans NAACP. His devotion to the blackout was tempered by his awareness of how difficult it would be to persuade the New Orleans black population to give up Carnival. One of the organizers of the 1961 boycott, he was nonetheless realistic—or cynical—about the 1964 opposition to Zulu. First, white liberals loved Zulu. "The jazz buffs, and all, see it as part of a culture, something artistic." Second, he had "no real quarrel with Zulu." He would prefer to have black participation in Carnival integrated into white Carnival, specifically into the Elks Krewe of Orleanians, and indeed Morial would have preferred to have no Zulu parade. But, he confessed, there were things more important than desegregating Carnival or blocking the Zulu parade. "If we accelerate our efforts in the areas that present real problems—voting, jobs, school dropouts, getting more people to use the facilities we've desegregated—the Zulu parade will become passe."[21]

The call for a new parade separate from Zulu failed. Infiltrating the krewe was the method ultimately adopted. Leonard Burns proposed that "respectable Negroes" join Zulu in the spring of 1964. Then both the positive goal of creating a new, dignified black parade and the negative goal of eliminating the traditional parade could be achieved by substituting one for the other. By 1965, the Zulu traditionalists had been defeated by the reformers. With fanfare, a new Zulu was announced, one in which black people could take pride. In February, James L. Russell, president of Zulu, invited "all Negro citizens" to help "in this gigantic enterprise to build the pride of the Negro in their very own Carnival parade." Zulu proclaimed a "new look." The krewe gave up blackfacing and grass skirts. The parade depicted the culture of the Watusis, "children of the Lion." As an indication of new public support, bands from three local high schools, along with the Olympia Brass Band, paraded with the krewe. Indeed, Dr. Burns, longtime Zulu foe, participated in the crowning of that year's king, Milton Bienamee.[22]

Yet the "new look" received hostile criticism from some New Orleanians. A writer for the *Vieux Carre Courier,* an "alternative" newspaper, attacked the parade in a column headlined "Zulu Turns White." In 1966, one reader of the *Louisiana Weekly* wrote in to say, "I believe in tradition. This 'old way' was designed for fun and entertainment"—not to insult black aspirations. Another reader said, "Personally, I would rather see one of the old Zulu parades with floats and native costuming of their choice, in which they excelled, than the utter chaos that passed as a parade, but only served as a degradation such as I witnessed on Carnival Day." Of course, it didn't help that the floats to be used in the 1966 parade burned down before Mardi Gras.[23]

The new, respectable Zulu also displeased the old guard, including Milton Bienamee. Just a few years later, Zulu abandoned the "new look" and returned to their old ways. In 1967, Bienamee announced, "No more of that dignity stuff. We're going back to the old traditions—African face image, grass skirt, and earrings in the nose." Bienamee credited his election to the throne to his efforts to get "the real African parade back." In opposition to the "new look," Bienamee and the krewe advocated "the real Zulu." Bienamee was a deputy criminal sheriff for Orleans Parish—and a deacon at the Glory Land Mort Gilam Baptist Church. The queen, Venella Warren, was a sheriff's matron for Orleans Parish. They marched in what one reporter called "the old burlesque tradition," accompanied by a racially mixed brass band, and they passed out coconuts. Coconuts too would become a source of conflict, when it was discovered that Zulu's supply came ultimately from South Africa.[24]

The white community tried to aid Zulu in these hard times. The president of the New Orleans Jazz Club, an organization with problematic relations with the black community, founded a group of honorary members of Zulu. "Honorary" in this case meant "white." For a $2.50 initiation fee and $10 in yearly dues, one gave recognition to a "fine old Carnival group," helped ensure that their parade would continue, and received "a personal share in helping race relations here." Another advantage of membership was the chance "to get together with other *honorary* members [emphasis mine]." This, of course, was just the kind of white paternalism that tainted Zulu's image in the black community.[25]

In 1968, Bienamee was the Big Shot of Africa for the third time. He promised that Zulu would maintain tradition. "This is a time to relax and let your hair down," he said. "There'll be no pomp and pretense this year." There was almost no parade as well: the organization split into two factions and elected two kings, both of whom vied for the parade permit.[26]

The denunciations from the black community continued. In 1969 protesters included the African-American Cultural Foundation, the New Orleans Advancement Association, and the Nat Turner Theater. The king made the traditional boasts for the parade. Lighting a cigar he proclaimed, "The weather's great. The people's great. The parade's great. But most of all, I'm great." But the parade was followed by a truck float with young black protestors distributing anti-Zulu pamphlets. Behind the truck came a car—the newspapers noted that it had out-of-state plates—carrying Queen Mother Moore of the Universal Association of Ethiopian Women; she too had asked Zulu "to stop slandering the image of black people." (At the same time, in the *Times-Picayune*, columnist Howard Jacobs complained that "the Zulu parade which once was unique because it was different, has gone conventional." He added, "Its once ferocious headhunters had deteriorated into undernourished warriors who looked as though they had never tasted fricasseed missionary.") Furthermore, the squabbling within the club grew worse. By the end of the year, the two factions in Zulu had taken each other to court.[27]

Despite the internal bickering and the bad reputation it had acquired for many black New Orleanians, the Zulu Social Aid and Pleasure Club survived. By 1980, Ernest Morial, the lukewarm Zulu opponent of 1964, was not only New Orleans's first black mayor but also an honorary member of Zulu. In their printed program for that year, Zulu reproduced a letter from the mayor to the krewe, in which Morial observed, with who knows what mixture of sincerity and sarcasm, "King Zulu and his subjects have brought much merriment and pleasure to our citizens and deserve our deepest appreciation for being such an important part of Mardi Gras."[28]

Zulu had changed with the times. It became an integrated organization. Woody Herman, wearing blackface and grass skirts, rode on float number six in 1980. In 1988, George W. Storm rode as the first white Zulu character, the province prince. More important, the krewe had attracted the black middle class to its ranks. In the 1980s Zulu was larger than ever before—with more than 350 members in 1984—and more respectable. Lawyers, engineers, and other professionals began to predominate. They were far more willing to jettison the old ways than the spare, embattled, and bickering krewe of the late 1960s. This new Zulu could hold sitdown dinners for 7000 at the Rivergate, with food catered by Chez Helene. In the end, neither reformers nor revelers won the battle of Zulu. The krewe had become respectable without showing any more civic leadership than its white counterparts.[29]

Still, in 1986, when a proposed visit to South Africa by the floatbuilder Blaine Kern and Zulu's president, Roy Glapion, brought on a storm of protest, the krewe promptly voted to forbid Glapion's making the trip. In the face of this disapproval, Kern too stayed at home—and nothing came of either his plans for a Carnival float at Johannesburg's centennial celebration or his scheme to recruit Chief Mangosuthu G. Buthelezi of Africa's Zulus and fifty of his warriors to march in 1987 with the Zulu Social Aid and Pleasure Club: the final fantasy of a "real African parade."[30]

Epilogue

The New Orleans City Council,
December 19, 1991

IT WAS THE END of a long, uncomfortable session. The seven members of the New Orleans City Council made their final remarks before voting on Dorothy Mae Taylor's ordinance desegregating certain private clubs that served as public accommodations—specifically written to desegregate the parading Carnival krewes. Taylor had introduced the ordinance two weeks earlier. As a compromise the council amended it so that enforcement would be delayed for one year, during which a so-called Blue Ribbon Committee would examine the issue of segregation in Carnival and make recommendations to the council. Dorothy Mae Taylor, Johnny Jackson, Jim Singleton, and Lambert Boissiere are black; Peggy Wilson, Jacquelyn Clarkson, and Joseph Giarrusso are white.

Jackson, admitting that the ordinance was not perfect and that anxieties and fears were high on both sides of the issue, called on the council to pass it unanimously both to make a statement against discrimination and to begin a process by which segregation could be eliminated. Wilson called the ordinance "terrible." Singleton, arguing that the ordinance complied with federal laws, supported it as in the best interests of his district and the city as a whole.

Clarkson, after describing the ordinance as "socialistic," nonetheless indicated that she would vote for it if the two representatives of the Carnival krewes present thought the compromise acceptable. Boissiere complimented both Taylor and the krewe representatives for reaching a compromise. Giarrusso, who advocated a coalition approach to solving city problems, announced that he would vote for the ordinance.

Then Dorothy Mae Taylor, the author of the measure, spoke. "There may some day be a generation that will enjoy Carnival feeling they can participate in any and every aspect of the festivity among people from all backgrounds because they are looked upon simply as another person, not as a color, sex, or nationality. It really saddens me to hear some comments made today, boasting on the fact of how much money is generated through discriminating practices. I say that really saddens me—in 1991 we will boast on such efforts. We ought to hang our heads in shame. And I would think we are moving in the direction now, and as I stated earlier, the question is very simple: Why is there a need to discriminate?" The vote was taken, and the results were announced with some surprise. The ordinance had passed unanimously.[1]

⊗

Despite claims that the council passed the ordinance hastily, the first hearing on the relationship between public accommodations and Carnival krewes had in fact been held in 1988. The krewes hardly took that hearing seriously—only two sent representatives. Taylor let the matter rest for several years, but when the city council created an appropriate enforcement agency, the Human Relations Commission, she had a public accommodations ordinance ready.

The ordinance, prepared by the City Attorney's office at Councilwoman Taylor's request, was based on the decision of the U.S. Supreme Court in the case of *New York State Club Association, Inc., v. City of New York*, a 1988 case in which the court upheld a law against discrimination by private clubs against a facial challenge. This New York law and its success in the courts opened the way for a New Orleans ordinance that outlawed discrimination on the basis of race, creed, color, religion, national origin, ancestry, sex or sexual orien-tation, age, physical condition, or disability by private clubs that served as public accommodations. A private club would be classified as a public accommodation if it met three criteria: if it had more than seventy-five members; if its members paid their dues as a business expense or if it had received a Carnival parade permit; and if it provided regular meal service or used the public streets regularly. The first set of criteria—membership, business expenses, and meal service—was drawn directly from the New York case. The second set of criteria—Carnival parade permits and use of the streets—clearly represented attempts to find some grounds for desegregating Carnival krewes.

On December 19, 1991, the two council members most obvi-ously working at cross purposes were Taylor and Wilson. Wilson periodically spoke as if the principal goal of the council should be to find ways to exempt the Carnival krewes from the ordinance. She finally offered an amendment to the ordinance that would have gutted it entirely. Nonetheless, even Wilson voted in favor of the Taylor ordinance.

Passing the ordinance hardly ended the debate. The issues surrounding desegregation of Carnival continued to be argued throughout 1992. Three members of the council presented the Blue Ribbon Committee with proposed changes to the ordinance: Bois-siere's shifted the "burden of proof" from the krewes and other organizations to the person claiming discrimination; Clarkson's re-moved jail time from the original ordinance and exempted Carnival from it. Wilson's version simply repealed the earlier ordinance. The committee held a series of hearings. Its recommendations weakened the original ordinance, requiring primarily that krewes file affidavits attesting that they had no written or unwritten policy of discrimi-nation before they obtained their parade permits. Partly because of the protests of the traditionally all-female krewes, Carnival krewes were also allowed to discriminate on the basis of sex—leading to the amused observation that the male Carnival establishment apparently preferred associating with homosexual men to heterosexual women.

Meanwhile, Wilson initiated a petition campaign to amend the city charter so that the council could not regulate the policies of krewes. Comus and Momus canceled their 1992 parades and Proteus joined them later by announcing that it would not parade in 1993. Several other krewes declared that they would give up parading too, but for reasons that had to do with the current economic crisis, not the ordinance. The council held two more hearings on the ordinance, finally voting unanimously on May 7, 1992, to amend the ordinance according to the Blue Ribbon Committee's recommendations.[2]

What this account fails to convey is the emotional nature of the debate—on December 19, 1991, and later. Jackson addressed the fear and anxiety on both sides, but the most powerful emotion present was anger. During the December meeting, Shirley B. Porter of the New Orleans NAACP, speaking in support of the ordinance, observed, perhaps too mildly, that the council chamber was full of "bad, bad feelings." The next day, Peggy Wilson told a New York Times reporter, "I don't think I've ever seen such hatred released on the world than was unleashed in the City Council last night." Harry McCall, Jr., a member of two krewes and two private clubs, claimed that the ordinance "serves no purpose other than to increase racial tension." A black man who spoke in favor of the ordinance predicted that this would be the first of many clashes between white economic power and black political power. New Orleans now had a black majority: "We shall control the streets of our city." One black woman claimed that white spectators in the chamber had attempted to intimidate black people present; one white man made a similar claim about black intimidation of white people.

The atmosphere at other hearings was just as troubled, the debate in the public press just as mean. Some white New Orleanians saw the ordinance as a black attack on white people; some black New Orleanians saw opposition to the ordinance as simple racism.

"At a time when the city's political leaders should be taking steps to encourage people to move back to New Orleans, they have banded together to ensure that white flight will continue or grow worse by creating and sanctioning an atmosphere of hostility to whites," wrote one white man. He concluded, "Dorothy Mae Taylor is a classic example of what happens when ignorance and political power come together." Henry Julian, a black civil rights lawyer, said at the May hearing that the civil rights community must obtain copies of all the signatures on the charter amendment petition. "We want to know the names of all the segregationists and white supremacists who live in this city because they're going to hear from us. . . . We're going to bring this debate to you." And in the wake of recent riots in Los Angeles he announced, "Every community has its own symbol . . . This is our Rodney King."[3]

Despite the very real anger, there was some common ground. Many of those who defended traditional Carnival—and its segregated krewes—argued with apparent sincerity that Mardi Gras was a symbol of racial harmony. Beyond that, they asserted that any threat to Carnival as constituted at present was a threat to that racial harmony. Those who advocated desegregating the krewes and their parades desired that which conservatives believed already existed: a Mardi Gras that reconciled all New Orleanians and that could represent racial harmony. For them, the present Carnival manifestly did not do this—was not their own discontent proof?—but they rejected neither Carnival nor the hope that it might embody harmony. For those in opposition, the ordinance seemed to create racial discord. For its advocates, the ordinance addressed racial discord already existing.

Those who spoke passionately about "tradition" did not seem to realize that other New Orleanians viewed their traditions as racist and exclusionary. They were unfeignedly surprised to learn that these traditions could be a source of offense; they were shocked to learn that those offended might interfere with these traditions. For them, the essence of Carnival was these traditions, which they spoke of with seemingly no awareness of their origins in a past that many other New Orleanians had cause to detest. Unlike the Carnival historian Perry Young, who was perfectly cognizant of the relationship between white supremacy and the Carnival krewes, the 1991 Carnival defenders divorced traditions from social context. They wanted to celebrate tradition and deny history.

The question is simple enough: Would a city with a black majority continue to do business with predominantly white krewes the old way? Failing to recognize that the existing arrangements in regard to krewes, parades, balls, and public accommodations were political in nature, conservatives viewed the ordinance as an unprecedented intrusion of city government into Carnival affairs. They counterattacked by claiming that the krewes were protected by the First Amendment right of freedom of association, that the krewes through Carnival subsidized the city, and that the city's economy depended on Carnival—hence Taylor's remark that she was saddened by the boasting over Carnival profitability—and that the ordinance exacerbated racial hostility. Those opposed to the legislation advanced arguments that undercut their case, as when John Charbonnet maintained that Carnival was the city's symbol throughout the world. If that was so, then the need to integrate Carnival was all the greater. The argument of Charbonnet and others that the ordinance would "kill" Mardi Gras was met with the obvious retort that, if the krewes refused to parade under the ordinance, the krewes would be Carnival's executioner, not the city.

Yet this was hardly the first public debate over the desirability of Carnival. The antebellum era had witnessed fears that Carnival in the street had become too rowdy, too violent, and too political, and various newspapers both predicted and demanded its abolition. Likewise, many turn-of-the-century New Orleanians had worried that Carnival had grown so disorderly as to be unmanageable—pointing to what they perceived as rising black assertiveness, but to general sexual display and prevalent violence among all races as well. In the 1950s there was widespread concern over juvenile delinquency and Carnival; in the 1970s Carnival rowdiness was blamed on an annual influx of "hippies." Indeed, debate over Carnival might be considered another one of its traditions. Nineteen ninety-one, like most other years of public concern over Carnival, was also a time of heightened social tensions; for example, the former Klansman David Duke had just run for governor of Louisiana. As at many other times in New Orleans's past, Carnival had far less to do with creating social tensions than it had with displaying them.

Besides the renewal of public debate, the 1991–1992 controversy exhibited many others features that had characterized Carnival. If the acrimony of the debate provoked fears of violence, violence, as we have seen, might be called a Carnival tradition. Its appearance in Carnival, in New Orleans and elsewhere, frequently reveals social tensions—and in New Orleans, these social tensions most often have been racial tensions as well. Sadly, there is little reason to be surprised that a sense of the threat of violence underlay the debate over the ordinance.

There is even less reason to be surprised that yet another story of Carnival was also a story of race. If Carnival has been how the city shows itself to itself, one of the things most often shown was racial separation. One may hope that, by whatever process, Carnival will be transformed so that it can be a symbol of not only racial harmony, as its supporters now claim, but a symbol of racial inclusiveness as well.

Beyond race, the Carnival controversy also represents the general cultural clashes that Carnival has long exhibited. Although the principal focus of testimony over the ordinance was on black-white relations, the ordinance also addressed religious and ethnic prejudice—in particular, the prejudice against Italians and Jews. One wonders what Councilman Joseph Giarrusso or city attorney Bruce Naccari thought while "tradition" was being defended. How long are the memories of the 1891 lynching? Did either of them know that Perry Young, who attributed the lynching to the leadership of members of Comus, acclaimed it as "possibly the most salutary lesson in Americanism that ever has been pronounced"? When Sanford Perez testified in front of the council a few months later he certainly remembered watching a krewe captain refuse an Italian orchestra leader ball tickets for his out-of-town guests—even though the orchestra was playing the ball—because they would not admit Italians or Jews. Perez also remembered the musician telling the captain to "shove the ball up his ass."[4]

Perez's father, a musician in that orchestra, would have been refused tickets if he had asked for them, because he was Jewish. Perez asked his father why he didn't say anything to the captain, only to be told, "You can't win." The anti-Semitism of much of New Orleans society had long been a dirty secret. Even though the original mystic societies had Jewish members, by the twentieth century most of the so-called elite krewes excluded them. The story was told that during the 1920s, a queen of Comus was one-quarter Jewish. When she came out for the grand march, she was received with scattered cries of "Jew, Jew." After World War II, the dirty secret became an embarrassing one as well. In 1972, City Councilman Peter H. Beer had raised the issue of Carnival anti-Semitism. At a public forum at the Jewish Community Center, he pointed to the heavy demands that Mardi Gras placed on the city, singling out the use of the municipal auditorium by the krewes. Their discrimination against Jews and others was so notorious that their use of public facilities almost constituted a municipal endorsement of anti-Semitism. Beer confided in his sympathetic audience. "Every guy in here has been through what I've been through," he said. "You sort of experience a change in the air about a week before Mardi Gras, when a good many of your friends seem preoccupied with something they don't want to discuss."[5]

Peter Beer raised his questions at places other than the Jewish Community Center. He also tried to get the rest of the city council interested in the costs of Carnival. Beer argued that ultimately the city government, as reluctant as it might be to admit it, was responsible for Carnival and what it meant for the city's image. In 1991, Dorothy Mae Taylor raised questions similar to those of Peter Beer, but with much more force.

And in 1991, once again, New Orleanians struggled over access to the central festive spaces of the city. The supporters of the ordinance wished to deny access to that central space to parades that, to them at least, represented inequality and prejudice. To those who protested the ordinance, this denial seemed an innovation. But of course issuing permits to one group denied access to that space for that time to all other groups. If Comus paraded down St. Charles Avenue and Canal Street Mardi Gras night, then no other krewe could do so. Furthermore, certain spaces and times had symbolic superiority. Rex's time and route symbolized its role as leader of "civic" Carnival, and Comus's time and route its role as leader of "social" Carnival; their preemptive claims to this space made them the focal point of parading Carnival.

The tug was over ownership of Carnival. Rex and the old-line krewes, those who staked the most on "tradition," claimed, "We own Carnival." The city council claimed, "No, the city owns Carnival and we represent the city." To which responses varied from "No, we, the krewes, own Carnival and without the krewes there will be no Carnival," to "No, nobody owns Carnival and it must not be regulated." The compromise, as of May 1992, was that of the Blue Ribbon Committee, in which the krewes and the city government (including representatives of the mayor as well as the council) negotiated at least a temporary settlement of the Carnival controversy by practically recognizing both the krewes' and the government's claims while leaving the legal aspects of "who owns Carnival" unclear. Thus people on both sides of the controversy viewed the Blue Ribbon Committee compromise as a victory and people on both sides viewed it as a defeat.

Some of those who believed in the city's right to regulate Carnival saw the original ordinance as having established the principle that the government controlled Carnival; they saw the compromise as the start of almost voluntary compliance with integration: the redefining of Carnival had begun. Some of those who believed in the city's right and obligation to desegregate Carnival saw the compromise as a retreat from the principle of the original ordinance. Conversely, those representing the krewes viewed the compromise as the product of negotiations in which they had taken part—reestablishing their role in Carnival—and the weakening of the enforcement procedures as a significant victory. Others who were associated with the krewes and their traditions saw even the compromise as an affront first to their good faith and civic leadership ("We own Carnival") and second to freedom of association ("Nobody owns Carnival"). Thus, while they practically favored weakening the ordinance, they hoped for its ultimate repeal—either by the council or by the courts—and rejected the principle behind the ordinance.[6]

In the midst of this debate, Carnival 1992 took place. Protesting the ordinance, neither Momus nor Comus rolled. Mardi Gras, however, drew the largest crowds yet in the history of New Orleans Carnival. Old krewes who accepted the ordinance and new krewes who declared their inclusiveness requested the times and routes that the old-line krewes had long used, just as Proteus had taken Comus's Tuesday night slot in the late nineteenth century. None of the old-line krewes had an uninterrupted tradition of parading during Carnival season. Meanwhile, other krewes considered parading in the suburbs of New Orleans, beyond the city's jurisdiction. And Rex invited three black men to join the krewe.[7]

Carnival has long served New Orleans not only as an arena for competition but also as a ritual of civic self-definition. Instead of being timeless, it has constantly been reworked throughout the city's history. Carnival will endure, no matter what criticisms are heaped on Rex, Comus, and Zulu or what decisions are made by them, not because Rex, Comus, and Zulu are immortal, but because they are incidental. Carnival existed before their appearance; when they change or die out or withdraw from the public realm, Carnival will change—just as it changed when they appeared. As it mutates, Carnival will nonetheless remain a source of contention. It always has been. Rather than "killing" Mardi Gras, the 1991 ordinance and its successors will be another episode in the ongoing contest over the meaning of New Orleans Carnival.

BIBLIOGRAPHIC NOTE

NOTES

ACKNOWLEDGMENTS

INDEX

Bibliographic Note

The principal primary sources for the study of New Orleans Carnival are newspapers. Although they may be supplemented by memoirs, travelers' accounts, popular histories, or private correspondence, in the end they provide the overwhelming bulk of descriptive evidence. No reading of secondary literature or travel accounts can substitute for research in local newspapers.

New Orleans historiography remains underdeveloped. Some important works are Donald H. Usner, Jr., "From African Captivity to American Slavery: The Introduction of Black Laborers to Colonial Louisiana," *Louisiana History* (Winter 1979), vol. 20, no. 1, 25–48, as well as his *Indians, Settlers, and Slaves in a Frontier Exchange Economy: The Lower Mississippi Valley before 1783* (Chapel Hill, 1992); Arnold Hirsch and Joseph Logsdon, eds., *Creole New Orleans: Race and Americanization* (Baton Rouge, 1992); Gwendolyn Midlo Hall, *Africans in Colonial Louisiana: The Development of Afro-Creole Culture in the Eighteenth Century* (Baton Rouge, 1992); Jerah Johnson, "New Orleans's Congo Square: An Urban Setting for Early Afro-American Culture Formation," *Louisiana History* (Spring 1991), vol. 32, no. 2, 117–157; Robert C. Reinders, *End of an Era: New Orleans, 1850–1860* (New Orleans, 1964); Joseph G. Tregle, "Early New Orleans Society: A Reappraisal," *Journal of Southern History*, 18 (February 1952), 23; George Dargo, *Jefferson's Louisiana: Politics and the Clash of Legal Traditions* (Cambridge, Mass., 1975); Earl F. Niehaus, *The Irish in New Orleans, 1800–1860* (Baton Rouge, 1965); Michael Doorley, "The Irish and the Catholic Church in New Orleans," master's thesis, University of New Orleans, May 1987; John W. Blassingame, *Black New Orleans, 1860–1880* (Chicago, 1973); Joy J. Jackson, *New Orleans in the Gilded Age: Politics and Urban Progress, 1880–1896* (Baton Rouge, 1969); Al Rose, *Storyville, New Orleans* (Alabama, 1974); Edward F. Haas, "John Fitzpatrick and Political Continuity in New Orleans, 1896–1899," *Louisiana History* (Winter 1981), vol. 22, no. 1, 7–29; Brian Garry Ettinger, "John Fitzpatrick and the Limits of Working-Class Politics in New Orleans, 1892–1896," *Louisiana History* (Fall 1985), vol. 26, no. 4, 341–367; William Ivy Hair, *Carnival of Fury: Robert Charles and the New Orleans Race Riot of 1900* (Baton Rouge, 1976); George M. Reynolds, *Machine Politics in New Orleans, 1897–1926* (New York, 1936); Edward F. Haas, *DeLesseps S. Morrison and the Image of Reform* (Baton Rouge, 1974). Although its scope is not limited to New Orleans, Dena J. Epstein's *Sinful Tunes and Spirituals: Black Folk Music to the Civil War* (Urbana, Ill., 1977) offers much material on Louisiana folk culture. The various volumes in *New Orleans Architecture* are a wonderful introduction to both the appearance and the layout of the city as well as its social history.

Earlier histories of New Orleans Carnival include J. Curtis Waldo, *History of the Carnival in New Orleans from 1857 to 1882* (New Orleans, 1882); T. C. DeLeon, *Our Creole Carnivals, Their Origins, History, Progress, and Results* (Mobile, 1890); George Soule, *The Carnival in New Orleans: Its Story and Its Sentiment* (n.d., circa 1910); George Soule, *The New Orleans Carnival: What It Is* (New Orleans, n.d., circa 1905); G. W. Nott, *Mardi Gras in New Orleans and the Mistick Krewe of Comus* (n.p., 1924); *Reminiscences of the First Balls of the Mystic Krewe of Comus and Two Previous Affairs: Author Unknown (Copied from an old Manuscript found in the Archives? of the Pickwick Club by C. Robert Churchill)* (New Orleans, Mardi Gras, Tuesday, February 12, 1929); Myron Tassin, *Bacchus* (Gretna, La., 1975). Perry Young, *The Mistick Krewe: Chronicles of Comus and His Kin* (New Orleans, 1931), is the best introduction. An exciting recent study that relies heavily on secondary literature is Samuel Kinser, *Carnival, American Style: Mardi Gras at New Orleans and Mobile* (Chicago, 1990). For elite organizations, see

Rosary Hartel O'Brien, "The New Orleans Carnival Organizations: Theatre of Prestige" (Ph.D. diss., University of California, Los Angeles, 1973), and Phyllis Hutton Raabe, "Status and Its Impact: New Orleans Carnival, the Social Upper Class and Upper-Class Power" (Ph.D. diss., Penn State University, 1973). For the study of women in Carnival, see the work of Karen Trahan Leathem, "Women on Display: The Gendered Meanings of Carnival in New Orleans, 1870–1900," *Locus* (Fall 1992), vol. 5, no. 1, 1–18; and "Yama-Yama Girls, Nuns, and Hussies: Mardi Gras Pleasures and Dangers in New Orleans, 1910–1941." Paper delivered at the 1993 Annual Meeting of the Organization of American Historians. For the Mardi Gras Indians, see David Elliott Draper, "The Mardi Gras Indians: The Ethnomusicology of Black Associations in New Orleans" (Ph.D. diss., Tulane University, 1973).

Eric Hobsbawm and Terence Ranger, *The Invention of Tradition* (Cambridge, 1983), reveals a pattern of cultural invention into which "organized" Carnival in New Orleans fits. Henry Louis Gates, Jr., *The Signifying Monkey: A Theory of African-American Literary Criticism* (New York, 1988), will be useful for any consideration of black Carnival.

The literature on Carnivals, festivity, and popular culture throughout the world is extensive. The following works, organized by region, provide some points of entry for cultural studies.

Europe: Mikhail Baktin, *Rabelais and His World* (Cambridge, Mass., 1968); Emmanuel Le Roy Ladurie, *Carnival in Romans* (New York, 1979); Natalie Zemon Davis, *Society and Culture in Early Modern France* (California, 1975); Edward Muir, *Civic Ritual in Renaissance Venice* (Princeton, 1981); Robert M. Isherwood, *Farce and Fantasy: Popular Entertainment in Eighteenth-Century Paris* (New York, 1986); Robert A. Schneider, *Public Life in Toulouse, 1463–1789: From Municipal Republic to Cosmopolitan City* (Ithaca, 1989).

Africa: Margaret Thompson Drewal, *Yoruba Ritual: Performers, Play, Agency* (Bloomington and Indianapolis, 1992); Dominique Zahan, *The Bambara* (Leiden, 1974); Patrick R. McNaughton, *Secret Sculptures of Komo: Art and Power in Bamana (Bambara) Initiation Associa-*

tions. Working Papers in the Traditional Arts, 4 (Philadelphia, 1979); Pascal James Imperato, *Buffoons, Queens, and Wooden Horsemen: The Dyo and Gouan Societies of the Bambara of Mali* (New York, 1983); David Birmingham, "Carnival at Luanda," *Journal of African History,* 29 (1988).

Latin America and the Caribbean: John W. Nunley and Judith Bettelheim, *Caribbean Festival Arts: Each and Every Bit of Difference* (Seattle, 1988); Robert Dirks, *The Black Saturnalia: Conflict and Its Ritual Expression on British West Indian Slave Plantations.* University of Florida Monographs in Social Sciences, 72 (Gainesville, Fla., 1987); Sandra Lauderdale Graham, *House and Street: The Domestic World of Servants and Masters in Nineteenth-Century Rio de Janeiro* (Cambridge, England, 1988); the essays in Institute of Social and Economic Research, *The Social and Economic Impact of Carnival: Seminar Held at the University of the West Indies, St. Augustine, Trinidad, on November 24–26, 1983* (St. Augustine, Trinidad, 1984); Ana Maria Alonso, "Men in 'Rags' and the Devil on the Throne: A Study of Protest and Inversion in the Carnival of Post-Emancipation Trinidad," *Plantation Society in the Americas* (1990), 73–120; Roberto Da Matta, "Carnival in Multiple Planes," in John J. MacAloon, ed., *Rite, Drama, Festival, Spectacle: Rehearsals Toward a Theory of Cultural Performance* (Philadelphia, 1984).

Notes

Introduction

1. *Daily States*, February 20, 1901, February 25, 1903; *Times-Democrat*, March 4, 1908; Rev. J. Chandler Gregg, *Life in the Army, in the Departments of Virginia and the Gulf, including Observations in New Orleans* (Philadelphia, 1866), 156–157.

2. Emmanuel Le Roy Ladurie, *Carnival in Romans* (New York, 1979); Natalie Zemon Davis, "The Rites of Violence," in *Society and Culture in Early Modern France* (Stanford, Calif., 1975), 152–187.

3. Victor Turner, "Liminality and the Performance Genres," in John J. Mac-Aloon, ed., *Rite, Drama, Festival, Spectacle: Rehearsals Toward a Theory of Cultural Performance* (Philadelphia, 1984), 19–41.

4. John J. MacAloon, "Olympic Games and the Theory of Spectacle in Modern Societies," in MacAloon, *Rite, Drama, Festival, Spectacle*, 241–280. Margaret Thompson Drewal, *Yoruba Ritual: Performers, Play, Agency* (Bloomington and Indianapolis, 1992), traces the relationship of ritual structure and ritual practitioners.

5. Eric Hobsbawm and Terence Ranger, *The Invention of Tradition* (Cambridge, England, 1983). Bacchus, created in 1968, is one example of a wealthier organization outdoing older krewes in Carnival display. For an account of the founding of Bacchus, see Myron Tassin, *Bacchus* (Gretna, La., 1975). For a shrewd account of Bacchus and the competition written at the time, see Mel Leavitt, "Nothing Like Carnival," *Clarion Herald*, February 13, 1969; and see also Letters to the Editor, March 6, 1969. An earlier krewe that rivaled the old-line krewes was Cynthius, which paraded in the late 1940s.

6. Henry Louis Gates, Jr., *The Signifying Monkey: A Theory of African-American Literary Criticism* (New York, 1988).

7. For a discussion of "plural societies," see M. G. Smith, *The Plural Society in the British West Indies* (Berkeley and Los Angeles, 1965), especially vii–xvii, 1–9, 75–91. Following J. S. Furnivall, Smith defines a plural society as "a unit of disparate parts which owes its existence to external factors, and lacks a common social will" (vii).

New Orleans certainly started as a plural society. When it ceased to be one is a question that deserves consideration. For New Orleans at its beginning, see Donald H. Usner, Jr., *Indians, Settlers, and Slaves in a Frontier Exchange Economy: The Lower Mississippi Valley before 1783* (Chapel Hill, 1992); Jerah Johnson, "Colonial New Orleans: A Fragment of the Eighteenth-Century French Ethos," and Gwendolyn Midlo Hall, "The Formation of Afro-Creole Culture," both in Arnold Hirsch and Joseph Logsdon, *Creole New Orleans: Race and Americanization* (Baton Rouge, 1992), 12–87. Hall develops her argument at greater length in *Africans in Colonial Louisiana: The Development of Afro-Creole Culture in the Eighteenth Century* (Baton Rouge, 1992).

8. Samuel Kinser, *Carnival, American Style: Mardi Gras at New Orleans and Mobile* (Chicago, 1990).

1. Creoles and Americans

1. Dunbar Rowland, ed., *Official Letter Books of W. C. C. Claiborne, 1801–1816* (Jackson, Miss., 1917), vol. 1, 331, 351–352, 354–355; Pierre Clement de Laussat, *Memoirs of My Life: to My Son During the Years 1803 and After, Which I Spent in Public Service in Louisiana as Commissioner of the French Government for the Retrocession to France of That Colony and for Its Transfer to the United States,* trans. Sister Agnes-Josephine Pastwa (Baton Rouge, 1978), 92–96; *Louisiana Gazette,* January 22, 1805.

2. Joseph G. Tregle, "Early New Orleans Society: A Reappraisal," *Journal of Southern History,* 18 (February 1952), 23.

3. See, for example, the listings of balls in *L'Ami des Lois,* February 14, 1817; *Bee,* February 2, 1828; *Picayune,* January 5, 1840; *Daily Delta,* March 1, 1851. M. Perrin du Lac, *Travels through the Two Louisianas and among the Savage Nations of the Missouri* (London, 1807), 90; Amos Stoddard, *Sketches Historical and Descriptive of Louisiana* (Philadelphia, 1812), 221; *Official Letter Books of W. C. C. Claiborne,* vol. 1, 327; vol. 3, 357.

4. Albert J. Pickett, *Eight Days in New-Orleans in February, 1847* (1847), 38. Copy in Louisiana Collection, Tulane University. Robert C. Reinders, *End of an Era: New Orleans, 1850–1860* (New Orleans, 1964), 154; Herbert Asbury, *The French Quarter: An Informal History of the New Orleans Underworld* (New York, 1936); *Daily True Delta,* February 9, 1853.

5. *Bee,* February 1, 1828.

6. *Picayune,* January 28, 1837; *Louisiana Gazette,* March 10, 1824; *L'Abeille de la Nouvelle Orleans (Bee),* February 18, 1833, March 16, 1841.

7. "Letters of Nathaniel Cox to Gabriel Lewis," *Louisiana Historical Quarterly* (April 1919), vol. 2, no. 2, 187; George W. Morgan to David Rees, January 24, 1805. David Rees Papers, Tulane University.

8. This account of American-Creole rivalry is drawn largely from Joseph Tregle, "Creoles and Americans," in Arnold Hirsch and Joseph Logsdon, eds., *Creole New Orleans: Race and Americanization* (Baton Rouge, 1992), 131–185. For additional

discussion of intermarriage between Creoles and Americans, see Paul F. Lachance, "The Foreign French," in the same volume, 101–130. For further discussion of American-Creole legal and political conflict, see George Dargo, *Jefferson's Louisiana: Politics and the Clash of Legal Traditions* (Cambridge, Mass., 1975).

9. Samuel Wilson, Jr., ed., *Impressions Respecting New Orleans by Benjamin Henry Boneval Latrobe: Diary and Sketches, 1818–1820* (New York, 1951), 32.

10. *Daily Delta*, February 21, 22 [misdated February 28], 1849.

11. Charles Lyell, *A Second Visit to the United States of North America* (New York, 1850), vol. 2, 91–92.

12. *Daily Delta*, February 26, 1852; *True Delta*, February 26, 1852; Pickett, *Eight Days in New-Orleans*, 17–40; John Dunlap to Mrs. Beatrice A. Dunlap, January 12, 1845. Dunlap Manuscripts, Tulane University.

13. Emmanuel Le Roy Ladurie, *Carnival in Romans* (New York, 1979); Robert M. Isherwood, *Farce and Fantasy: Popular Entertainment in Eighteenth-Century Paris* (New York, 1986); Edward Muir, *Civic Ritual in Renaissance Venice* (Princeton, 1981), 156–181.

14. G. W. Nott, *Mardi Gras in New Orleans and the Mistick Krewe of Comus* (n.p., 1924); *L'Abeille de la Nouvelle Orleans (Bee)*, February 8, 1842; Samuel Kinser, *Carnival, American Style: Mardi Gras at New Orleans and Mobile* (Chicago, 1990), 9.

15. Natalie Zemon Davis, "The Reasons of Misrule," in *Society and Culture in Early Modern France* (Stanford, Calif.,1975), 97–123; Ladurie, *Carnival in Romans*, 295–298; Robert A. Schneider, *Public Life in Toulouse, 1463–1789: From Municipal Republic to Cosmopolitan City* (Ithaca, 1989), 83.

16. *Official Letter Books of W. C. C. Claiborne*, vol. 2, 47–408; A. Oakey Hall, *The Manhattaner in New Orleans: or Phases of "Crescent City" Life* (New York and New Orleans, 1851); *Carollton Star*, January 3, 1852. If Herbert Asbury is correct, charivaris had a long existence in New Orleans, dating back at least as far as the Spanish regime. Asbury, *The French Quarter*, 116–117.

17. *Picayune*, February 8, 1837, January 31, February 28, 1838, February 13, 1839; Nott, *Mardi Gras in New Orleans*.

18. *Picayune*, March 3, 1840; *Bee*, March 2, 1840.

19. Lloyd Vogt, *New Orleans Houses: A House-Watcher's Guide* (Gretna, La., 1989), 15–19, 33–43; Samuel Wilson, Jr., "Early History of Faubourg St. Mary" and "Julia Street's Thirteen Sisters," in Mary Louise Christovich, Roulhac Toledano, Betsy Swanson, and Pat Holden, *New Orleans Architecture: The American Sector: Faubourg St. Mary* (Gretna, La., 1984), 3–48, 174–176.

20. *Daily Delta*, February 24, 1857; see also *Bee*, February 24, 1857. Six men signed the invitation to the original meeting to plan the Comus parade. They were S. M. Todd, L. D. Addison, J. H. Pope, F. Shaw, Jr., Joseph Ellison, and William P. Ellison. *Daily Picayune*, February 2, 1913. Todd was a dealer in art supplies; Addison worked for the firm of Bullitt, Miller, and Co., commission merchants and cotton factors; Pope and Joseph Ellison owned Pope, Ellison, and Co., commission merchants; Shaw was a commission merchant; and William P.

Ellison was a partner in the cotton brokerage firm of Starke and Ellison. *Cohen's New Orleans Directory for 1855* (New Orleans, 1855); *Kerr's General Advertiser and City Directory for the Year 1856* (New Orleans, 1856).

21. Charles Mackay, *Life and Liberty in America: Or, Sketches of a Tour in the United States and Canada, in 1857–8* (London, 1859), vol. 1, 254–277; *L'Abeille de la Nouvelle Orleans (Bee)*, February 16, 17, 1858. See also *Reminiscences of the First Balls of the Mystic Krewe of Comus and Two Previous Affairs: Author Unknown. . . .* (New Orleans, Mardi Gras, Tuesday, February 12, 1929); Perry Young, *The Mistick Krewe: Chronicles of Comus and His Kin* (New Orleans, 1931), 69.

22. For further discussion of Comus's methods, see Kinser, *Carnival, American Style,* 88–97.

23. *Daily Delta,* March 1, 6, 9, 10, 1859.

24. *L'Abeille de la Nouvelle Orleans (Bee)*, February 16, 1858; *Daily Delta,* March 6, 1859.

25. Young, *The Mistick Krewe,* 67–68; Clement A. Miles, *Christmas Customs and Traditions: Their History and Significance* (New York, 1976; reprint of 1912 edition); Herbert Halpert, "A Typology of Mumming," in Herbert Halpert and G. M. Story, eds., *Christmas Mumming in Newfoundland* (Toronto, 1969), 35–61. Early-nineteenth-century festivities and burlesque parades in Philadelphia are analyzed in Susan G. Davis, *Parades and Power: Street Theatre in Nineteenth-Century Philadelphia* (Philadelphia, 1986). Dena J. Epstein, *Sinful Tunes and Spirituals: Black Folk Music to the Civil War* (Urbana, Ill., 1977), 66–68. For the entry of Americans into New Orleans, see Hirsch and Logsdon, *Creole New Orleans,* 91–100.

2. African-Creoles

1. Timothy Flint, *Recollections of the Last Ten Years, Passed in Occasional Residences and Journeyings in the Valley of the Mississippi* (New York, 1968; reprint of 1826 edition, Boston), 140. This passage gives no date for Flint's observation of the dance. As he visited in 1823, arriving sometime in January and staying into March, I assume that the dance occurred at that time; however, Flint returned to the city that autumn. For other discussions of the great Congo-dance described by Flint, see Dena J. Epstein, *Sinful Tunes and Spirituals: Black Folk Music to the Civil War* (Urbana, Ill., 1977), 133, and Samuel Kinser, *Carnival, American Style: Mardi Gras at New Orleans and Mobile* (Chicago, 1990), 35. Kinser argues that the great Congo-dance took place during Carnival. For a brief discussion of African drumming in the Old and New World, see H. S. Farel Johnson, "Carnival Drumming and African Oral Tradition," *Plantation Society in the Americas* (1990), 63–71.

2. Donald H. Usner, Jr., "From African Captivity to American Slavery: The Introduction of Black Laborers to Colonial Louisiana," *Louisiana History* (Winter 1979), vol. 20, no. 1, 25–48; Epstein, *Sinful Tunes and Spirituals,* 84–85; Gwendolyn Midlo Hall, "The Formation of Afro-Creole Culture," in Arnold Hirsch and Joseph

Logsdon, *Creole New Orleans: Race and Americanization* (Baton Rouge, 1992), 58–87; see also her *Africans in Colonial Louisiana: The Development of Afro-Creole Culture in the Eighteenth Century* (Baton Rouge, 1992).

3. Dominique Zahan, *The Bambara* (Leiden, 1974); Patrick R. McNaughton, *Secret Sculptures of Komo: Art and Power in Bamana (Bambara) Initiation Associations.* Working Papers in the Traditional Arts, 4 (Philadelphia, 1979); Pascal James Imperato, *Buffoons, Queens, and Wooden Horsemen: The Dyo and Gouan Societies of the Bambara of Mali* (New York, 1983).

4. See John W. Nunley and Judith Bettelheim, *Caribbean Festival Arts: Each and Every Bit of Difference* (Seattle, 1988), for an introduction to Carnival and Christmas festivals. See Paul F. Lachance, "The Foreign French," in Hirsch and Logsdon, *Creole New Orleans,* 101–130, for a discussion of Saint Domingue refugees.

5. Henry C. Castellanos, *New Orleans as It Was: Episodes of Louisiana Life* (Gretna, La., 1990), 294–298.

6. Christian Schultz, Jr., *Travels on an Inland Voyage Through the States of New York, Pennsylvania, Virginia, Ohio, Kentucky and Tennessee, and Through the Territories of Indiana, Louisiana, Mississippi, and New-Orleans; Performed in the Years 1807 and 1808; Including a Tour of Nearly Six Thousand Miles* (New York, 1810; reprint, Ridgewood, N.J., 1968), vol. 2, 197.

7. Castellanos, *New Orleans as It Was,* 158–159. For Congo Square, see Jerah Johnson, "New Orleans's Congo Square: An Urban Setting for Early Afro-American Culture Formation," *Louisiana History* (Spring 1991), vol. 32, no. 2, 117–157.

8. Kinser, *Carnival, American Style,* 36; Martin R. Delany, *Blake; or the Huts of America* (Boston, 1970), 98–108.

9. See, for example, *Bee,* March 3, 1829 [Mardi Gras], February 22, 23, 1830, February 7, 1842.

10. *Daily Orleanian,* March 5, 1851, February 28, 1854, February 20, 1855, February 5, 1856, February 25, 1857.

11. Robert Dirks uses this term in quite another fashion; see Dirks, *The Black Saturnalia: Conflict and Its Ritual Expression on British West Indian Slave Plantations.* University of Florida Monographs in Social Sciences, 72 (Gainesville, Fla., 1987).

3. Americans and Immigrants

1. *Bee,* February 7, 1856.

2. See Alun Hawkins, *Whitsun in Nineteenth-Century Oxfordshire.* History Workshop Pamphlets, 8 (1973), for a discussion of forfeits during May Day celebrations in early-nineteenth-century England. For Ireland, see Robert Jerome Smith, "Festivals and Calendar Customs," in Harold Orel, ed., *Irish History and Culture: Aspects of a People's Heritage* (Lawrence, Kans., 1976), 129–145.

3. Joseph Tregle, "Creoles and Americans," in Arnold Hirsch and Joseph Logsdon, *Creole New Orleans: Race and Americanization* (Baton Rouge, 1992), 131–185.

4. Earl F. Niehaus, *The Irish in New Orleans, 1800–1860* (Baton Rouge, 1965); Michael Doorley, "The Irish and the Catholic Church in New Orleans," master's thesis, University of New Orleans, May 1987.

5. Smith, "Festivals and Calendar Customs," 129–145.

6. *L'Abeille de la Nouvelle Orleans (Bee)*, February 5, 1845; *Daily Delta*, February, 22, 1849, March 6, 1851, February 21, 1855, February 27, 1857; *Daily True Delta*, February 17, 1858; Charles Mackay, *Life and Liberty in America: Or, Sketches of a Tour in the United States and Canada, in 1857–8* (London, 1859), vol. 1, 254–277.

7. *Bee*, February 23, 1855, March 9, 10, 1859.

8. Albert J. Pickett, *Eight Days in New-Orleans in February, 1847* (1847), 17–40. Copy in Louisiana Collection, Tulane University. Pickett also said maskers on foot were hounded by boys who pelted them with sticks and mud; he saw one reveler stripped of his mask and old woman's clothes by a jeering crowd. *Bee*, February 10, 1853; see also the case of Charles Hynes, *Daily True Delta*, February 6, 1856; *Daily Delta*, February 21, 1855, March 9, 1859. For a general discussion of entrudo, see Sandra Lauderdale Graham, *House and Street: The Domestic World of Servants and Masters in Nineteenth-Century Rio de Janeiro* (Cambridge, England, 1988), 66–71.

9. Tregle, "Creoles and Americans," 131–185. The story of the masker disguised as a priest can be found in the *Daily Orleanian*, February 21, 22, 1855.

10. John S. Kendall, "The Municipal Elections of 1858," *Louisiana Historical Quarterly* (July 1922), vol. 5, no. 3, 357–376; Francis P. Burns, "Charles M. Waterman, Mayor of New Orleans: His Defense of His Conduct in the Municipal Election of 1858," *Louisiana Historical Quarterly* (July 1924), vol. 7, no. 3, 466–479; Niehaus, *The Irish in New Orleans*, 84–97; W. Darrell Overdyke, "History of the American Party in Louisiana, Chapter I," *Louisiana Historical Quarterly* (October 1932), vol. 15, no. 4, 581–588.

11. *Bee*, February 7, 1856; and see *Daily Delta*, February 6, 1856.

12. *Republican*, March 1, 1870; *Bee*, February 18, 1858.

13. *Bee*, February 18, 1858.

14. *Daily Orleanian*, February 25, 1857; *Bee*, March 1, 1854; *Daily Crescent*, February 13, 1850; see also *Daily Delta*, February 13, 1850.

15. Errol Hill, "The History of Carnival," in Institute of Social and Economic Research, *The Social and Economic Impact of Carnival: Seminar Held at the University of the West Indies, St. Augustine, Trinidad, on November 24–26, 1983* (St. Augustine, Trinidad, 1984), 6–39. Newspaper quotations are from page 14. See also Ana Maria Alonso, "Men in 'Rags' and the Devil on the Throne: A Study of Protest and Inversion in the Carnival of Post-Emancipation Trinidad," *Plantation Society in the Americas* (1990), 73–120; Susan G. Davis, *Parades and Power: Street Theatre in Nineteenth-Century Philadelphia* (Philadelphia, 1986), 38–48, 73–111; Louis P. Masur, *Rites of Execution: Capital Punishment and the Transformation of American Culture, 1776–1868* (New York, 1989).

16. *Times-Picayune*, March 5, 1933.

17. *Daily Creole*, December 3, 9, 1856.

18. *Louisiana Gazette*, February 7, 8, 1825. The *Louisiana Gazette* was opposed to masking on general principle; its editor called the practice of masking "this rotten relict [*sic*] of European degeneracy." *Louisiana Gazette*, February 11, 1825. *New Orleans as It Is: Its Manners and Customs—Morals—Fashionable Life—Profanation of the Sabbath—Prostitution—Licentiousness—Slave Markets and Slavery, & c. & c. & c. By a Resident* (Utica, N.Y., 1849).

19. *L'Abeille de la Nouvelle Orleans (Bee)*, February 2, 1828, March 3, 1829, February 22, 23, 1830, February 3, 1838, February 20, 1855.

20. *Daily Creole*, December 3, 9, 1856.

21. *Bee*, February 18, 1858, March 10, 1859.

4. Rex

1. *Republican*, February 14, 1872; *Louisianian*, February 15, 1872; *Daily Picayune*, February 14, 1872.

2. *Louisianian*, February 4, 15, 1872; *Daily Picayune*, February 14, 1872.

3. "Handbook of the Carnival containing Mardi Gras. . . ." (New Orleans, 1873). Copy in Rosemonde E. and Emile Kuntz Collection, Tulane University; *Republican*, February 14, 1872.

4. "Handbook of the Carnival containing Mardi Gras. . . ."; *Republican*, February 14, 1872; *Daily Picayune*, February 14, 1872.

5. *Republican*, February 14, 1872.

6. *His Imperial Highness the Grand Duke Alexis in the United States of America during the Winter of 1871–72* (Cambridge, Mass., 1872). Copy at Tulane University.

7. *Louisianian*, February 15, 1872; Colonel Francis C. Kajencki, "The Louisiana Tiger," *Louisiana History* (Winter 1974), vol. 15, no. 1, 49–58.

8. For Lydia Thompson, see Robert G. Allen, *Horrible Prettiness: Burlesque and American Culture* (Chapel Hill, 1991), particularly 3–21.

9. "First Rex Tells How It Began," *Times-Picayune*, February 25, 1938.

10. J. Curtis Waldo, *History of the Carnival in New Orleans from 1857 to 1882* (New Orleans, 1882).

11. *L'Abeille de la Nouvelle Orleans (Bee)*, March 4, 1862; United States War Department, *The War of the Rebellion: A Compilation of the Official Records of the Union and Confederate Armies*, series 1, vol. 6, 720. For an account of the Confederacy's declaring martial law in New Orleans after Carnival 1862, see pp. 857–858.

12. For these and other balls, see *Era*, February 15, 19, 1863, February 4, 9, 1864; *L'Abeille de la Nouvelle Orleans (Bee)*, February 6, 16, 1863, February 1, 3, 4, 8, 1864. For "The Streets of New York," see *L'Abeille de la Nouvelle Orleans (Bee)*, February 28, 1865.

13. Kenneth E. Shewnaker and Andrew K. Prinz, "A Yankee in Louisiana: Selections from the Diary and Correspondence of Henry R. Gardner, 1862–1866," *Louisiana History* (Summer 1964), vol. 5, no. 3, 290; *L'Abeille de la Nouvelle Orleans*

(*Bee*), February 19, 1863, February 10, 1864; *Era,* February 18, 1863, February 9, 10, 1864. The *Times* agreed with the *Era's* assessment, saying, "The mummeries of Mardi Gras were more extensively observed yesterday than for many years in this city." *Times,* February 10, 1864.

14. I am indebted to Dr. Richard Sommers for this reference. Nathan B. Middlebrook to Sue, February 12, 1864. Nathan B. Middlebrook, Second Connecticut Light Battery, letters to wife and other family members. Civil War Miscellaneous Collection, U.S. Army Military History Institute, Carlisle Barracks, Pa.

15. *L'Avenir: Journal di Dimanche,* March 3, 1867; Greville John Chester, *Transatlantic Sketches in the West Indies, South America, Canada, and the United States* (London, 1869), 208–211; *Republican,* March 2, 1870. See also *Republican,* February 14, 1872, March 1, 1876.

16. *Republican,* February 14, 1872, February, 17, 1877.

17. *Orleanian,* March 5, 1876; *Times,* March 6, 1881.

18. *Republican,* February 12, 1874, February 3, 14, 1877; *Bulletin,* February 24, 1876; *Democrat,* February 29, 1876.

19. Waldo, *History of the Carnival in New Orleans,* 16.

20. *Republican,* February 17, 1874; *Daily Picayune,* February 17, 1874; *Bulletin,* February 24, 1876.

21. Eric Hobsbawm and Terence Ranger, *The Invention of Tradition* (Cambridge, England, 1983).

5. Comus

1. *Daily Picayune,* February 26, 1873. Some images die hard. In the March 2, 1962, edition of Tulane University's student paper, the *Hullabaloo,* the Missing Link cartoon from 1873 was reproduced to illustrate an article on the history of Carnival. For the fullest discussion of the 1873 parade, and indeed of Carnival during Reconstruction, see Perry Young, *The Mistick Krewe: Chronicles of Comus and His Kin* (New Orleans, 1931). Young was the pioneer historian of New Orleans Carnival, and he carefully made explicit many of the connections between Carnival and Reconstruction politics. A New Orleans white man of his era, Young was supportive of the earlier white supremacists and disdainful of both radical Reconstruction and black civil and political rights.

2. *Daily Picayune,* January 4, 1874, February 10, 1875.

3. *Republican,* February 28, 1873, March 6, 1873; Ted Tunnell, *Crucible of Reconstruction: War, Radicalism, and Race in Louisiana, 1862–1877* (Baton Rouge, 1984), 171; Joseph G. Dawson, *Army Generals and Reconstruction: Louisiana, 1862–1877* (Baton Rouge, 1982).

4. *Times,* February 14, 1866; *Daily Picayune,* February 14, 15, 1866. I follow Perry Young in saying they had no police guard, but the account in the *Daily Picayune* suggests otherwise.

5. William H. Forman, Jr., "William P. Harper in War and Reconstruction," *Louisiana History* (Winter 1972), vol. 13, no. 1, 47–70. See also his "William P. Harper and the Early New Orleans Carnival," *Louisiana History* (Winter 1973), vol. 14, no. 1, 41–47.

6. *Daily Delta*, February 22, 1860. Henry Clay was memorialized more permanently a few months later; in April a statue of him was dedicated at the intersection of St. Charles and Canal. The Clay statue became a central meeting place for New Orleanians until 1901, when it was removed to Lafayette Square.

7. For a description of the political situation in Louisiana in 1873, see Tunnell, *Crucible of Reconstruction*, 171, and Dawson, *Army Generals and Reconstruction*, 112–163. For a description of "The World Of Audubon," see Young, *The Mistick Krewe*, 107–110, and the *Daily Picayune*, January 7, 1873.

8. *Republican*, February 25, 1873.

9. *Republican*, February 26, 1873.

10. Eric Foner, *Reconstruction: America's Unfinished Revolution, 1863–1877* (New York, 1988), 262–264; Joseph Logsdon and Caryn Cossé Bell, "The Americanization of Black New Orleans, 1850–1900," in Arnold Hirsch and Joseph Logsdon, *Creole New Orleans: Race and Americanization* (Baton Rouge, 1992), 201–261.

11. Paul Andrew Hutton, *Phil Sheridan and His Army* (Lincoln, Neb., 1985), 262–281; Tunnell, *Crucible of Reconstruction*, 202–205; Young, *The Mistick Krewe*, 137.

12. *Bulletin*, January 6, 1875, January 7, 9, 1875; *Daily Picayune*, February 9, 1875.

13. *Bulletin*, February 9, 10, 1875; *Republican*, February 4, 10, 11, 1875.

14. *Bulletin*, January 7, 1876; *Democrat*, January 7, 1876.

15. *Republican*, February 10, 1877; *Daily Picayune*, February 9, 12, 1877.

16. *Republican*, February 14, 1877.

17. Natalie Zemon Davis, "The Rites of Violence," in *Society and Culture in Early Modern France* (Stanford, Calif., 1975), 152–187, discusses the link between religious organization and popular violence.

18. *Republican*, February 26, 1873, January 7, 1876.

19. *Republican*, January 8, 1870, February 21, 1871, February 11, 1872.

20. *Louisianian*, February 11, 1872.

21. Henry Clay Warmoth, *War, Politics, and Reconstruction: Stormy Days in Louisiana* (New York, 1930).

22. See Tunnell, *Crucible of Reconstruction*; Warmoth, *War, Politics, and Reconstruction*; and Dawson, *Army Generals and Reconstruction*. See also Lawrence N. Powell, "The Centralization of Local Government in Warmoth's Louisiana: Machine Politics, Black Power, and Republican Factionalism" (unpublished ms.).

23. Errol Hill, "The History of Carnival," in Institute of Social and Economic Research, *The Social and Economic Impact of Carnival: Seminar Held at the University of the West Indies, St. Augustine, Trinidad, on November 24–26, 1983* (St. Augustine, Trinidad, 1984), 6–39. See also Ana Maria Alonso, "Men in 'Rags' and the Devil on the Throne: A Study of Protest and Inversion in the Carnival of Post-Emancipation Trinidad," *Plantation Society in the Americas* (1990), 73–120.

24. *Republican,* February 25, 1873. The literature on Carnival inversion is enormous. Among many possibilities, see Mikhail Baktin, *Rabelais and His World* (Cambridge, Mass., 1968); Natalie Zemon Davis, "The Reasons of Misrule," *Society and Culture in Early Modern France* (Stanford, Calif., 1975), 97–112; Sandra Lauderdale Graham, *House and Street: The Domestic World of Servants and Masters in Nineteenth-Century Rio de Janeiro* (Cambridge, England, 1988), 66–71; Kim Johnson, "The Social Impact of Carnival," Institute of Social and Economic Research, *The Social and Economic Impact of Carnival: Seminar Held at the University of the West Indies, St. Augustine, Trinidad, on November 24–26, 1983* (St. Augustine, Trinidad, 1984), 171–207; David Birmingham, "Carnival at Luanda," *Journal of African History,* 29 (1988), 93–103; Joseph V. Guillotte, III, "Every Man a King: Reflections on the Aesthetics of Ritual Rebellion in Mardi Gras," *Plantation Society in the Americas,* 33–46. None of these writers would have been in sympathy with former masters and white supremacists no matter how oppressed they felt themselves, but the symbolic inversion and festive behavior they describe can be applied in some ways to conservative white New Orleanians.

25. *Royal Herald,* February 22, 1898.

26. The *Daily Picayune* did not agree with the *Bee.* According to the *Picayune,* two maskers were stabbed at Corkery's Saloon. *Daily Picayune,* February 15, 1877. Prosper Jacotot, "The Voyage of a Laborer in the Mississippi Valley" (1877), trans. S. Fucich and F. Peterson (1939). Copy at Tulane University.

6. Northerners

1. John R. Cowan, *A New Invasion of the South: Being a Narrative of the Expedition of the Seventy-First Infantry, National Guard, through the Southern States to New Orleans, February 24–March 7, 1881* (New York, 1881), 7. See also *Louisianian,* February 18, 1881, March 5, 1881.

2. Cowan, *A New Invasion of the South,* 68.

3. Ibid., 86–87.

4. *Louisianian,* February 23, 1871, February 14, 1880; *Bulletin,* February 29, 1876.

5. Cowan, *A New Invasion of the South,* Appendix F; *Times,* February 25, 1879, March 1, 1881.

6. J. Curtis Waldo, *History of the Carnival in New Orleans from 1857 to 1882* (New Orleans, 1882). The last float represented "Turks, Servians, Herzegovinians, and Montenegrains." Waldo described them as "a motley crowd, but one of the most interesting in the display"—as, indeed, it should have been. I cannot resist complimenting whoever the 1877 designer was who foresaw the origins of World War I as part of the military progress of the world.

7. *Times-Democrat,* February 9, 1891.

8. George Soule, *The Carnival in New Orleans: Its Story and Its Sentiment* (n.d., circa 1910). See also George Soule, *The New Orleans Carnival: What It Is* (New Orleans, n.d., circa 1905).

9. Frank L. Loomis, *A History of the Carnival and New Orleans Illustrated* (New Orleans, 1903). See also the 1904–1905 edition. *Times-Democrat*, February 15, 1893; Soule, *The Carnival in New Orleans*.

10. Mark Twain, *Life on the Mississippi* (Penguin Books, 1984), 302, 326–327.

11. Charles L. Dufour and Leonard V. Huber, *If Ever I Cease to Love: One Hundred Years of Rex, 1872–1971* (New Orleans, 1970); Krewe of Rex, "Rex Carnival Edition, Mardi Gras, New Orleans, Louisiana, February Twenty-Seven, MDCCCC" (New Orleans, 1900). In 1891, Mayor Shakespeare fell off his horse in the Monday Rex parade. *Times-Democrat*, February 10, 1891.

12. *Sunday Figaro*, January 21, 1894; Chris C. Socola, publisher, *Souvenir: New Orleans Mardi Gras and Rex's Merry Season* (New Orleans, 1900).

13. This description of New Orleans in the last fifth of the nineteenth century is based on Joy J. Jackson, *New Orleans in the Gilded Age: Politics and Urban Progress, 1880–1896* (Baton Rouge, 1969). See also Edward F. Haas, "John Fitzpatrick and Political Continuity in New Orleans, 1896–1899," *Louisiana History* (Winter 1981), vol. 22, no. 1, 7–29; Brian Garry Ettinger, "John Fitzpatrick and the Limits of Working-Class Politics in New Orleans, 1892–1896," *Louisiana History* (Fall 1985), vol. 26, no. 4, 341–367. The letters to Mayor Shakespeare are in the Joseph Shakespeare Collection, Historic New Orleans Collection: [illegible] to Hon. Jos. A. Shakespeare, April 20, 1888; Robert A. Holland to Hon. Jo. Shakespeare, March 15, [1891]; J. H. Portfield et al. to Shakespeare, March 17, 1891. For Italians in Louisiana, see Ethelyn Orso, *The St. Joseph Altar Traditions of South Louisiana* (Lafayette, La., 1990); Joel Gardner, ed., *A Better Life: Italian-Americans in South Louisiana* (1983); Russell M. Magnaghi, "Louisiana Italians Prior to 1870," *Louisiana History* (Winter 1986), vol. 27, no. 1, 41–68; Barbara Botein, "The Hennessy Case: An Episode in Anti-Italian Nativism," *Louisiana History* (Summer 1979), vol. 20, no. 3, 261–279. On Comus and the lynching, see Perry Young, *Carnival and Mardi Gras in New Orleans* (New Orleans, 1939), 58–59. Young called the lynching "possibly the most salutary lesson in Americanism that ever has been pronounced."

14. Waldo, *History of the Carnival in New Orleans*, 41; *Times*, January 15, 1879; *Louisianian*, January 11, February 15, 1879; Frederic Trautmann, ed., *Travels on the Lower Mississippi, 1879–1880: A Memoir by Ernst von Hesse-Wartegg* (Columbia, Mo., 1990), 174.

15. Bernard Lemann, "City Timescape—The Shifting Scene," and Betsy Swanson, Mary Louise Christovich, Roulhac Toledano, and Pat Holden, "Architectural Inventory," in Mary Louise Christovich, Roulhac Toledano, Betsy Swanson, and Pat Holden, *New Orleans Architecture: The American Sector: Faubourg St. Mary* (Gretna, La., 1984), 49–63, 93–105.

16. "Comus edition," *Daily-Picayune*, February 19, 1901.

17. *Herald*, February 6, 1913, March 2, 1916. For a discussion of Behrman, see Robert W. Williams, Jr., "Martin Behrman and New Orleans Civic Development, 1904–1920," *Louisiana History* (Fall 1961), vol. 2, no. 4, 373–400. New Orleans Public Service, "A Special Service Dedicated to the Convenience of Our Carnival

Visitors." Copy in Louisiana Historical Association Collection, box 12, folder 24, Tulane University. Flyer entitled "Life Begins at Forty" (1975), Christopher Valley, Sr., Papers, Record Group 59, Louisiana State Museum. *Times-Picayune and New Orleans States Magazine*, week of February 19, 1950.

18. Cowan, *A New Invasion of the South*, 65–66.

19. T. C. DeLeon, *Our Creole Carnivals, Their Origins, History, Progress, and Results* (Mobile, 1890); *Democrat*, February 25, 1879.

20. Waldo, *History of the Carnival in New Orleans*. A copy of the broadside *Welcome to Strangers*, January 26, 1884, can be found in Louisiana Historical Association Collection, box 13, folder 6, Tulane University. *Weekly Pelican*, February 26, 1887; *Mardi Gras: Letters to the Commercial Advertiser by W. G. Bowdoin*, February 17, 1901. Copy in Historic New Orleans Collection; *Times*, February 5, 8, 15, 1880.

21. Reports of earl marshall to Carnival court, March 20, 1899. Major H. H. Isaacson study file, Historic New Orleans Collection.

22. Major H. H. Isaacson study file, Historic New Orleans Collection.

23. *Times-Democrat*, February 24, 1900; reports of earl marshall to Carnival court, March 15, 1901. Major H. H. Isaacson study file, Historic New Orleans Collection; *Daily States*, February 28, 1906, February 9, 1910.

7. High Society

1. *Times-Democrat*, February 4, 1891. See also *Item*, February 4, 1891; *Picayune*, February 3, 1891; *States*, February 4, 1891.

2. *Times-Democrat*, February 4, 9, 1891, February 19, 1895, February 4, 1896, February 13, 25, 1897.

3. *Times-Democrat*, February 14, 1901.

4. *Times-Democrat*, February 2, 1894, February 20, 27, 1895. See Perry Young, *Carnival and Mardi Gras in New Orleans* (New Orleans, 1939), 72–75, for a discussion of Jewish exclusion.

5. James Zacharie, *New Orleans Guide, With a Description of the Routes to New Orleans, Sights of the City Arranged Alphabetically, and Other Information Useful to Travellers* (New Orleans, 1885).

6. Eric Hobsbawm and Terence Ranger, *The Invention of Tradition* (Cambridge, England, 1983).

7. *Times-Democrat*, February 26, 1884, March 8, 9, 1886; *Picayune*, February 14, 1888.

8. *Daily Picayune*, March 21, 1886.

9. For additional discussion, see Karen Trahan Leathem, "Women on Display: The Gendered Meanings of Carnival in New Orleans, 1870–1900," *Locus* (Fall 1992), vol. 5, no. 1, 1–18.

10. *Times-Democrat*, March 2, 1884; Young, *Carnival and Mardi Gras in New Orleans*, 166–167.

11. *Times-Democrat*, February 19, 1890, January 29, 30, 1898.

12. *Times-Democrat*, March 2, 1892. See Varina Davis to Mr. "Secor," June 13, 1886. Davis Family Papers, Historic New Orleans Collection. Winnie Davis was born in 1864 and died in 1898.

13. *Times-Democrat*, February 1, 1891; Sue Bryan, "Lovely Bessie Behan One of Youngest Queens to Reign Over Carnival Festival" (n.d., 1953?). Queens of Carnival Scrapbooks, Historic New Orleans Collection.

14. Mary Orme Markle, *My Memoires* (1972). Markle Family Papers, Tulane University. Aunt Serena to Mary [J. Hosmer], January 12, 1904. Jones-Hosmer-Buck Family Papers, Tulane University. Herman Drezinski, "1911 Queen Here; Recalls Being Late" (n.d.). Queens of Carnival Scrapbooks, Historic New Orleans Collection.

15. Young, *Carnival and Mardi Gras in New Orleans*, 78. According to Pie Dufour, however, Howard was the only Rex who married his queen. Clipping entitled "Father-Daughter Royal Line Trace." Queens of Carnival Scrapbooks, Historic New Orleans Collection. See obituary for Frank T. Howard in the *Daily Picayune*, October 25, 1911, *Daily States*, October 25, 1911. On the wedding, see "Society Notes," *Times-Democrat*, January 29, February 5, 1899.

16. Rose Kahn, "Carnival Queen of 1904 Returns Each [word missing]" (n.d., 1953?). Queens of Carnival Scrapbooks, Historic New Orleans Collection.

17. For further discussion of elite balls, see Rosary Hartel O'Brien, "The New Orleans Carnival Organizations: Theatre of Prestige" (Ph.D. diss., University of California, Los Angeles, 1973).

18. The phrase "Babylonian Period" appears in a flyer for an exhibition held by the Historic New Orleans Collection in 1974. Copy of the flyer in Louisiana Collection, Tulane University. See Edward W. Said, *Orientalism* (1978), for a book-length treatment of Western attitudes toward the "Orient." *Weekly Pelican*, February 19, 1887.

19. George Soule, *The Carnival in New Orleans: Its Story and Its Sentiment* (n.d., circa 1910); Henri Schindler, "The Golden Age of Carnival," *Dixie*, March 4, 1984; Ceneilla Bower Alexander Papers. In Alexander-McClure Family Papers, Historic New Orleans Collection. Aubrey Starke, "Richard Henry Wilde in New Orleans and the Establishment of the University of Louisiana," *Louisiana Historical Quarterly* (October 1934), vol. 17, no. 4, 605–624; "What the Woman in the Moon Saw in the Crescent City," *States*, February 16, 1896.

20. Perry Young, *The Mistick Krewe: Chronicles of Comus and His Kin* (New Orleans, 1931), 161; *The Ramayana: The Iliad of the East, Illustrated by the Knights of Momus, February 16, 1882* (New Orleans, 1882).

21. Mistick Krewe of Comus, *Scenes from the Metamorphoses of Ovid* (New York, 1878); Young, *The Mistick Krewe*.

22. "The business depression in the middle of the past decade made the annual dues to many an unwelcome burden. The Mystic Krewe withdrew itself until more

prosperous times." *Times-Democrat*, February 19, 1890. Proteus was reluctant to give up Tuesday night parading, which Comus regarded as its prerogative. In 1891 and 1892, both Comus and Proteus paraded on Tuesday, and it was Proteus that held its ball at the traditional French Opera in 1891. *Times-Democrat*, February 18, 1890, February 11, 1891.

23. T. C. DeLeon, *Our Creole Carnivals, Their Origins, History, Progress, and Results* (Mobile, 1890), 22; *Times-Democrat*, February 11, 1891.

24. George Soule, *The Carnival in New Orleans: Its Story and Its Sentiment* (n.d., circa 1910). See also George Soule, *The New Orleans Carnival: What It Is* (New Orleans, n.d., circa 1905).

25. New Orleans is hardly the only place where people agreed to act out the fantasies of outsiders. See Nathan Irvin Huggins, *Harlem Renaissance* (New York, 1971), particularly chapter 3, "Heart of Darkness," 84–136, for a discussion of how white interest in black culture affected Harlem.

26. *Times-Democrat*, February 15, 1896.

8. Mardi Gras Indians

1. *Times-Democrat*, March 4, 1908.

2. This account of the Mardi Gras Indians is drawn from David Elliott Draper, "The Mardi Gras Indians: The Ethnomusicology of Black Associations in New Orleans" (Ph.D. diss., Tulane University, 1973); Maurice M. Martinez, Jr., "Two Islands: The Black Indians of Haiti and New Orleans," *Arts Quarterly* (July/August/September 1979), 5–7, 18; Maurice M. Martinez, Jr., "Delight in Repetition: The Black Indians," *Wavelength* (February 1982); Jason Berry, Jonathan Foose, and Tad Jones, *Up from the Cradle of Jazz: New Orleans Music since World War II* (Athens, Ga., 1986), 203–219; Michael P. Smith, "New Orleans' Carnival Culture from the Underside," *Plantation Society in the Americas* (1990), 11–32. For comparisons with other masquerading traditions, see Robert Dirks, *The Black Saturnalia: Conflict and Its Ritual Expression on British West Indian Slave Plantations.* University of Florida Monographs in Social Sciences, 72 (Gainesville, Fla., 1987); John W. Nunley and Judith Bettelheim, *Caribbean Festival Arts: Each and Every Bit of Difference* (Seattle, 1988); Institute of Social and Economic Research, *The Social and Economic Impact of Carnival: Seminar Held at the University of the West Indies, St. Augustine, Trinidad, on November 24–26, 1983* (St. Augustine, Trinidad, 1984).

3. Draper, "The Mardi Gras Indians," 10; Martinez, "Repetition"; Berry, Foose, and Jones, *Up from the Cradle of Jazz*, 203–213; Anita Schrodt, "Indians Parade in Regalia, Ritual," *Times-Picayune*, February 8, 1975; "The Beat of the Wild Magnolias," *States-Item*, April 20, 1977; Smith, "New Orleans' Carnival Culture from the Underside," 11–32. Lyle Saxon, "Creole Masker of 1885 to Don Domino This Year,"

Times-Picayune, February 23, 1941, an interview with Mrs. Paul Michinard, discusses going to Canal and Claiborne to see Mardi Gras Indians in the late nineteenth century. Mrs. Michinard claimed, "My grandmother remembered the Indian costumes in her girlhood, and do you know that the Indian tribes of Negro maskers are still appearing at Mardi Gras now."

4. *Times-Democrat*, February 15, 1899; *Times-Democrat*, February 12, 1902. See also *Times-Democrat*, February 25, 1903.

5. Smith, "New Orleans' Carnival Culture from the Underside," 11–32. For Indians in the islands, see Nunley and Bettelheim, *Caribbean Festival Arts*.

6. John W. Blassingame, *Black New Orleans, 1860–1880* (Chicago, 1973), 1. See also Joseph Logsdon and Caryn Cossè Bell, "The Americanization of Black New Orleans, 1850–1900," in Arnold Hirsch and Joseph Logsdon, *Creole New Orleans: Race and Americanization* (Baton Rouge, 1992), 201–261.

7. Errol Hill, "The History of Carnival," in Institute of Social and Economic Research, *The Social and Economic Impact of Carnival: Seminar Held at the University of the West Indies, St. Augustine, Trinidad, on November 24–26, 1983* (St. Augustine, Trinidad, 1984), 6–39; Errol Hill, *The Trinidad Carnival: Mandate for a National Theatre* (Austin, 1972); Gordon Rohler, "An Introduction to the History of the Calypso," *The Social and Economic Impact of Carnival*, 40–120; Ana Maria Alonso, "Men in 'Rags' and the Devil on the Throne: A Study of Protest and Inversion in the Carnival of Post-Emancipation Trinidad," *Plantation Society in the Americas* (1990), 73–120; Anthony deVerteuil, C.S. Sp., *The Years of Revolt: Trinidad, 1881–1888* (Port-of-Spain, 1984); Brereton quote in deVerteuil, 60.

8. Alice Zeno interviews, November 14, December 12, 1958. Hogan Jazz Archive, Tulane University; Jerah Johnson, "Colonial New Orleans: A Fragment of the Eighteenth-Century French Ethos," in Arnold Hirsch and Joseph Logsdon, *Creole New Orleans: Race and Americanization* (Baton Rouge, 1992), 12–57; Draper, "The Mardi Gras Indians," 134; Martinez, "Two Islands," 5–7, 18. For a description of the Choctaws at the turn of the century, see David I. Bushnell, Jr., "The Choctaw of St. Tammany," *Louisiana Historical Quarterly* (January 8, 1917), vol. 1, no. 1, 11–20.

9. *Item*, February 24, 1925; *Times-Picayune* Mardi Gras supplement, February 1932.

10. *Times-Picayune* Mardi Gras supplement, February 1932; Draper, "The Mardi Gras Indians," 469.

11. Draper, "The Mardi Gras Indians," 152; *Times-Democrat*, March 4, 1908; Schrodt, "Indians Parade in Regalia, Ritual."

12. Martinez, "Repetition"; *Daily States*, February 28, 1900; Berry, Foose, and Jones, *Up from the Cradle of Jazz*, 212; Jeff Hannusch a.k.a. Almost Slim, *I Hear You Knockin': The Sound of New Orleans Rhythm and Blues* (Ville Platte, La., 1985), 262. For brief accounts of fighting among Indians during Carnival, see the *Times-Picayune*,

February 18, 1920, February 14, 1923; *Item*, February 14, 1923; *States*, February 18, 1920.

13. Berry, Foose, and Jones, *Up from the Cradle of Jazz*, 216.

14. Those interested in lyrics to black Indian songs can consult several sources. In "The Mardi Gras Indians," Draper transcribes the lyrics of many Indian songs. Wild Tchoupitoulas, *Wild Tchoupitoulas* (Island Records, AN 7052), has traditional Mardi Gras Indian songs set to the music of what was fundamentally the Meters. Because the Wild Tchoupitoulas were the first to record many of these tunes, the writer credits are given to their big chief, George Landry. In fact, many of the lyrics are traditional. The recording that best demonstrates how the Indians sound is The Golden Eagles, "Lightning and Thunder" (Rounder Records, 2073).

15. Henry Louis Gates, *The Signifying Monkey: A Theory of African-American Literary Criticism* (New York, 1988), xxiv. See also Martinez, "Repetition."

16. In his discussion of Signifyin(g), Gates cautions, "It is curious to me how very many definitions of Signifyin(g) share this stress on what we might think of as the black person's symbolic aggression, enacted in language, rather than upon the play of language itself, the meta-rhetorical structures in evidence. 'Making fun of' is a long way from 'making fun,' and it is the latter that defines Signifyin(g)" (*The Signifying Monkey*, 68). Perhaps Gates—like Berry, Foose, and Jones—would reject my emphasis on violence and assertion and concentrate on the Indians' performance as a form of play. However, as confrontations among the Indians frequently did end in violence, it seems that more than Signifyin(g) occurred when Indians met.

17. There was a general attempt on the part of the black community to reduce Carnival violence. See, for example, the *Louisiana Weekly*, February 14, 1931, March 4, 1933, February 10, 1934.

18. "The Beat of the Wild Magnolias"; Draper, "The Mardi Gras Indians," 54; *Times-Picayune*, March 1, 1979.

19. Draper, "The Mardi Gras Indians," 45, 384; "The Beat of the Wild Magnolias"; Michael P. Smith, *Spirit World: Pattern in the Expressive Folk Culture of Afro-American New Orleans* (New Orleans, 1984); Claude F. Jacobs and Andrew J. Kaslow, *The Spiritual Churches of New Orleans: Origins, Beliefs, and Rituals of an African-American Religion* (Knoxville, 1991); Alonso, "Men in 'Rags,'" 83; Leslie G. Desmangles, *The Faces of the Gods: Vodou and Roman Catholicism in Haiti* (Chapel Hill, 1992).

20. William Ivy Hair, *Carnival of Fury: Robert Charles and the New Orleans Race Riot of 1900* (Baton Rouge, 1976), 79.

21. *Times-Democrat*, February 23, 1909. See *Times-Democrat*, February 24, 1911, for a similar story.

22. *Daily States*, February 12, 1902.

23. *Times-Democrat*, March 1, 1911.

24. Joel Williamson, *Crucible of Race: Black-White Relations in the American South since*

Emancipation (New York, 1984). See almost any New Orleans newspaper of the period, particularly the *Times-Democrat*, for examples of highlighting of black crime and editorial defenses of white supremacy.

25. *Times-Picayune*, March 2, 1927.

9. Mardi Gras Queens

1. *Times-Picayune*, February 22, 1928.

2. *Times-Picayune*, February 22, 1928; *Item*, February 21, 1928.

3. *Sunday Sun*, February 25, 1906; Henry H. Solomon, publisher, *Mardi Gras 1891: How to Enjoy Yourself: Where to Make Purchases during the Carnival* (New Orleans, 1891); Barney Bigard, *With Louis and the Duke: The Autobiography of a Jazz Clarinetist*, ed. Barry Martyn (New York and Oxford, 1986), 23; Frank L. Loomis, *A History of the Carnival and New Orleans Illustrated* (New Orleans, 1903). See also the 1904–1905 edition. William Ivy Hair, *Carnival of Fury: Robert Charles and the New Orleans Race Riot of 1900* (Baton Rouge, 1976), 79. Samuel Kinser, *Carnival, American Style: Mardi Gras at New Orleans and Mobile* (Chicago, 1990), 129–131, is a discussion of the relationship between prostitution and Carnival. The best account of prostitution in New Orleans is Al Rose, *Storyville, New Orleans* (University, Alabama, 1974).

4. *Times-Picayune*, February 18, 1925, February 14, 17, 1926, February 22, 1928; *Item*, February 21, 22, 1928.

5. *Times-Picayune*, February 9, 1921; *Item*, February 17, 1926, February 20, 1927. Yama-yama costumes, very popular for Carnival, looked like loose-legged pajamas, with a gigantic bow at the collar and large, fuzzy buttons. They had been popularized by Bessie McCoy, a performer whose song about the yama-yama man was also wildly popular. For a sketch of Bessie McCoy, see "Tragic Romance of the Yama Yama Girl," *Times-Picayune*, February 12, 1933.

6. See Natalie Zemon Davis, "Women on Top," *Society and Culture in Early Modern France* (Stanford, Calif., 1975), 124–151, for a general discussion of women and of cross-dressing in European festivity. See Edward Muir, *Civic Ritual in Renaissance Venice* (Princeton, 1981), 156–181, for a discussion of Carnival in Venice and of the practice of prostitutes dressing as men. For the Yoruba, see Margaret Thompson Drewal, *Yoruba Ritual: Performers, Play, Agency* (Bloomington and Indianapolis, 1992). For New Orleans, see *Bee*, February 22, 1860; *Daily Delta*, February 26, 1857; *Daily Crescent*, February 27, 1857; Greville John Chester, *Transatlantic Sketches in the West Indies, South America, Canada, and the United States* (London, 1869); *Republican*, February 14, 1872; *Bulletin*, February 10, 1875; *Republican*, February 10, 1875. For further discussion of the role of women in New Orleans Carnival, see the work of Karen Trahan Leathem, "Women on Display: The Gendered Meanings of Carnival in New Orleans, 1870–1900," *Locus* (Fall 1992), vol. 5, no. 1, 1–18, and "Yama-Yama Girls, Nuns, and Hussies: Mardi Gras Pleasures and Dangers in

New Orleans, 1910–1941." Paper delivered at the 1993 Annual Meeting of the Organization of American Historians.

7. Davis, "Women on Top."

8. *Daily Delta*, February 22, 1855.

9. *Republican*, February 22, 23, 1870; Perry Young, *The Mistick Krewe: Chronicles of Comus and His Kin* (New Orleans, 1931), 159.

10. *Times-Democrat*, February 15, 1893.

11. *Times-Democrat*, February 28, 1906, February 21, 1908, February 25, 1914; letter to the editor, *Times-Democrat*, March 5, 1911; Letters from the People, *Times-Democrat*, February 25, 1912.

12. *States*, February 18, 1920.

13. *Times-Picayune*, February 18, 1920.

14. *Times-Picayune*, February 9, 1921.

15. *States*, February 18, 1920.

16. *Times-Democrat*, March 4, 1908; *Times-Picayune*, February 21, 1917.

17. *Times-Picayune*, March 5, 1924.

18. *Times-Picayune/States-Item*, February 13, 1983.

19. Lucy J. Fair, "New Orleans," in Wayne R. Dynes, ed., *Encyclopedia of Homosexuality* (New York and London, 1990), 892.

20. Fair, "New Orleans." For black female impersonators, see also Jason Berry, Jonathan Foose, and Tad Jones, *Up from the Cradle of Jazz: New Orleans Music since World War II* (Athens, Ga., 1986), 54–64, 88–91.

21. Lucy J. Fair, "Mardi Gras and Masked Balls," in *Encyclopedia of Homosexuality*, 765–767; Calvin Trillin, "U.S. Journal: New Orleans: Mardi Gras," *New Yorker*, March 9, 1968, 143–144; Jim West, "The Mardi Gras Mystique," *Impact*, Carnival supplement, February 1979.

22. *Impact*, February 1978.

23. Calvin Trillin, "U.S. Journal," 138–144; *Impact*, February 1979; *Mardi Gras Madness: New Orleans Style* (Gretna, La., 1982). Copy at Louisiana Collection, Tulane University.

24. *Times-Picayune/States-Item*, February 13, 1983; Kathy Caruso, "Gay Balls," *Courier*, February 2, 1978; *Impact*, Carnival supplement, February 1979.

25. *Times-Picayune/States-Item*, February 13, 1983; Fair, "Mardi Gras," 767.

26. *Impact*, Carnival supplement, February 1979.

27. Fair, "New Orleans," 896.

28. See Millie Ball, "For the Fun of It," *Dixie*, March 1, 1981; *Times-Picayune/States Item*, February 13, 1983; Fair, "New Orleans," 896; Charlene Schneider, "Speaking Out," *Impact*, March 1979.

29. See "Readers' Opinions," *Impact* (November 1978), vol. 2, no. 11; *Impact*, February 1978; *Times-Picayune*, March 5, 1924.

30. Jim West, "Up Front," *Impact*, February 1978.

31. Ball, "For the Fun of It."

10. Louis Armstrong's Mardi Gras

1. Lee Collins interview, June 2, 1958; Albert Warner interview, January 8, 1959. Hogan Jazz Archive, Tulane University. Gilbert Millstein, "Africa Harks to Satch's Horn," New York *Times*, November 20, 1960, from an undated article in *Time* in the Louis Armstrong vertical file at the Hogan Jazz Archive, Tulane University. *Times-Picayune*, March 2, 1949; Louis Armstrong to Jane Holder, February 2, 1952. Copy in Louis Armstrong vertical file, Hogan Jazz Archive, Tulane University. *Times-Picayune*, March 1, 1949; *State-Item*, July 12, 1971. See also "Louis the First," *Time*, February 21, 1949.

2. Richard Meryman, *Louis Armstrong—A Self Portrait: The Interview by Richard Meryman* (New York, 1971); *States-Item*, July 14, 1971.

3. Max Jones, "Louis Blasts Jim Crow," *Melody Maker*, December 12, 1959. See also *Jet*, November 26, 1959, 56–58.

4. "'Satchmo' Cancels N.O. Date," *Louisiana Weekly*, October 18, 1958.

5. Steel Arm Johnny's real name was Ferdinand Poree; he was killed New Year's Eve 1919. *States*, January 1, 1920. The account of Armstrong's 1918 Carnival is taken from Louis Armstrong, *Satchmo: My Life in New Orleans* (New York, 1954). Armstrong customarily gave his birthdate as July 4, 1900; we now know that he was born August 4, 1901. Photocopy of Certificate of Baptism, Sacred Heart of Jesus Church, Louis Armstrong vertical file, Hogan Jazz Archive. For a discussion of the African-American vernacular aesthetic, see Henry Louis Gates, *The Signifying Monkey: A Theory of African-American Literary Criticism* (New York, 1988). This account of Zulu is assembled from three sources that do not agree on all particulars: John E. Rousseau, "Historical Role of Negroes in Gay Mardi Gras Recalled," *Louisiana Weekly*, March 3, 1962; "'Real African Parade' Planned by Zulu Group," *States-Item*, February 3, 1967; *Dixie*, February 19, 1984. For example, Rousseau claims that Willie Stark wore his lard-can crown as king of the Tramps and that James Robertson was the first Zulu king. The 1967 story has the first Zulu parade in 1909, with William Story the first king, wearing the lard-can crown and carrying a scepter made from a banana stalk. The *Dixie* account claims that the organization disbanded between 1917 and 1920, which does not jibe with Armstrong's memoirs. According to Calvin Trillin, in 1964, the Zulu organization took 1916 as their official date of organization. Calvin Trillin, "A Reporter at Large: The Zulus," *The New Yorker*, June 20, 1964, 41–119. The Sunny Henry quotation comes from Sunny Henry interview, October 21, 1959, Hogan Jazz Archive, Tulane University.

6. Minor "Ram" Hall interview, September 2, 1958, Hogan Jazz Archive, Tulane University; *Daily States*, February 11, 1902.

7. *Times-Picayune*, March 1, 1925. Once again, there is a significant parallel with other Carnival cultures. In Trinidad, for example, both the rise of calypso and the creation of steel bands was very much a part of Carnival.

8. Jack Laine interview, April 21, 1951, Hogan Jazz Archive, Tulane University.

9. William J. Schafer, with assistance from Richard B. Allen, *Brass Bands and New Orleans Jazz* (Baton Rouge, 1977), traces the evolution of New Orleans brass bands and their relationship to the development of jazz. It is the indispensable introduction to the subject. Schafer relies heavily, as do I, on the interviews in the Hogan Jazz Archive at Tulane University—the indispensable source.

10. Charles "Sunny" Henry interview, October 2, 1959; Percy Humphrey interview, November 4, 1965. Hogan Jazz Archive, Tulane University.

11. John Casimir interview, January 17, 1959; Sunny Henry interview, October 21, 1959. Hogan Jazz Archive, Tulane University. And see Willie Parker interview, March 29, 1960, and Barney Bigard, *With Louis and the Duke: The Autobiography of a Jazz Clarinetist*, ed. Barry Martyn (New York and Oxford, 1986), 7.

12. John Casimir interview, January 17, 1959, Hogan Jazz Archive, Tulane University.

13. Arnold Loyacano interview, September 29, 1956. Hogan Jazz Archive, Tulane University.

14. Monk Hazel interview, July 16, 1959, Hogan Jazz Archive, Tulane University.

15. Danny Barker, *A Life in Jazz*, ed. Alyn Shipton (New York and Oxford, 1986), 62–63; John Casimir interview, January 17, 1959, Hogan Jazz Archive, Tulane University.

16. Barker, *A Life in Jazz*, 34. When such police tactics were used against predominantly white crowds, they drew public condemnation. See *Times-Democrat*, February 22, 1912; Letters from the People, February 3, 1913.

17. Bigard, *With Louis and the Duke*, 7; Barker, *A Life in Jazz*, 23.

18. George Justin interview, June 1, 1958; Jack Laine interview, March 26, 1957; Alice Zeno interviews, November 14, December 10, 1958. Hogan Jazz Archive, Tulane University. Pianist Isidore "Tuts" Washington also followed parades as a child. Jeff Hannusch a.k.a. Almost Slim, *I Hear You Knockin': The Sound of New Orleans Rhythm and Blues* (Ville Platte, La., 1985), 5–6. On the question of following parades, there are some dissenting voices. Dave Bailey said in his interview, "Never did follow no parades when I was a kid; never followed no parades around; just go and look at them. On Carnival Day I hardly go and see Carnival parades. I don't like to be in amongst a gang of people." Dave Bailey interview, October 25, 1959, Hogan Jazz Archive, Tulane University.

19. Percy Humphrey interview, November 4, 1965, Hogan Jazz Archive, Tulane University.

20. Schafer, *Brass Bands and New Orleans Jazz*, 87–95.

21. Sidney Bechet, *Treat It Gentle* (New York, 1960); Bigard, *With Louis and the Duke*, 8; Charles Love interview, May 10, 1960, Hogan Jazz Archive, Tulane University.

22. Lee Collins interview, June 2, 1958, Hogan Jazz Archive, Tulane University; Barker, *A Life in Jazz,* 57–59.

23. Peter Bocage interview, January 29, 1959; John Joseph interview, November 26, 1958; John Casimir interview, January 17, 1959. Hogan Jazz Archive, Tulane University.

24. Ernest "Punch" Miller interviews, September 1, 1959, August 23, 1960, Hogan Jazz Archive, Tulane University.

25. "Louis the First," *Time,* February 21, 1949.

26. John Joseph interview, November 26, 1958, Hogan Jazz Archive, Tulane University.

27. Steve Brown interview, April 22, 1958, Hogan Jazz Archive, Tulane University.

28. Willie Parker interview, November 7, 1958, Hogan Jazz Archive, Tulane University; Barker, *A Life in Jazz,* 5.

29. Lee Collins interview, June 2, 1958; Monk Hazel interview, July 16, 1959. Hogan Jazz Archive, Tulane University.

30. Punch Miller interview, August 20, 1959, Hogan Jazz Archive, Tulane University.

31. Jack Laine interview, March 26, 1957. See also Nick LaRocca interviews, May 21, June 2, 1958. Hogan Jazz Archive, Tulane University.

32. Jack V. Buerkle and Danny Barker, *Bourbon Street Black: The New Orleans Black Jazzman* (New York, 1973), 181–182; *Times-Picayune,* February 18, 1969.

11. New Orleanians

1. *Times-Picayune,* February 11, 1934; Perry Young, *Carnival and Mardi Gras in New Orleans* (New Orleans, 1939), 50–51; *Catholic Action of the South,* February 21, 1935; Elsie Martinez and Margaret LeCorgne, *Uptown/Downtown: Growing Up in New Orleans* (Lafayette, La., 1986), 148.

2. *Times-Picayune,* February 11, 1934, February 19, 1939; *Louisiana Weekly,* February 17, 1934.

3. *Times-Picayune,* February 12, 1918.

4. *Times-Picayune,* February 8, 13, 15, 17, 18, 1920; *L'Abeille de la Nouvelle-Orleans (Bee),* February 17, 24, 1920; *Item,* February 13, 15, 16, 17, 1920; *States,* January 18, 22, February 13, 15, 17, 18, 1920.

5. *Times-Picayune* (editorial), February 11, 1931.

6. Thomas DiPalma, *New Orleans Carnival and Its Climax Mardi Gras* (New Orleans, 1953); *Times-Picayune,* February 3, 4, 5, 6, 1937.

7. *Louisiana Weekly,* February 22, 1936, January 30, 1937; *Item and Tribune,* February 21, 1941.

8. *Times-Picayune*, February 21, 24, 1941, February 14, 1988; *Item*, February 24, 1941.

9. *Times-Picayune*, February 19, 1929, March 1, 1933; Herman Drezinski, "Captain of Elks Krewe Retiring," *States-Item*, March 22, 1965. Box 1, "Entry for Carnival Parade Mardi Gras Day"; Box 1, "History Highlights, folder 1935." Christopher Valley, Sr., Papers, Record Group 59, Louisiana State Museum.

10. Drezinski, "Captain of Elks Krewe Retiring." Box 1, "History Highlights, folder 1935." Christopher Valley, Sr., Papers, Louisiana State Museum.

11. Box 1, Data Sheet [1935?]; Christopher Valley letter, February 25, 1938. And see Valley's letter of February 9, 1939: "Any truck driver with liquor on his breath or person will be barred from the parade. . . ." Christopher Valley, Sr., Papers, Record Group 59, Louisiana State Museum.

12. Box 1, folder "First Years Entries." Christopher Valley, Sr., Papers, Record Group 59, Louisiana State Museum; Marina E. Espina, *Filipinos in Louisiana* (New Orleans, 1988), 14, 19–33.

13. "Elks Krewe Most Democratic of Carnival Parades," *Times-Picayune*, February 21, 1941; Drezinski, "Captain of Elks Krewe Retiring"; letter of Walter Lebreton to Christopher Valley, Sr., March 10, 1965, reproduced in newsletter, copy in box 1. Christopher Valley, Sr., Papers, Louisiana State Museum. The success of the Krewe of Orleanians led to imitation. After the Second World War, a new parade was "organized." There were more truck floats than could be included in the Krewe of Orleanians. The city still kept truck floats off the main boulevards. Civic leaders suggested that another parade of truck floats be organized to march before the Rex parade. They argued that the city owed its returning veterans the chance to ride truck floats on Canal Street, and so the Krewe of Crescent City held its first parade on Mardi Gras morning 1946. *Times-Picayune*, February 4, March 2, 3, 5, 6, 1946; see also *Item*, March 1, 2, 3, 4, 5, 6, 1946.

14. Registration form, 1965. Christopher Valley, Sr., Papers, Record Group 59, Louisiana State Museum.

15. Roger Mitchell interview, January 19, 1972; Tony Sbarbaro and Emile Christian interview, February 11, 1959. Hogan Jazz Archive, Tulane University.

16. This account of 1946 Carnival is taken from the *Times-Picayune* for February and March, particularly the issues of February 4, March 2, 3, 5, 6, 1946; see also *Item*, March 1, 2, 3, 4, 5, 6, 1946.

17. *Louisiana Weekly*, March 11, 1933; *Times-Picayune*, February 4, March 2, 3, 5, 6, 1946; see also *Item*, March 1, 2, 3, 4, 5, 6, 1946.

12. Zulu

1. *States-Item*, December 7, 1960. For an account of Louisiana politics in the era of desegregation, see A. J. Liebling, *The Earl of Louisiana* (Baton Rouge, 1970). For New Orleans politics from the 1940s through the early 1960s, see Edward F. Haas,

DeLesseps S. Morrison and the Image of Reform (Baton Rouge, 1974), and Arnold R. Hirsch, "Simply a Matter of Black and White: The Transformation of Race and Politics in Twentieth-Century New Orleans," in Arnold R. Hirsch and Joseph Logsdon, *Creole New Orleans: Race and Americanization* (Baton Rouge, 1992), 262–319.

2. *Times-Picayune*, January 22, 1961. The fullest account of the Zulu controversy is Calvin Trillin, "A Reporter at Large: The Zulus," *The New Yorker*, June 20, 1964, 41–119.

3. *Times-Picayune*, January 30, 1961; "Worker Gives Up Zulu Crown," *Times-Picayune*, February 1, 1961; *States-Item*, February 2, 1961; "Advance Protests Made to Zulu," *States-Item*, February 11, 1961. See also "Boycott Talk Forces Zulu King to Quit," *States-Item*, January 31, 1961.

4. *Times-Picayune*, February 5, 1961.

5. *Times-Picayune*, February 4, 1961; Royal B. Stein, letter to the editor, *States-Item*, February 22, 1961.

6. Davie Snyder, "Zulu Runs His Usual Wild Course," *States-Item*, February 16, 1961; Vincent Randazzo, "Floats of Zulu Met by Cheers," *Times-Picayune*, February 15, 1961; Jerry Hopkins, "Mardi Gras: Boycott on Bourbon Street," *Rogue* (June 1961), 53–58, 76–78.

7. Hopkins, "Mardi Gras: Boycott on Bourbon Street," 53–58, 76–78.

8. "Citizens Cheer Top Mardi Gras," *Time-Picayune*, February 17, 1961.

9. Hopkins, "Mardi Gras: Boycott on Bourbon Street," 53–58, 76–78.

10. *Times-Picayune*, February 22, 1974; *Louisiana Weekly*, February 28, 1931; *Times-Picayune*, February 2, 1940; Nineteen forty-one Zulu Program. Copy at Louisiana Collection, Tulane University.

11. *Louisiana Weekly*, March 12, 1938; *Times-Picayune*, February 15, 1947. See also Edward J. J. Sorrell, letter to the editor, *Times-Picayune*, February 22, 1950, and "Louis the First," *Time*, February 21, 1949.

12. Nathan Irvin Huggins, *Harlem Renaissance* (New York, 1971), chapter six, "White/Black Faces—Black Masks," 244–301, is an incisive discussion of travesty and African-American humor that pays particular attention to black performers acting out white stereotypes of black people.

13. *Louisiana Weekly*, May 14, 1938; Virginia R. Dominguez, *White by Definition: Social Classification in Creole Louisiana* (New Brunswick, N.J., 1986); Trillin, "A Reporter at Large," 66.

14. *Times-Picayune*, February 5, 1961; advertisement in *Louisiana Weekly*, cited in *States-Item*, February 19, 1961.

15. "Charges 'Intelligentsia' Aims to Destroy Zulu Parade," undated article from *Louisiana Weekly* [1966?] in Zulu, vertical file, Hogan Jazz Archive, Tulane University. See also *States-Item*, February 19, 1961.

16. *Louisiana Weekly*, March 10, 1962.

17. "Zulu Spokesman Sounds Off about New 'Route,'" *Louisiana Weekly*, March 17, 1962.

18. "Anent King Zulu," *Louisiana Weekly,* March 17, 1962; Trillin, "Reporter at Large," 58–61.

19. Elgin Hychew, "Dig Me!" *Louisiana Weekly,* June 29, 1963; *Louisiana Weekly,* October 12, 26, November 23, 1963.

20. Trillin, "Reporter at Large," 47.

21. Ibid., 56–58.

22. Trillin, "Reporter at Large," 61; "Zulus to Parade with 'New Look' Mardi Gras," *Louisiana Weekly,* February 20, 1965. See also *Times-Picayune,* March 5, 1965, February 23, 1966; John E. Rousseau, "Thousands Await New Look of Zulus Mardi Gras Day," *Louisiana Weekly,* February 27, 1965; *Louisiana Weekly,* March 6, 1965.

23. Ormonde Plater, "Zulu Turns White," *Vieux Carre Courier,* March 5, 1965; *Louisiana Weekly,* March 12, 1966.

24. Thomas Griffin, "Lagniappe," *States-Item,* January 26, 1967; *States-Item,* February 3, 8, 1967; "Bienamee Big Zulu Winner for Fifth Time," *States-Item,* February 23, 1968; *Times-Picayune,* February 4, 8, 1967; "'Big Shot of Africa' Role Is Awaited by Bienamee," *Times-Picayune,* February 12, 1968.

25. Hermann Deutsch, "Late But Important Information Offered," *States-Item,* February 28, 1967. The *Louisiana Weekly* described the New Orleans Jazz Club as "so-called liberal minded whites, with a Negro or two thrown in (maybe) for color." *Louisiana Weekly,* November 13, 1965.

26. "Bienamee Big Zulu Winner for Fifth Time," *States-Item,* February 23, 1968; "'Big Shot of Africa' Role Is Awaited by Bienamee," *Times-Picayune,* February 12, 1968; *States-Item,* February 8, 1973.

27. *States-Item,* February 12, 19, 1969, January 1, 1970; *Times-Picayune,* February 19, December 7, 1969.

28. *Zulu Official 1980 Program* (New Orleans, 1980).

29. *States-Item,* February 2, 1980; *Times-Picayune,* February 9, 1975, February 12, 1988; *Times-Picayune/States-Item,* March 5, 1984.

30. *Times-Picayune/States-Item,* July 16, 22, 1986.

Epilogue

1. Videotaped minutes of City Council Meeting, December 19, 1991. See also *Times-Picayune,* December 20, 1991; New York *Times,* December 21, 1991. For additional explanation of Clarkson's vote, see her letter to the editor, *Times-Picayune,* January 19, 1992.

2. Obviously, this account is only a brief summary. Readers wishing to know more about this debate should consult the local newspapers, which were full of discussion throughout this period. The newspapers must be supplemented by public documents: Blue Ribbon Committee on Carnival, final report, May 7, 1992; videotape, City Council Meeting, Public Hearing on Public Accommodations,

held on February 6, 1992; videotape, City Council Meeting, Public Accommodations Hearing, May 7, 1992.

3. R. Raymond Lang, Letters to the Editor, *Times-Picayune*, January, 20, 1992; videotape, City Council Meeting, Public Accommodations Hearing, May 7, 1992.

4. Perry Young, *Carnival and Mardi Gras in New Orleans* (New Orleans, 1939), 58–59; videotape, City Council Meeting, Public Hearing on Public Accommodations, held on February 6, 1992.

5. *Vieux Carre Courier*, February 11–17, 1972; Calvin Trillin, "U.S. Journal: New Orleans: Mardi Gras," *New Yorker*, March 9, 1968, 138–144; *Times-Picayune*, March 29, 1972.

6. For a discussion of "who owns Carnival?"—in this case in Brazil—see Roberto Da Matta, "Carnival in Multiple Planes," in John J. MacAloon, ed., *Rite, Drama, Festival, Spectacle: Rehearsals Toward a Theory of Cultural Performance* (Philadelphia, 1984), 208–240. For the range of responses to the Blue Ribbon Compromise, see City Council Meeting, Public Accommodations Hearing, May 7, 1992, with particular attention to the remarks of Dorothy Mae Taylor, James Singleton, Carl Galmon, Henry Julian, John Charbonnet, Blaine Kern, Harry McCall, Jr., and Henri Schindler. See also op-ed piece by Schindler: Henri Schindler, "The Gods Depart—Carnival Losing Old-Time Magic," *Times-Picayune*, September 4, 1992, and McCall's letters to the editor, *Times-Picayune*, January 22, October 11, 1992.

7. *Times-Picayune*, January 12, March 8, 20, September 4, 21, 1992; Charles W. Kreher, president of the Krewe of Triton, to Peggy Wilson, February 11, 1992. Copy in Blue Ribbon Committee report.

Acknowledgments

Various people and institutions helped me write *All on a Mardi Gras Day*. At the Historic New Orleans Collection John Barbry, Carol Bartels, and Jon Kukla made my research enjoyable and productive. The Collection helped fund my research by making me a Williams Senior Research Fellow, as well as generously providing illustrations for the book.

My undergraduate institution, the University of New Orleans, provided me with a set of scholars whose comments on an early draft of the manuscript were most useful: Jerah Johnson, Joseph Logsdon, and my mentor, Joseph G. Tregle, Jr. Thanks too to Lucy J. Fair.

People at Tulane University also deserve thanks, particularly the staff at the Hogan Jazz Archive, the Louisiana Collection, and the Manuscripts Division at its Howard-Tilton Memorial Library; Lawrence Powell, who read an early draft of the manuscript and shared work-in-progress with me; and the Tulane History Department, which, by making me an unsalaried and unduticd adjunct professor, facilitated my access to the university's holdings.

All my friends in New Orleans helped, but particular thanks go to Wendy Boldizar, Douglas Guth, Karen Milner, David Muth, and Bruce E. Naccari.

At Princeton University, several of the senior faculty read an early draft of this book: Peter Brown, Natalie Zemon Davis, Laura Engelstein, Gerald Geisson, Anthony Grafton, William Chester

Jordan, James McPherson, Daniel Rodgers, and Robert Tignor. Brown and Jordan also read and commented on a second draft, as did two graduate students, Jane Dailey and David Nirenberg. Grafton offered me much useful advice, as did Phil Katz and Rachel Weil. Princeton University funded some of the research for this book simply by paying my salary; they were also generous with sabbaticals and summer funding.

Other friends who helped me at one stage or another were E. A. Buurma, Edward Haas, Richard F. Hamm, Karen Leathem, and Richard J. Sommers. Aïda Donald, my editor at Harvard University Press, and Christine Thorsteinsson also made useful suggestions for revision.

Finally, let me thank the city of New Orleans.

Index

African-Americans: political empowerment of, 64, 116, 183; competition with African-Creoles, 116, 159, 184–185; assertion during Carnival, 126–129; middle class of, 160; as flambeaux carriers, 175–176; boycott of Carnival, 178–182; cultural differences among, 182–186

African-Creoles, 30–31; festival traditions of, 3, 29–35, 115–116, 135; assertion during Carnival, 7, 113; during Reconstruction, 72; competition with African-Americans, 116, 159, 184–185. *See also* Creoles; Mardi Gras Indians

Alexander, Ceneilla Bower, 108, 109

Alexis, grand duke of Russia, 52, 54–55

American Party, 42, 43–44

Anglo-Americans: competition with Creoles, 5, 7, 10–12, 27; at Carnival balls, 10, 14, 16–17; accounts of antebellum Carnival, 18–19, 31–33; Carnival clubs of, 23; influence in Carnival, 25–27; festival traditions of, 26; and Irish immigrants, 43

Anti-Catholicism, 43–44, 76. *See also* Catholics

Anti-Semitism, 56, 198, 199

Apollo, Mystic Krewe of, 141, 143, 144

Armory ballroom, 16–17, 48

Armstrong, Louis: as king of Zulu, 147–148, 149, 151–152, 163; in Parish Prison, 149–150, 151; on jazz, 159

Atlanteans, Krewe of, 96–97, 99, 107, 108, 112; debut of, 98

Bacchus, Krewe of, 172

Ballrooms: disorderly conduct at, 5, 10–13, 40, 47–49, 50; cultural pluralism in, 14, 16–17; regulation of, 48–49; during federal occupation, 58; late-nineteenth-century, 97; as theater, 98

Balls. *See* Carnival balls (late-nineteenth-century); Masked balls; Quadroon balls

Bands, 21, 152–153; black, 153–157, 164; white, 155, 162; competition among, 157–158; brass, 158–159, 164, 180. *See also* Musicians; Second line (of parades)

Bambaras, 30, 31

Barker, Danny, 156, 161, 164

Begue's restaurant, 1

Behrman, Martin, 92, 167

Bienamee, Milton, 189, 190

Bigard, Barney, 156, 158

Black Bottom (dance), 131–132, 134

Blue Ribbon Committee on desegregation, 192, 194, 195, 200

Blues, 159

Boissiere, Lambert, 192, 193, 194

Boosterism, 92, 111; role of Carnival in, 57

Bucking contests, 157–158

Buffalo Bill Wild West Show, 114, 123

Burns, Leonard, 179, 184, 188

Butler, General Benjamin, 59, 65

Buzzards (marching group), 162

Calypso, 118, 122

Caribbean area: immigration from, 31–32; Christmas celebrations of, 32; festivals of, 113–114

Carnival: European, 3, 8, 9, 142; social conflict in, 3, 7–8, 198; violence during, 3–4, 113–114, 120–122, 197, 198;

Carnival (*continued*)
  competitive aspects of, 4–5, 8, 200, 201;
  women in, 5, 73, 120, 137–140; as symbol
  of racial harmony, 5–6, 196, 198; gentrification of, 6, 98–101, 107; reform of,
  6, 60–64, 182, 185–191; class distinction
  in, 6–7, 101; English folklore in, 24–25,
  26; anti-Semitism in, 56, 198, 199; regulation of, 57, 200–201; during Civil War,
  57–59; as means of reconciliation, 82–86,
  95; civic leadership of, 85–88, 104, 200;
  audience of, 86, 95, 166; commercial
  value of, 88, 90–95, 162–163; "Babylonian
  Period" of, 107; segregation of, 127–128,
  161–162, 165–167, 171, 173–177, 188;
  during "jazz age," 133–141; gay participants in, 141–146; and spread of jazz,
  162; children in, 165–166; during
  World War I, 167; during Prohibition,
  167–169; during Depression, 169–174,
  177; strikes against, 176; boycott by
  blacks, 178–182, 187–188; during civil
  rights era, 178–191; desegregation of, 192–
  201; and juvenile delinquency, 197; "ownership" of, 200–201
    antebellum, 17–26; and American an-
    nexation, 10; Anglo-American influence
    on, 25–27; racial equality in, 28, 34–37;
    pluralism of, 34; disorderly conduct at, 36–
    37, 49, 197; violence in, 36–42, 44–45,
    49–50; class distinction in, 42, 45–46
      Reconstruction-era, 51–57, 59–68, 97,
      168; commercialism in, 53, 62; political
      satire in, 53, 68–70; reform by Krewe of
      Rex, 60–64; and tourist trade, 63, 77; use
      of tradition, 63–64; political aspects of,
      64, 65–66, 79; boycott of, 72, 73; vio-
      lence during, 75; prohibition of, 76; as
      theater of protest, 79. *See also* Reconstruc-
      tion
  Carnival balls (late-nineteenth-century), 97–
    107; women's role in, 98; exclusivity of,
    98–101, 107; audience of, 99, 100; formal-
    ity of, 101–102, 112; courts of, 102–107;
    themes of, 107–112; gay, 144. *See also*
    Masked balls
  Carnival clubs: origins of, 20–21; Anglo-
    American, 23; restrictions of, 24; in Rex
    parade, 56; in Reconstruction era, 66, 68;
    white supremacists in, 66; nonparading,
    98, 99; gay, 143–144. *See also* Krewes

Carpetbaggers, satirization of, 59, 65, 76
Carrie Nation Club, 1, 5
Casimir, John, 154, 156, 159
Catholics, ethnic differences among, 43.
  See also Anti-Catholicism
Chance, Krewe of, 172
Charivaris, 21; origin of, 20; prohibition of,
  47
Chickasaw tribe (Mardi Gras Indians), 121
Children: in second line, 156–157; segrega-
  tion of, 165–166
Christmas celebrations, 24, 25, 26; Carib-
  bean, 32, 117; masking at, 46
Citizens' Council of Gentilly, 181
Civil rights activism, 178–191
Civil War: Carnival during, 57–59; effect on
  Comus, 67–68
Claiborne, Governor W. C. C., 50; corre-
  spondence with James Madison, 10–11;
  and Louisiana culture, 12, 15–16, 18
Clara Street Jelly Role Club, 134
Clarkson, Jacquelyn, 192, 193, 194
Class distinction, 6–7; in antebellum era, 42,
  45–46; role of tableaux in, 101; and jazz,
  159
Collins, Charles L., 2, 5
Collins, Lee, 158, 161
Commercialism, 53; bans on, 62, 172
Comus, Mystic Krewe of: origins of, 3, 21,
  23–24; tableaux of, 24, 67, 83; English traditions of, 24–25; membership of, 25; during Reconstruction, 56, 65–69, 75, 151;
  during Civil War, 57; costumes of, 65, 68–
  69; Confederate veterans in, 67, 68, 75;
  support of Unionism, 68–69; violence by,
  90, 198; Carnival balls of, 100, 101, 102,
  103–104; parades of, 108, 200; themes of,
  109, 110; after World War I, 167, 168;
  protest of desegregation, 201
Confederate veterans: in Carnival, 54, 67,
  68, 75, 85; daughters of, 102
Congo-dance, 3, 7, 29, 30, 35, 122; origins
  of, 31, 32–33. *See also* Dancing
Consumer League, 187
Consus (Carnival society), 98; balls of, 1–3
Costume balls. *See* Masked balls
Costumes: of Parisian Carnival, 19; antebellum, 20, 21–22, 24; Anglo-American, 26;
  African-Creole, 29–30; postbellum, 50, 53–
  54; of Reconstruction era, 59–60, 81; of
  Rex parade, 61, 63; of Comus, 65, 68–69;

commercial success of, 95; of Mardi Gras
Indians, 116, 118–119, 123; yama-yama,
134; of women, 138–140; of Jolly Boys,
170
Cotton trade, 17–18; in Reconstruction era,
69
Cowan, John R., 82, 92–93, 95
Cowbellion societies, 21
Cox, Nathaniel, 14, 15
Creole Onward Brass Band, 155–156, 164
Creoles: competition with Anglo-Americans,
5, 7, 10–12, 14–15, 27; antebellum, 11–
12; Spanish, 19; and Irish immigrants, 43.
See also African-Creoles
Creole Wild West tribe, 114
Custom House faction, 77, 78–79

Dancing: role in antebellum culture, 10–13,
16–17; at Carnival balls, 107; erotic, 131–
132, 133–135; of second lines, 154, 155.
See also Congo-dance
Davis, Natalie Zemon, 3, 136
Davis, Varina (Winnie), 102, 103–104
Democratic Party, antebellum, 42; immi-
grants in, 43
Depression, 169–174, 177
Disorder, public, 7–8, 38–42, 197; at ball-
rooms, 47–49; Rex's treatment of, 60; dur-
ing Reconstruction, 71–72; of Mardi Gras
Indians, 126–127. *See also* Violence
Drug use, during Carnival, 3
Drumming, parade, 159, 161, 164
Dueling, 41
Dufour, Pierre, 41, 136
Dunican, Peter, 38, 42
Dyow (African societies), 31

Elks, Order of, 171–175, 188
Elves of Oberon, 98
English folklore, in Carnival, 24–25, 26, 67
Europe, Carnivals of, 3, 8, 19, 142
Evolution, 65, 74
Exoticism, in Carnival, 108, 110–111

Fair, Lucy J., 141–142, 144
Female impersonators, 142–143
Flambeaux carriers, 175; strikes by, 176
Flanders, Mayor Benjamin F., 52, 54
Flint, Timothy, 3, 7, 29, 30, 32, 33, 34
Floats, 92; commercial success of, 95; design-
ers of, 108, 109; of Orleanians, 171

Flour throwing (*entrudo*), 17, 36–37, 41–42,
59; prohibition of, 62
France, Carnival traditions of, 19, 20–21
"French balls," 133
French Opera House, 98
French Quarter: parade routes in, 22, 25, 91;
architecture of, 23; immigrants in, 39; gay
culture of, 142–143; Italian population of,
161
"Funky Butt" (song), 158, 160

Gar, Papa, 151, 152
Gates, Henry Louis, Jr., 7, 122–123, 151
Gay beauty pageant, 143, 145
Gay rights movement, 144, 145–146
Gertrude Stein Society, 144
Giarrusso, Joseph, 179, 192, 193, 198
Globe Ball Room, 58
Gombey dancers, 115
Grant, Ulysses S., 65, 79, 84

Hazel, Monk, 155, 161
Hermes, Krewe of, 169–170, 176
Hobsbawm, Eric, 6, 63–64, 101
Homosexuals, in Carnival, 141–146
Hood, John Bell, 84, 91
Humphrey, Percy, 154, 157

"If Ever I Cease to Love" (song), 54, 55,
152
Immigrants: German, 39; Catholic, 43; Italian, 89, 161, 198
    Irish: violence by, 38–42; festival tradi-
tions of, 40; effect on New Orleans society, 42–43
Indians. *See* Mardi Gras Indians
Industrial Parade, 92
Intoxication, during Carnival, 4, 172–
173
Irish Channel, 39, 162

Jackson, Johnny, 192, 195
Jazz, 5; influence of Carnival on, 149, 152–
153; and class conflict, 159; white players
of, 160–161; commercial value of, 162–
163; songs, 163. *See also* Bands; Musicians
"Jazz age," Carnival during, 133–141
Jesse, George, 143, 146
Jews, prejudice against, 56, 198, 199
Jim Crow laws, 8, 126, 127, 167; breakdown
of, 129; and Louis Armstrong, 148–149

Kellog, Governor William Pitt, 70, 73

King NOR, 3, 165

King of the Wake, 7, 29, 30, 35, 122; origins of, 31, 32–34; as king of Zulu, 150

King of Zulu, 122; Louis Armstrong as, 147–148, 149, 151–152, 163; parody of Rex, 151; in 1961 boycott, 180; queens of, 189. See also Zulu, Krewe of

Kinser, Samuel, 8, 34

Knights of the White Camellia, 78

Know-Nothings, 42; anti-Catholicism of, 43–44

Krewes: gay, 143; female, 170, 194; segregation of, 171; desegregation of, 192–196; and "ownership" of Carnival, 200–201. See also Carnival clubs

Ku Klux Klan, 53, 56, 68

Laine, Jack, 153, 162

Levee Shed bill, 78

Lions Club, 134

Lords of misrule, 26, 74, 79, 80; black, 151

Lost Cause, 102

Louisiana: Reconstruction politics of, 70–74, 75–80; race relations in, 81

Louisiana Ball Room, 36

Louisiana Gay Political Action Committee, 144

Louisiana National Guard, 73

Louisiana State Legislature: during Reconstruction, 70; arrests in, 79; move from New Orleans, 89; segregation legislation of, 178

Lundi Gras, 63

Lynching, 90, 198

Mackay, Charles, 41, 49

Mansion House Ball Room, 48

Mardi Gras Indians, 5, 7, 185; competition among, 113–114, 116, 120–121, 123; violence by, 113–116, 120–122, 124–125, 126; origins of, 114–117; costumes of, 116, 118–119, 123; music of, 122, 123–124, 125. See also African-Creoles

Masked balls: antebellum, 13–14, 16–17, 19, 97; racial disguise in, 35–36, 47, 49; during federal occupation, 58; of Reconstruction era, 72, 73. See also Carnival balls (late-nineteenth-century)

Masking: antebellum, 19, 20; racial disguise

in, 35–36, 37; in British tradition, 38; and violence, 44; at Christmas celebrations, 46; during Civil War, 58–59; regulation by Rex, 60, 62; reform of, 86–87; of African-Creoles, 115; by women, 137–138; during World War I, 167

May Day celebrations, 24, 25

Memphis, Carnival of, 66

Merry Widows Social Club Ball, 153

Midsummer's Eve celebrations, 24, 25

Miller, Punch, 159, 162

Ministerial Alliance, 187

Mobile (Alabama), 110, 183

Momus, Knights of: organization of, 68; political satire by, 74–75, 76; parades of, 95, 99, 108; tableaux of, 99–100; themes of, 109; after World War I, 167, 168; during Depression, 169; flambeaux carriers of, 176; protest of desegregation, 201

Morial, Ernest, 188, 190–191

Morrison, Mayor Chep, 148, 179

Mummers, 26, 87

Musicians, 156–164; black, 156–157, 162; competition among, 157–158; white, 160–161. See also Bands

Mystic Krewe of Comus. See Comus, Mystic Krewe of

Mystic societies, 98, 99. See also Carnival clubs; Krewes

NAACP, 184, 187, 188; in 1961 boycott, 181; and desegregation of Carnival, 195

Nativism, 8, 42

Nereus, 98, 105

New Orleans: prostitution in, 2, 53, 73, 132–133, 137; race relations in, 5–6, 126–129, 175, 198; class distinction in, 6–7, 8, 97; desegregation ordinance of, 7, 192–197, 198, 200, 201; multiculturalism of, 8, 123, 166, 198; architecture of, 23, 91–92; during Civil War, 57–59; benefit of Carnival to, 88, 90–95; commerce in, 88–89, 91–95, 111; population of, 88–89, 117; financial problems of, 89; lawlessness in, 89–90; yellow fever in, 89–91; hedonistic image of, 111, 163; segregation in, 116, 127–128, 148–149; gay community of, 141–146; Louis Armstrong's dislike of, 149–150; musical tradition of, 163–164; Filipino community of, 173; desegregation of schools in, 178; city council of (1990s),

192–195, 200; Human Relations Commission of, 193

antebellum: African-Creole traditions of, 3, 29–35; American annexation of, 10, 11, 14–15; cultural life of, 10, 11–17, 30–31; ballrooms of, 13–14; multiculturalism of, 15, 16–17, 26, 34, 43; role of balls in, 16–17; racial divisions in, 27–28; Caribbean immigrants to, 31–32; race relations in, 35–36; immigration to, 39–40, 89; class distinction in, 42; effect of Irish immigration on, 42–43; Vigilance Committee of, 44; regulation of holidays, 46–47, 49; regulation of ballrooms, 48–49

Reconstruction-era: federal occupation of, 57–58; tourist trade in, 63; social change in, 64; Metropolitan Police of, 66, 73, 79; support of Constitutional Union Party, 69; riots in, 71–72, 84

New Orleans Jazz Club, 189

New Orleans Mardi Gras Association, 87

New Orleans Public Service Company, 92, 162

New York Seventy-first Infantry, 82–83, 95

NOR parades, 165–166

Orientalism, 107–108, 109, 110, 111

Original Dixieland Jazz Band, 162

Orleanians, Krewe of, 3, 35, 188; founding of, 171–172; ethnic diversity in, 173–175

Orleans Ball Room, 48, 58

"The Pack" (maskers), 52

Parades: European origin of, 19, 20; antebellum, 21–26; themes of, 23, 108–110; routes of, 25–26, 91, 170, 200; during Civil War, 57; educational function of, 108; designers of, 108–109; of Mardi Gras Indians, 119–122; bands in, 152–153; second line of, 153–156; children in, 165. See also Rex parades; Zulu parades

Paris, Carnival traditions of, 19, 20

Patron saints' days, 40

Perrin du Lac, M., 12, 15

Peter Clavier, Knights of, 179

Phorty Phunny Phellows, 112

Pickwick Club, 23, 66, 68

Priests of Mithras, 98

Processions. See Parades

Prohibition, 5, 141, 167; satirization of, 1

Prostitutes, 2, 73, 132; in Rex parade, 53; transvestism of, 58, 133, 135–136

Proteus, Krewe of, 176, 201; Carnival balls of, 101, 103; parades of, 108; themes of, 109, 110; after World War I, 167

Quadroon balls, 13

Queens: of Carnival balls, 103–105, 106; of Mardi Gras Indians, 120, 125; of Zulu, 180, 189

Racism, 27–28, 175; of antebellum Carnival, 36–37; violent, 84, 127–130; protests against, 116. See also White supremacists

Ragtime, 160

Railroads, role in promoting Carnival, 93, 94

Raphael, Alex T., Jr., 182–183, 185, 186, 187

"Ratty" music, 150, 159

Reconciliation, Carnival as means of, 82–86, 95

Reconstruction, 5; opposition of Comus to, 69; African-Creoles during, 72. See also Carnival, Reconstruction-era

Red, White, and Blue tribe, 121

Reformers, 1–2; and gay Carnival, 146; civil-rights era, 180, 182, 185, 186, 187

Republicans, black, 77–78

Republicans, radical, 80; criticism of Carnival, 60, 61; satirization of, 65–66, 68, 69–70, 74, 76, 151; and New Orleans culture, 76–77

Rex, Krewe of: formation of, 54; reform of Carnival, 60–64; and Momus, 75; tableaux of, 83; civic leadership of, 85–88, 104, 200; role in reconciliation, 85–86; and yellow fever, 90–91; and tourism, 94; Carnival balls of, 101–102, 106; integration of, 201

Rex parades: origin of, 3, 52–57; costumes of, 61, 81, 107–108; political aspects of, 64, 70–71, 80; Northern attendees of, 83; themes of, 84–85, 109–110, 111–112; prostitutes in, 135; bands in, 152–153; after World War I, 167, 168; and Krewe of Orleanians, 174

Ritual, 8; and violence, 3, 117; Carnival as, 4

Royal Host of New Orleans, 63, 82–83; membership of, 84, 94, 95; expenditures of, 93

Russell, James L., 188, 189

St. Augustine boys school, 185, 186
St. Charles Theatre, 58
St. Louis ball, 16–17; violence at, 40
St. Patrick's Day celebrations, 39
St. Philip Street Ball Room, 48
Salomon, Lewis J., 52, 55–57
Second line (of parades), 153, 160, 163; competition among, 154, 156; dancing by, 154, 155; children in, 156–157; influence on musicians, 157, 158
"Self-Reconstruction," 71
Sexuality, expression during Carnival, 4, 131–132, 135–139, 197
Shakespeare, Joseph, 88, 89
Sheet Iron Band, 21
Sheridan, General Philip H., 72, 73
Shriners, 95
Shrove Tuesday, 40
Slave societies, 30, 31
Smith, Michael P., 114, 115
Social Darwinism, 65–66
Soule, George, 85–86, 108, 109, 111
South Louisiana Citizens' Council, 181
Stein, Royal B., 180, 181
Stickfighting, 117
Stoddard, Amos, 12, 15
Storyville, 132, 167

Tableaux: of Comus, 24, 67, 83; of Atlanteans, 96–97; of Carnival balls, 96–98, 105–106, 107, 108, 112; of Momus, 99–100; audience of, 101; parodies of, 112; homosexual, 141, 144
Taylor, Dorothy Mae, 192, 193, 194, 196, 197, 199
Thugs, white, 36–37, 38–40, 42
Tourism, 63, 77, 83–84; role in reconciliation, 85, 86; commercial value of, 88, 93–95; during Depression, 170
Tradition: in Reconstruction Carnival, 63–64; invention of, 101, 115
Tramps (marching club), 151
Transvestism: male, 22, 139–141; in Rex parade, 53; of prostitutes, 58, 133, 135–136; commercialization of, 142–143
Trinidad: Carnival in, 45–46, 79, 122, 126; festival traditions of, 114, 115, 117, 118
Twain, Mark, 87–88
Twelfth Night celebrations, 24–25, 26, 27; during Reconstruction, 68, 69–70, 74, 76

United Clubs, 179, 187

Valley, Chris, 5, 171–172, 174, 177
Venice, Carnival traditions of, 19, 20, 135
Venus, Krewe of, 170
Vietnam War era, Carnival during, 8
Violence, 3–4, 197, 198; ritualized, 3, 117; in antebellum Carnival, 36–39, 44–45; by Irish immigrants, 38–42; political, 43–44; and masking, 44, 46; during Reconstruction, 71–72, 75; racial, 84, 127–130; of late nineteenth century, 89–90; by Mardi Gras Indians, 113–116, 120–122, 124–125, 126; among second lines, 154–156; reflection in music, 164. See also Disorder, public
Voodoo, 126

Waldo, J. Curtis, 56, 91
Warmouth, Governor Henry Clay, 52, 54, 79; black Republican support of, 77
Weddings, and Carnival balls, 106
White Citizens' Council, 181
White League, 66, 75, 90; in 1874 riot, 72, 73, 84
White supremacists, 5, 76, 128; Comus's support of, 67; use of Carnival, 80; during civil rights era, 182; and desegregation of Carnival, 196, 197. See also Racism
Wild Squat Toulas tribe, 120
Williams, Black Benny, 156, 159
Wilson, Peggy, 192, 194, 195
Women: participation in Carnival, 5, 73, 120; in Carnival balls, 98, 102–107; assertion during Carnival, 134, 135, 137; transvestism by, 135–136; masking by, 137–139; cigarette-smoking, 139; krewes of, 170, 194. See also Prostitutes
World Wars, effect on Carnival, 167, 175–176

Yellow fever, 81, 89; epidemics, 90–91
Yellow Pocahontas tribe, 114
Young, Perry, 106, 165, 197, 198
Yuga, Krewe of, 143

Zeno, Alice, 118, 119
Zulu, King of. See King of Zulu
Zulu, Krewe of, 5, 30; boycott of, 3, 178–182, 187, 188; origins of, 151; during Depression, 177; and civil rights movement,

182–191; black criticism of, 183–184, 189, 190; fiftieth anniversary of, 187–188; white members of, 189–190

Zulu Aid and Pleasure Club, 190, 191; and Louis Armstrong, 150, 151–152

Zulu parades: Louis Armstrong in, 147–148, 149, 150, 151–152, 177; music of, 159; audience of, 176–177; reform of, 188–191